Spiritualism's Place

Spiritualism's Place

*Reformers, Seekers, and Séances
in Lily Dale*

Averill Earls, Sarah Handley-Cousins,
Marissa C. Rhodes, and
Elizabeth Garner Masarik

☰ THREE HILLS
AN IMPRINT OF CORNELL UNIVERSITY PRESS
ITHACA AND LONDON

Copyright © 2024 by Cornell University

All rights reserved. Except for brief quotations in a review, this book, or parts thereof, must not be reproduced in any form without permission in writing from the publisher. For information, address Cornell University Press, Sage House, 512 East State Street, Ithaca, New York 14850. Visit our website at cornellpress.cornell.edu.

First published 2024 by Cornell University Press

Printed in the United States of America

Library of Congress Cataloging-in-Publication Data

Names: Earls, Averill, 1986– author. | Handley-Cousins, Sarah, 1984– author. | Rhodes, Marissa C., 1987– author. | Masarik, Elizabeth Garner, author.
Title: Spiritualism's place : reformers, seekers, and séances in Lily Dale / Averill Earls, Sarah Handley-Cousins, Marissa C. Rhodes, and Elizabeth Garner Masarik.
Description: Ithaca : Cornell University Press, 2024. | Includes bibliographical references and index.
Identifiers: LCCN 2024011459 (print) | LCCN 2024011460 (ebook) | ISBN 9781501777264 (hardcover) | ISBN 9781501777288 (epub) | ISBN 9781501777271 (pdf)
Subjects: LCSH: Women and spiritualism—New York (State)—Lily Dale—History. | Spiritualism—New York (State)—Lily Dale—History. | Feminism—New York (State)—Lily Dale—History. | Lily Dale (N.Y.)—History—19th century. | Lily Dale (N.Y.)—History—20th century.
Classification: LCC BF1275.W65 E17 2024 (print) | LCC BF1275.W65 (ebook) | DDC 133.908209747/9—dc23/eng/20240424
LC record available at https://lccn.loc.gov/2024011459
LC ebook record available at https://lccn.loc.gov/2024011460

Dedicated to Ron Nagy and our listeners

Contents

Acknowledgments	ix
Abbreviations	xi
Introduction: Messages at the Stump	1
1. Welcome to Lily Dale	14
2. Little Victorian Cottages	39
3. The Fox Cottage	65
4. The Auditorium	89
5. The Maplewood Hotel	116
6. The Indian Village	142
Epilogue: The Lily Dale Museum	168
Notes	179
Bibliography	203
Index	215

Acknowledgments

Even though we've been friends for over a decade and have worked together on our podcast for years, we never considered writing a book together—until Michael McGandy, former editorial director of Three Hills, approached us with an idea. So this project would not have happened without him. And like all historians, we owe a lot to the archivists, experts, loved ones, and editors who brought this book to life. We're grateful for the labor and attention of our final editor, Mahinder Kingra, and acquisitions assistant India Miraglia at Three Hills, and for the formative feedback provided by the two reviewers; one of them remains unknown to us, but the other, Spencer McBride, has been enthusiastic and encouraging throughout this process. We couldn't have done any of this work without Ron Nagy at the Lily Dale Museum, as well as the folks in the front office and on the Lily Dale Assembly board of directors, who gave us access to the board meeting minutes, and the volunteers who gave us access to the special collections of the Marion Skidmore Library. We were also aided by a bevy of helpful folks: Elizabeth Graham and Jennifer

Mills, who graciously shared their research on Oskenonton, including providing us with some of his letters; Chautauqua County historian Michelle Henry; Jamestown Community College professor Traci Langworthy; Pomfret town historian Todd Langworthy; and Darwin R. Barker Library director Graham Tedesco-Blair about Lily Dale's connection to the temperance movement. We're especially thankful for all of our Patreon supporters, whose monthly and annual generosity funded research trips, book acquisitions, and a Zoom account, which allowed us to make group trips to Lily Dale, get texts we couldn't access through our various libraries, and of course meet, plan, and record podcast episodes over the years. And finally, we are nothing without the support and love of our families and friends.

Abbreviations

AAS	American Association of Spiritualists
AIM	American Indian Movement
AIRFA	American Indian Religious Freedom Act
ASPR	American Society of Psychical Research
AWSA	American Woman Suffrage Association
CFI	Center for Inquiry
CLFA	Cassadaga Lake Free Association
IAPSOP	International Association for the Preservation of Spiritualist and Occult Periodicals
LDM	Lily Dale Museum
NAWSA	National American Woman Suffrage Association
NSAC	National Spiritualist Association of Churches
NWSA	National Woman Suffrage Association
SPIRIT	Support and Protection of Indian Religions and Indigenous Traditions
UAS	Universal Association of Spiritualists
WCTU	Women's Christian Temperance Union

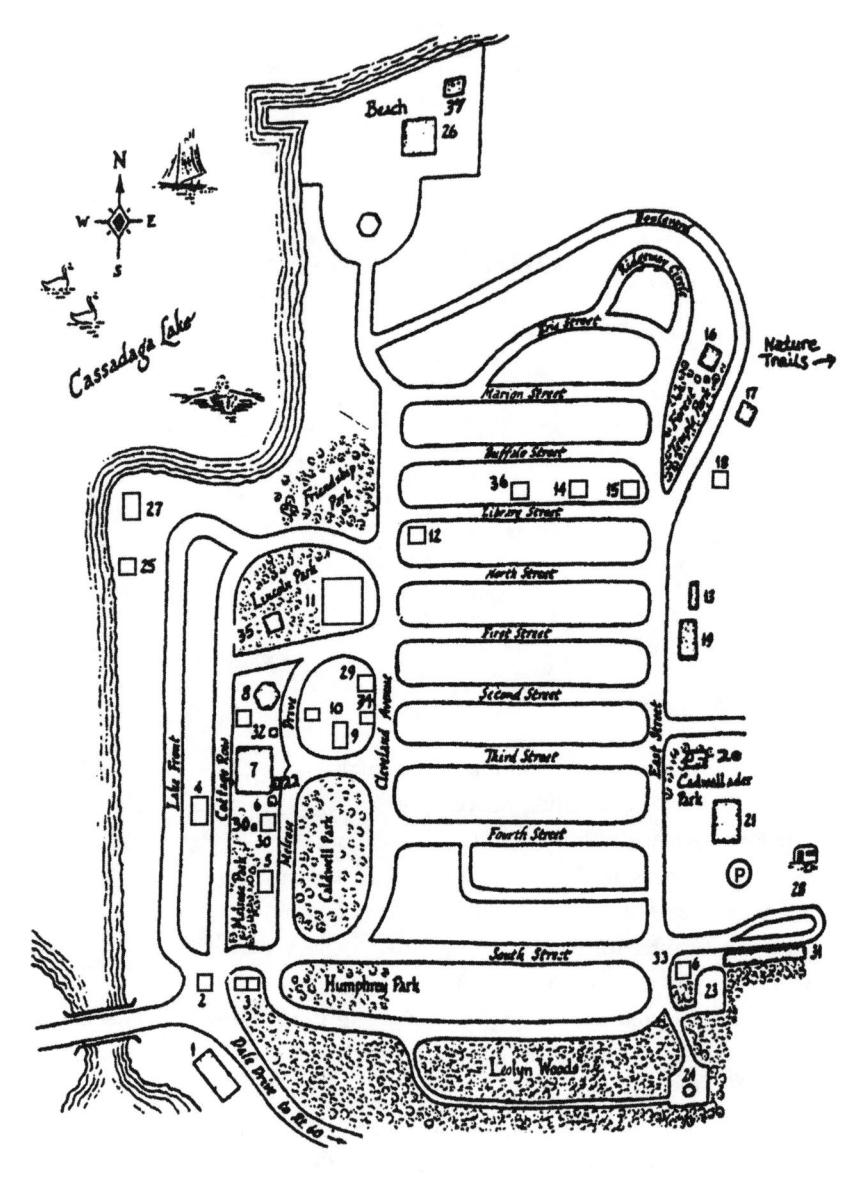

Figure 1. Map of Lily Dale grounds from the 1995 Camp Program. Lily Dale Museum, Lily Dale, New York.

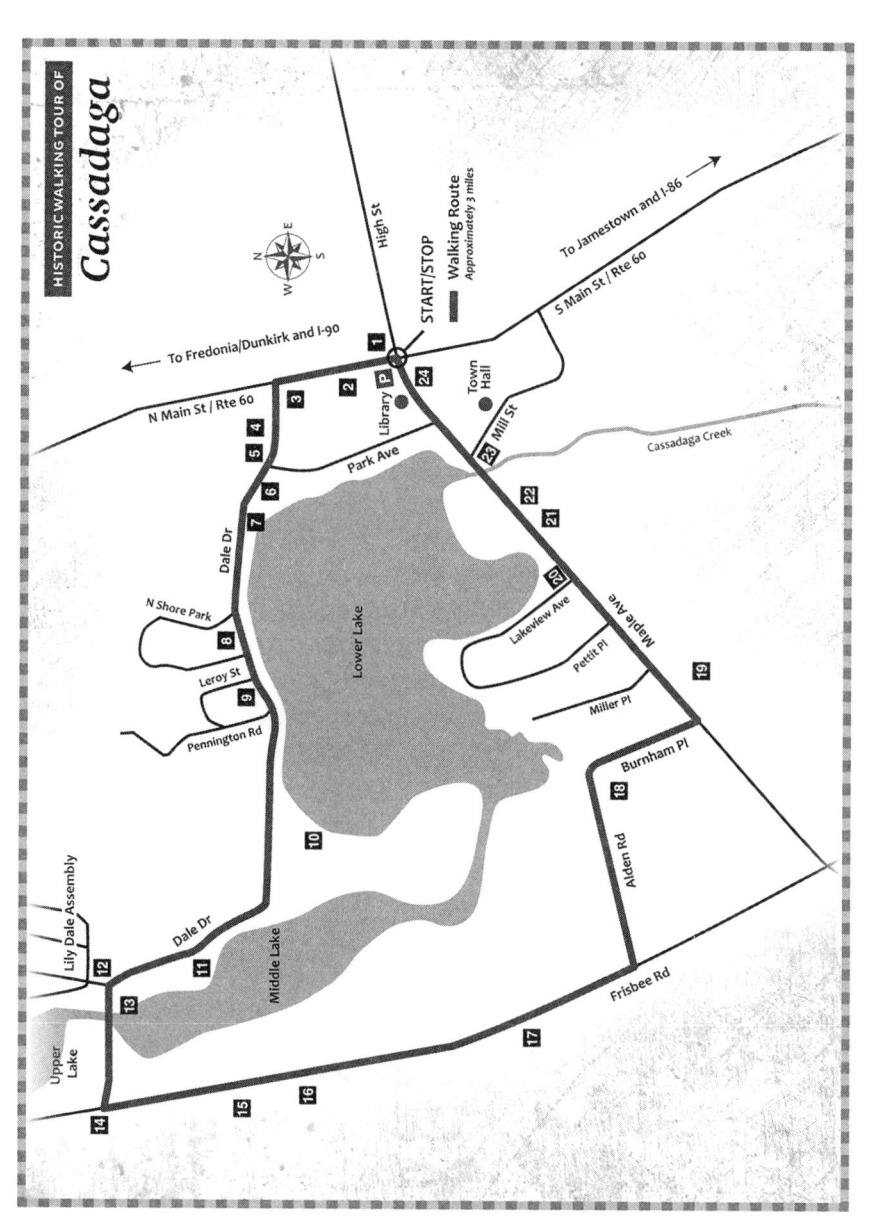

Figure 2. Map from the "Cassadaga Walking Tour" pamphlet developed by the Citizens for a Better Cassadaga, Chautauqua County Health Network, funded by the New York State Department of Health. Cassadaga Walking Tour Map, 2016, Lily Dale Museum.

Spiritualism's Place

Introduction

Messages at the Stump

Averill

During our first visit to Lily Dale as a group, Marissa, Elizabeth, Sarah, and I did all the things visitors do: we stayed in one of the historic homes, toured the library and the museum, ate breakfast at the coffee shop and lunch at the Lily Cafeteria, had individual readings with licensed mediums, went to the daily messages at the Stump, attended a church service, and even did the ghost walk on our first night there. It was the summer of 2021, and though we'd met many times over Zoom for writing dates, virtual painting tutorials with the ArtSherpa, and podcast recordings, we hadn't been in the same room for over a year. We were giddy with the thrill of the research project and the chance to spend time together after the emotional turbulence of the COVID-19 lockdown.

That first night, the ghost walk of Lily Dale turned out, to our delight, to be more of a historic tour of the town than an immersion in the grisly ghost stories you usually get on these tours.[1] Our guides led the group of twenty or so visitors through the town. We learned a little about all the places that would, eventually, ground this book: the beautiful sprawling

Victorian house in which we were staying on that trip; the auditorium that hosted speakers like Susan B. Anthony and Cora L. V. Scott; the Maplewood Hotel, constructed to house the thousands of visitors who made their way to Lily Dale each summer; the site of Mohawk opera singer Oskenonton's home; the location of the Fox Cottage; the Lily Dale Museum; and the final stop of the evening, "Inspiration Stump" in the Leolyn Woods.

The guides led us on a relaxed walk through the dark wood, narrated only by the sounds of quiet conversations and shoes crunching fallen twigs and decaying vegetation. Though it was August, it was cool enough that we'd all put on sweatshirts and were thankful that the buzzing mosquitoes that plague Lily Dale at this point in the season couldn't get at our arms and necks. It wasn't a long walk, and soon we were invited by our tour guides to find a comfortable seat on one of the benches that encircle the Stump. The four of us slid into a pew together and let the weight of a dark night (there was a waning crescent moon just barely illuminating the clearing) press down upon us. It was our very first visit to Lily Dale together, and after nearly a year in our various isolations because of the pandemic, it was good to be reunited.

Lily Dale, New York, is a gated community on the shores of Cassadaga Lake, surrounded by ten acres of thick old-growth forest. The town was founded in 1879 as an intentional Spiritualist community. Even today, residency in the community requires membership in a Spiritualist church and the Lily Dale Assembly, as well as the approval of the town's board of directors. The hamlet of Pomfret, New York, enjoys close proximity to Seneca Falls and the Chautauqua Institution, both foundational sites of the women's rights movement. It also rests at the western end of what historians have called the "Burned Over District," a region that experienced wave after wave of religious revival during the mid-nineteenth century. The region gave rise to several new religions, was home to myriad socialist utopian communities, and cultivated a reputation as fertile ground for religious radicalism and reform. Though it was founded well after the peak of religious experimentation in New York State, Lily Dale, as a Spiritualist community, captured this historical nexus at its founding in 1879 and has preserved its treasures for over a century.

For some people, Lily Dale is a special place. Those who seek to connect with lost loved ones and work through their pain in conversation with the dead flock there every summer during "camp" season. Its setting, with the lake on one side and the Leolyn Woods on the other, gives the outdoor space of the town a meditative ambiance. Once, when Spiritualism was in its heyday and the town attracted more families, you would have heard the laughter of children from the Lyceum building.[2] Now there's not much that will keep kids entertained, so walks along the lakeshore, through the woods, or down the narrow Victorian-lined residential streets are quiet. There are no bars for people to spill out of at night, so the long ghost tours are the only kind of late-night activity that you'll encounter. There are no longer demonstrations of physical mediumship rattling the walls of the Victorian cottages or reverberating out of the auditorium; the controversial séances involving spirit trumpets, materialization, and table tipping have been banned in Lily Dale since the 1950s.[3] Even though it's a little quieter than it was one hundred years ago, and the number of visitors has declined, it's still a place where you can find solace in both the peace of nature and the offices of working mediums who promise to connect you with your dead.

Of course, the aesthetic and the environment were cultivated by the Spiritualists who founded the town. The Lily Dale board of directors has always marketed the town as both a summer resort and a religious camp.[4] Lily Dale lore says that this place is special, that it was spiritually significant for the Seneca, and that its specialness drew Spiritualists to it in the 1840s, when people first started meeting there on Willard Alden's farmland.[5] Alden, "an ardent Spiritualist," eventually selected Sunday, June 15, 1877, as the day reserved for local Spiritualists to picnic in a grove on his farm, which the Spiritualists started calling the "June Picnic and Sunday Assembly."[6] After his death, the Spiritualists who'd gathered at Alden's Grove got together to form a society, the Cassadaga Lake Free Association, and purchased land about a half mile from Alden's property. They built up the town much like any other Victorian resort, with cottages for rent and communal buildings that would host speakers, feed visitors, and cater to the various entertainment needs of summer crowds.[7] But in the style of the religious revivalists like the Methodists, it was also a religious "camp," where services were available daily, and one could pray—and commune with the dead—in just about every space on the property.

In most ways, we four are the demographic typically drawn to Lily Dale. Like the mediums who have historically practiced in the town, the visitors are predominantly white, wealthier, middle-aged women. Our whiteness and gender presentation mean we can blend in easily when we sit down in the readings at the Stump or walk through the town. We've collectively lost three fathers and a mother, all too young, and all in ways that were too fast and yet painfully prolonged. Marissa and Sarah are from the Burned Over District, and had visited Lily Dale with family and friends many times before we conceptualized this project.[8] I am from Vermont, like so many of the religious radicals who set central and western New York on fire.[9]

Historians are, in some ways, like mediums seeking answers from the dead. Academic historians like us take pride in our rigorous research standards and careful interpretations of the past. But as women and as feminists, we seek to correct the biases built into traditional historical methodologies. When archives are compiled and cataloged by men for men, historians of women must, out of necessity, go beyond the archive to access the lived experiences of ordinary women from the past. For this project, that means approaching Lily Dale as a space on its own terms. Each chapter of this book is anchored to an iconic space in the community. After colorfully describing a specific place at Lily Dale, we take a deep dive into the historical context that gives the site special meaning for women historians. Here in this introduction, we're starting at Inspiration Stump, the site of twice-daily public "message services." We use this space as a point of entry into the historical world of communing with the dead, seeking to uncover what this activity meant to people of the past, and the circle it helps us draw around the four of us, this town, and you, our reader.

The Stump is all that remains of what was once a massive tree. If its rings were ever counted to determine its age at death, I've yet to find a record, and now it's too late, because the original stump is encased in cement. In the 1890s, the Stump was leveled off to make it easier to stand on, and then cemented over. Steps were added in the 1930s.[10] For decades, mediums have climbed up on the Stump and delivered messages to those gathered around. According to records in the Lily Dale Archive and Museum, a "trail from the Alden House . . . was used to walk through the peace and tranquility to the 'Inspiration Stump' as early as 1873."[11] Over

Figure 3. Inspiration Stump, pre-1899. Image is a photocopy of the original on a loose sheet of paper in the "Places and Spaces" folder, Lily Dale Museum.

Figure 4. Women at the Stump, early 1900s. "Places and Spaces" folder, Lily Dale Museum.

Figure 5. The Stump with its first cement covering, early 1900s. "Places and Spaces" folder, Lily Dale Museum.

the years the Stump naturally decayed, and so Lily Dale's leaders shored it up, first with a sturdier platform on which to stand, and eventually with a full cement makeover.

The Stump is perhaps the most religiously significant site in Lily Dale, in that there are twice-daily message services held there. Messages from the dead—or, as believers say, from "Spirit"—are the core of Spiritualism. Spiritualist newspapers from the late nineteenth century, such as *The Sunflower* or *The Banner of Light,* all include lengthy sections titled "Messages" or "The Messenger." These are printed messages purportedly from dead people, written in the first person, much as one would encounter in a live session with a trance medium. While one could visit Lily Dale and expect to get direct messages when attending a séance or meeting for a private reading with a medium in her home/office, receiving the messages at the Stump service is a different kind of thrilling experience. Visitors sit or stand in a big group, and mediums take turns plucking messages out of the ether. The medium will experience a touch or a voice, indicating to them that a spirit would like to connect to someone in the audience. Then the medium will deliver the message, and any number of spirits might choose to communicate to specific members of the audience. Plus, unlike readings in private homes, the messages at the Stump were included in the gate fee, so you didn't have to pay extra. The same is true today.

As the Lily Dale board expanded the resort-like amenities of the camp season over the years, they built on the traditions that were cultivated by the folks who pilgrimaged to the Leolyn Woods each summer. They built rafts for floating dances on the lake, and bandstands to host performers. They erected a picnic pavilion to accommodate hundreds dining alfresco. They pruned and primped the clearing surrounding the massive Inspiration Stump. According to a 1931 camp program, Inspiration Stump was located in "a virgin forest on the Lily Dale assembly grounds." The program focuses on the spirituality of place and space:

> Many of the mediums who have blessed the world with the ministrations received their first contact from the spirit world at this sacred spot. It's a secure haven to all who seek rest and quiet, as well as those who strive for psychic development. Public meetings are held at the Stump at regular intervals each day during the season, at which mediums demonstrate their gifts, and there are also addresses and exchanges of thought.[12]

In describing the Leolyn Woods, the Lily Dale leaders of 1931 made clear what they found important. In omitting questions about whose land this was and where their ideas about the "sacredness" of the spot came from, they also made clear the biases of the early Spiritualists. As a religious movement, Spiritualism was often deeply reflective and critical of power structures in the modern world. Spiritualist leaders were feminists and suffragists, embraced temperance and the abolition of slavery, and contemplated the negative impact of industrialization and urbanization. But, as we'll discuss in chapter 2, the first formal Spiritualist organizations were not welcoming to Black practitioners and were ultimately hierarchical and male-dominated. And as we'll demonstrate in chapter 6, Spiritualists were sometimes guilty of appropriating Native American religious practices and spaces without the cultural authority to do so—and some even pretended to *be* Native American to seize that authority. Like so many of the social and religious movements of the nineteenth century, Spiritualism was radically freeing and unintentionally problematic, prodding at some social boundaries while reinforcing others.

We knew before our first research trip to Lily Dale that we'd encounter those kinds of messy contradictions and ideas. As our nighttime history tour came to an end on that first trip, the guides invited us to find a seat, switch off our flashlights, and take in the ambience of the near-midnight woods: the creaking of the trees, the breathing of our fellow travelers, the chirping of night creatures. This space, which is by day the site of group readings during "camp" season in Lily Dale, is rich with life. Isn't it ironic, when this place is the heart of a town famed for speaking to the dead?

Sarah, Elizabeth, Marissa, and I arranged ourselves on a bench, and like the others in the group, we turned off our tiny flashlights and let the darkness wash over us. The tour guides said a few words about letting the weight of the place settle into us, to clear our minds and open ourselves to this special place. I did as they bade. But the only time my mind is quiet and empty is when I am asleep. And sure enough, as I sat leaning back against those warm wooden benches, with nothing but even-breathing humans and the sounds of a forest in the night to anchor me to the world, I drifted off. Not for long (I think)—because I started awake, realizing that I'd fallen asleep, and felt only stillness around me. For one—panicked— moment, I thought I was alone. I felt utterly and totally abandoned in that black wood. But I reached out a hand, and there was Marissa, still on the bench not two feet away.

Though this is a collaboratively written book, we linked each chapter to one place in Lily Dale and mostly to one of us, except for chapter 3, which we wrote together. As with our podcast episodes, we've been drawn to topics and rabbit holes that reflect a little bit of who we are, professionally and personally. Marissa (the historian) studies and teaches radical religions, free love, and temperance as integral and compelling aspects of early feminist thought. Marissa's personal story also makes her uniquely qualified to write our chapter on temperance and Lily Dale's establishment as a dry town. Marissa (the person) is a born-again Christian turned agnostic, married to a committed teetotaler, and struggles with issues of spirituality and alcohol use in her adult life. Her father was an autodidact who passed on his voracious love of learning (and heavy drinking) to his daughter before his early death from alcohol-related stomach cancer. On a recent trip to Lily Dale, organized as a dry bachelorette party for a sober friend, Marissa experienced a powerful reading that revived old struggles between sobriety and substance use, atheism and spirituality, life and death.

Sarah, a native of rural northern New York, grew up in a family that placed great importance on the connection between heritage and place. Sarah's professional expertise in nineteenth-century American medicine is complemented by her unique experience with spiritualism. After her brother's sudden death, her family visited Lily Dale seeking comfort in their grief. Over time, several family members came to identify as Spiritualists, but while Sarah was always game for a trip to Lily Dale and is fascinated by upstate New York's radical history, she's never jumped into Spiritualism herself. A practicing Christian with a healthy sense of skepticism (yes, a weird combination), plus what Marissa terms her "emotional constipation," Sarah has a unique perspective on this tiny village of mediums. Her historical expertise is invaluable, but Sarah's lived experience of grief and her intimate knowledge of Spiritualist practice also informs her chapters on the Burned Over District and the connection between Lily Dale and Native American culture.

Before we started on this book project, neither Elizabeth nor I had ever been to Lily Dale. And yet we discovered more than we bargained for as we roamed the streets of this little town. Elizabeth, a native Texan who relocated to Buffalo as an adult, has had a lifelong interest in the occult and—as our resident goth—being "spooky." Shortly after our first group trip to Lily Dale, Elizabeth and her husband took another trip there for a romantic weekend getaway. None of us were surprised that Elizabeth fell in love with Lily Dale. As we took some air after a recent research trip down to Lily Dale Beach, she commented that she could easily see herself retiring in this beautiful place. It has all the history, mystery, and community spirit that she seeks in her life. She's a heavy skeptic, but she's open to talking with the dead and is known to wear a pendant that holds some of her father's ashes when she needs some life advice. Elizabeth is the first one to tell you that she's experienced ghosts, and the last one to believe that she actually has. Her expertise on American women's history and research on child death and its relation to women's political activism position her as the perfect one of us to craft our chapter on the women's rights movement.

I'm a historian of Ireland, gender, and sexuality. I also vacillate between immovable disbelief and hopeful openness when it comes to the "supernormal." When we first pitched the idea for this book, I had no idea what I could bring to the project (other than benevolent leadership, of course). But then I started tugging on threads and finding connections. Gender, domesticity, Victorian social constructs—all things I'd studied and thought about throughout my academic career. And then came these historical people who doubted and felt crushing loss and believed in confusing circles. Among the four of us, I am the least tethered to a belief system, and so perhaps both more and less likely to believe. I grew up with stories about my family's "pagan" roots and penchant for second sight. My dad swears he once laid hands on a puppy with parvo and cured it. And when I'm not trying to, I glimpse futures in my dreams that come to pass. But I don't trust people who seek to profit off others' pain. Like the countless skeptics who've come before me, in my first, and possibly last, sitting, I "tested" my medium; I gave a fake name with an email address I don't use much. Some thorough googling probably would have led the medium to the "real" me, and all my emotional baggage. But honestly, I went to that reading hoping that my mother, gone four years, would speak to me through this medium. When I was researching skeptics and fraud in early Spiritualism, I read Harry Houdini's words and felt them resonate through me: "I was willing to believe, even wanted to believe."[13] I walked away from my first sitting with a medium, tears streaming down my face, deeply disappointed and not the least surprised. My skepticism doesn't protect me from heartbreak when proof of an afterlife doesn't materialize.

In writing this book, we're thinking about place and space in both historical and personal ways. That means we'll take you to some of our favorite places in Lily Dale and sink deep into rabbit holes to discover what those places and spaces mean to the history of Spiritualism, women's history, and western New York State. We've spent the better part of a decade together here, and that's where we start this book. Sarah introduces us to a very brief history of the notorious Burned Over District in chapter 1, and the history of radical religions and movements founded in Rochester, Buffalo, and, of course, Lily Dale, in the nineteenth century. In chapter 2, I return us to the specific boundaries of Lily Dale through an exploration of the home and femininity in both Spiritualism and Victorian culture. In chapter 3, we all come together to write about the role of Spiritualism's origin story—the raps and knocks produced by the Fox sisters in 1848—in Lily Dale. The Fox sisters, like so many physical mediums in the nineteenth century, had to contend with accusations of fraud throughout their lives. They were tested by scientists and psychical investigators during their young adulthood. Their story—the challenges and the fame they accumulated—is a significant part of Spiritualism's history. In addition to taking on the stewardship of the physical Fox Cottage, Lily Dale, the self-described "largest Spiritualist camp in the world," has also had to contend with fame, fraudsters, and skeptics for most of its history. In chapter 4, Elizabeth takes us into the feminist core of Spiritualism as it manifested in the women's rights movement. Lily Dale was a hotbed of suffragist speakers and women's leadership at the end of the nineteenth century, and continued to be until women got the right to vote. In chapter 5, Marissa takes us for a stay at the Maplewood and Leolyn hotels. Like many Victorian intentional communities, Lily Dale was founded by people who embraced a number of radical social movements but were also practical businesspeople. The temperance movement made Lily Dale into a dry town, so that inside Lily Dale's gates, the Maplewood hosted spirits of the dead, but not the boozy kind. Just outside the gates, by contrast, the Iroquois Hotel served alcohol.[14] In chapter 6, Sarah takes us into the realm of cultural appropriation versus celebration, and the role (and use) of Native Americans in Spiritualism and in Lily Dale.

Our collective favorite place in Lily Dale is the museum and archive, run by our friend Ron Nagy, the historian of Lily Dale. Starting in the summer of 2021, Ron has generously shown us how to navigate the archives, answered our random one-off emailed questions, and opened the archive for us in the offseason so that we could photograph anything and everything we could get our hands on. (We sent him thumb drives with all the digitized material we generated as a modest thank-you for his time and knowledge.) In this book we return to the museum last, as it was often the last place we visited on our collective research trips to Lily Dale, and the reason we got to go to Lily Dale together at all. The history of Lily Dale is collected there in ephemera, knickknacks, newspaper clippings, photographs, and the business signs that used to hang outside now departed mediums' doors. Like every edifice in Lily Dale, it has its own storied past, and as the archive of the people, beliefs, and streets of Lily Dale, it is a special place all its own.

In our little foursome, I know that I am alone in some things. Marissa, Sarah, and Elizabeth all have children, and I chose long ago to remain child-free. Though we've all lost parents, only I have lost my mother, which I sometimes feel is a devastation on a different level, even though I know it's not. And after a decade of making a home and a life in Buffalo, fifty miles north of Lily Dale, I was the first of us to take a job outside western New York, though not the last, as Marissa accepted a position in Florida.[15] But my singleness in these things only ever brings a fleeting moment of panic, because all I've ever had to do is reach out, and these three—my closest friends, podcast cohosts, and coauthors of this book— are there.

Our hope in writing this book collaboratively is that our varying degrees of belief, skepticism, interest, and ambivalence toward Spiritualism, and thus Lily Dale's history and mission, will speak to our readers, who undoubtedly possess varying degrees of belief, skepticism, interest, and ambivalence too. We're glad you're here, and hope you enjoy this bridge to Lily Dale. We love this place, and we love its complicated, sometimes cringey history. We want to share a little of that with you in the pages of this book.

This is a book about the history of an intentional community of Spiritualists in western New York. Lily Dale was founded as the utopian movements of the nineteenth century were fizzling out, when the United States was still reeling from the destruction of the Civil War and upheaval of Reconstruction, and when women were demanding political participation and social change. It was born as the United States was eradicating the Indians of the western plains and as industrialization was ushering Americans into a Gilded Age. The history of this town, then, is all of those histories.

But in other ways, this book is also about us—four women who embarked together on a journey to bring history to the public, first in podcast form, and now (unexpectedly) in book form. We are all feminists, historians, and friends, and that carries us through the ways we are different. Christian or agnostic or atheist; parent or not; humanist or misanthrope; introvert or extrovert; western New Yorker or Vermonter or Texan. The threads of ourselves that we've woven into our teamwork and into this book may surface now and again, as they do when we're riffing and laughing on our podcast episodes. We hope that was what you were looking for when you picked up this book, but if not, welcome to you anyway. We're Averill Earls, Sarah Handley-Cousins, Marissa C. Rhodes, and Elizabeth Garner Masarik, and we are your historians for this story of Lily Dale, New York.

1

Welcome to Lily Dale

Sarah

As we rolled up to a little white gatehouse at the entrance to Lily Dale, the town looked like any other small campground. I had seen dozens of similar camps over the course of my life growing up on the shores of Lake Ontario. The lakeshore was littered with the places, slightly run-down campsites that served the summer people—or "uproms," as my dad called them, his slang for "up from," the phrase inevitably uttered when someone asked a visiting downstater where they were from. Even the metal entry gate, decorated with a large blue banner-style sign declaring the camp the "Lily Dale Assembly," didn't seem all that unusual. After all, I had grown up situated between a marina that styled itself Shangri-La and an evangelical Christian retreat center called The Braes, both with similarly exuberant names and entry gates. And like those camps, Lily Dale is situated next to the Cassadaga Lakes, a string of small, interconnected lakes in western New York's Southern Tier. The place looks like any other lakeside town in the state—gas stations full of trucks towing boats, seasonal businesses, little cottages built on the water's edge.

But as we paid the fee and made our way through the gate, I knew that, even though at first glance it may have seemed familiar, Lily Dale was very different. That blue sign on the gate, for instance, didn't just declare the town's name. In smaller text, the sign proclaims that Lily Dale is "the world's largest center for the religion of Spiritualism." Lily Dale isn't any old lakeside camp. It's a gated intentional community dedicated to the study and practice of Spiritualism, which blends many facets of world religions around the central principle of "continuous life," or the belief that the "existence and personality of the dead continue after the change called death."[1] It is also based on the foundational belief that humans have the capacity to communicate with the dead. According to Spiritualist belief, the spirits of the dead do not travel to some distant cosmic paradise, nor do they disappear entirely. Instead, as one practitioner described it to me, Spiritualists believe that the dead have simply stepped into the next room, out of sight, but not out of earshot. And, using the right tools, we can still talk with them.

That was why my mom and I were driving into the little village. My younger brother Michael died suddenly in the summer of 2008, and—trying to find a way out from the leaden blanket of grief—my mom had begun exploring the world of Spiritualism. It started when my aunt took her to see a trusted medium for a reading. That first reading was profound, and in short order, Spiritualism became a part of my family's experience of grief. We talked about spirituality until the wee hours of the morning, fueled by red wine and menthol cigarettes. (Don't worry, we've all quit now!) In one of these conversations, someone mentioned Lily Dale, and when we learned it was just a short drive from Buffalo, my mom and I decided to take a weekend trip to explore. I was apprehensive. Never as comfortable discussing emotions or spirituality as my mom, and far more skeptical about the idea of talking to ghosts, I found myself distancing myself by processing the experience as a historian. During that first visit, I had just finished work on a master's degree in history and was still reeling from a rejection from the doctoral program I had desperately hoped to get into. (Let's just say I wasn't in a good place.) Although I was unsure whether I had a future as a historian at all, I still thought like one. Spiritualism is, if nothing else, a *feeling* religion, in which emotions are at the center of nearly every interaction, so perhaps it's because I was so uneasy with the prospect of a weekend spent intensely examining my feelings that

I instead focused on trying to place Lily Dale within what I knew about the history of religion in rural upstate New York.

In many ways, the town seemed unlikely: an isolated intentional community of mediums, psychics, and other spirit practitioners tucked into a wooded grove on the shores of Cassadaga Lake. If it was anything like the rural upstate area I grew up in, the surrounding town of Cassadaga was likely conservative, more comfortable hunting and fishing than consulting spirit guides and tarot cards. Indeed, most of the writing on Lily Dale, ranging from articles in the *New York Times* and *Atlas Obscura* to books and scholarly papers, highlights the fact that the little town seems a little out of place.[2] But despite the fact that it did stand out from the community surrounding it, to my historian's mind, the town's existence actually made a lot of sense. Intentional communities, although somewhat unusual today, were much more commonplace in the nineteenth century, and upstate New York, smoke still rising from the famed religious revival circuit known as the Burned Over District, had been a hotbed of religious experimentation. In that context, it's actually completely natural that Lily Dale should be located in this quiet forested corner of western New York. What was actually remarkable was that it was still there.

In his early history of Lily Dale, writer (and likely member) Josh Ramsdell described the campgrounds of the Cassadaga Lake Free Association—one of the earlier names of what is now called the Lily Dale Assembly—not simply as a lovely lakeside getaway but as untouched wilderness, tamed only by the hands of its Spiritualist founders. The grounds of Cassadaga "were in the heart of the virgin forest," he wrote, waxing poetic, where "the squirrels chattered among the branches and the birds hardly paused in their song to harken to the strange sound of a man's merry making." And like the frontiering generations of Americans who had turned such "virgin wilderness" into an industrious young nation, Ramsdell turned the founders of Lily Dale into pioneers: "As the rough marble under the sculptor's skillful fingers, takes form and comes forth a finished ideal," he wrote, "so this wild and tangled forest, under the less elegant but no less effective stroke of the ax and scythe, wielded by hands whose aim was success and who had determined to have a place in which to worship in their own peculiar way, made the forest a park, the wilderness a dwelling place, out of chaos—order."[3] Indeed, Lily Dale residents still think of their founders as trailblazers akin to the early American settlers. Lily Dale archivist and historian Ron Nagy has also referred to the earliest founders as "sturdy pioneers" in his work.[4]

While Lily Dale's setting is incredibly lovely to this day, situated in a thick wood alongside one of New York's many beautiful lakes, it was not exactly carved out of virgin wilderness. The land wasn't remote or recently discovered but had belonged to a local farmer and Spiritualist, Willard Alden, who had allowed the Spiritualists of surrounding Chautauqua County to use it for their summertime gatherings. But more important than such details is the use of the term "virgin wilderness," suggesting

Figure 6. Illustrated cover of the first history of the Cassadaga Lake Free Association, written by Josh D. Ramsdell in 1889. The Association would later change its name to Lily Dale. Lily Dale Museum.

a new frontier, untouched by human hands. The land had been occupied and manipulated for many centuries, of course, by the Erie and later the Haudenosaunee peoples, who cleared the underbrush of the forests to facilitate hunting—but more on the Native American influence at Lily Dale later.[5] The language of pioneers, though, is part of a larger trend: in the latter half of the nineteenth century, in the midst of rapid industrialization, and as the nation celebrated its centennial, Americans were prone to reminding themselves that they were a people capable of pushing up their sleeves and doing the honest hard work of clearing new ground, literally and figuratively. The historian Laurel Thatcher Ulrich has called this the "mystique of the age of homespun," when Americans idealized and idolized the colonial era, when men cleared the land by hand and women produced the family's clothing on the loom.[6] The key is that it was largely nostalgic fiction.

By referring to the founders of the community as pioneers, Ramsdell was creating a past for Lily Dale that mirrored this humbly heroic vision of American history. The founders weren't just members of an organization creating a camp where they could gather with like-minded folks, but pilgrims exploring and taming a new frontier. But while the members of the Cassadaga Lake Free Association certainly did have to fell logs and clear underbrush to found the hamlet now called Lily Dale, it's more accurate to say that these founders were continuing a long tradition in New York State rather than breaking new ground. Western New York was the hub of religious revivalism during the nineteenth century, as well as home to the transportation and marketplace revolutions of the time.[7] This was a region where people founded new religions and built communities based on shared beliefs and ideals. Lily Dale, in that sense, fits right in.

To really situate the founding of Lily Dale, then, we need to zoom way out and explore why it was New York, and not some corner of Vermont or Ohio, that became "the world's largest center for the religion of Spiritualism." Within a decade of its founding, Spiritualism spanned the United States, Canada, Europe, and Australia, making it a truly international faith system—but its roots were firmly planted in the Empire State. No one is entirely sure where that nickname came from, but it does seem fitting. Its colonial ownership shifted between the Dutch and the English, two of the expansive European empire builders during the seventeenth and eighteenth centuries, and the region was also originally dominated by arguably the most powerful Native American empire of the era, the Haudenosaunee. The five tribes of Haudenosaunee people made up the Six Nations of the Iroquois Confederacy: the Mohawk, Seneca, Cayuga, Onondaga, and Oneida. (The Tuscarora, another Iroquoian-speaking tribe that migrated up from the Carolinas, joined the Confederacy in 1722.) The Haudenosaunee were formidable players in the imperialist wars of the colonial era, vying for control of the fur trade during the Beaver Wars against the French, the Huron, and the Algonquins, as well as other smaller tribes. By the late seventeenth century, the Confederacy commanded what was then called the New Netherland territory, as well as the Ohio River Valley and most of inland New England. In the late seventeenth century, when the colony became New York, the Iroquois allied themselves with the British. While this alliance did help bring about a British victory in the French and Indian War, the conflict weakened the unity of the Confederacy and resulted in a treaty that ceded Iroquois territories in Ohio to the Crown.[8]

The cracks in the Iroquois Confederacy became fractures during the American Revolution. The war posed a problem for the Six Nations, who had important trade relationships with both the British and the colonists. Ultimately, each nation decided for itself how to align: the Oneida and Tuscarora with the colonists, and the Mohawk, Seneca, Cayuga, and Onondaga with the British. After the Seneca war chief Cornplanter attacked an American fort in the Mohawk Valley, Americans began to see all of the Haudenosaunee as a threat. In 1779 George Washington tasked Generals John Sullivan and James Clinton with destroying the Haudenosaunee in a campaign that would start in central New York and end by taking British-held Fort Niagara. While the Americans never succeeded in seizing the fort, the Sullivan–Clinton campaign certainly met its objective of devastating the Haudenosaunee. Sullivan, Clinton, and their troops burned villages, destroyed crops, and turned the Haudenosaunee into refugees.[9] The United States government seized most of the Iroquois' homeland in upstate New York, and what land they retained was chipped away as Governor George Clinton encouraged them to sell to settlers or the state through the end of the eighteenth century.

Though the former Haudenosaunee territory was prime farming land, settlement by whites was slow. The state had no east–west rivers to facilitate travel, making the trek from the populated regions in the eastern part of the state to the prime farmland in central and western New York a long and arduous journey. Most early white settlement of central New York happened as Pennsylvanians moved north, using the Susquehanna River to establish farms and orchards in the Finger Lakes region. Slowly, New Englanders spread westward. Yankees from Massachusetts and Connecticut moved across the Hudson and into the Mohawk Valley, while Vermonters made their way around the Adirondack Mountains to settle the shores of the St. Lawrence River and Lake Ontario. Eventually, migrating New Englanders began to congregate in the Genesee River Valley, just west of the Finger Lakes.[10]

This area, commandeered from the Seneca for settlement by Revolutionary War veterans, was understood to be the most fertile ground in the state. The Yankee settlers in the Genesee River Valley tended to migrate in large family units to start their orchards and small farms, and occasionally even whole villages pulled up stakes and moved into the region, meaning that migrants often reconstructed their former communities, complete with customs and beliefs, in their new home. Despite its great farming soil, settlement in the Genesee Valley and points west was fairly small in the first quarter of the century. Population growth was slow for the same reason it had taken decades for the area to be settled in the first place: the state is wide, with no way across its east–west expanse except dirt roads using literal horsepower. The arduous journey didn't just slow down migration but also hampered economic development. Farmers and small businesses, such as flour mills, were limited in what they could produce for sale because of the huge expense of transporting their goods to the lucrative markets of larger cities like New York, Philadelphia, and Boston. Rochester (known colloquially as the "Flour City"), for instance, quickly established grain mills, powered by the mighty waterfalls of the Genesee River. But the only way to sell the flour in any quantity (other than selling it back to the wheat farmers in the countryside and folks in the city) was to load it on ships and perilously sail it across Lake Ontario, then up the St. Lawrence River to Montreal, all while hoping that the wheat farmers in Ontario and Quebec hadn't already saturated the market.[11]

But then came the canal. Begun in 1817, the "ditch" that was eventually named the Erie Canal radically transformed upstate New York. Based on a Haudenosaunee trail that had long connected the Hudson River and

Lake Erie, the canal was proposed in 1806 and would span some 363 miles across the state, with a natural southern extension, the Hudson, effectively connecting Buffalo—and the Great Lakes beyond—to New York City.[12] The ambitious plan seemed foolhardy to many, including President Thomas Jefferson, who declared that the scheme was "little short of madness."[13] Unsurprisingly, it took over a decade for the canal's main booster, Governor DeWitt Clinton, to secure the political support and funding needed to tackle the enormous project. Work on the canal officially began on July 4, 1817, in Rome, New York, with laborers digging the ditch more or less by hand. In 1825 the completed canal was opened with a truly extravagant celebration, with cannons set up along the entire length of the canal fired sequentially from Buffalo to the Atlantic Ocean and back again. The chain of explosions took over three hours to complete. As the first cannons began firing in western New York, Governor Clinton boarded a barge and traveled the entire length of the canal, a trip that took nine days. When he arrived in New York Harbor, he emptied a barrel of fresh water drawn from Lake Erie into the Atlantic, thereby "wedding the waters."[14] This inaugural trip was not particularly speedy by modern standards, but in the words of the historian Daniel Walker Howe, it represented the "first step in a transportation revolution."[15]

During 1826, just a year later, around seven thousand boats traveled the canal, and annual tolls were bringing in more than five times the interest due on the state's canal-related debts.[16] The state's economy boomed, and the formerly inconsequential towns that dotted the canal began to grow. Buffalo, which Clinton once described as containing "five lawyers and no church," expanded from 2,600 residents in 1824 to 42,000 in 1850.[17] Rochester, which was a small and industrious village of 1,600 in 1821, grew into a small and *very* industrious city of over twenty thousand within a decade.[18] New towns sprouted along the canal seemingly overnight. According to the historian Peter Bernstein, at least ten new towns suddenly appeared between Syracuse and Buffalo, all with the word "port" in their names. (Many are still there! The biggest is Lockport, but there's also Port Byron, Weedsport, Spencerport, Middleport, and Brockport, where Elizabeth teaches.) Within a few decades, as the canal made it possible for products from the Midwest to travel to New York City, it spurred the growth of other cities along the Great Lakes such as Cleveland, Detroit, and Chicago. The stretch of New York State that Thomas

Jefferson once considered wilderness was now a bustling line of steadily growing towns and small cities, centered on a corridor that transformed not only New York but the young nation as well.

The canal also facilitated a unique religious culture in central and western New York, the same culture that would eventually spark Spiritualism and provide it a permanent home in Lily Dale. Of the migrants who moved (laboriously in the decades before the canal) to western and central New York, many were the young sons and daughters of New England farming families with too little land to subdivide into inheritance plots. The fertile stolen lands of the Haudenosaunee offered a fresh start. The newcomers' formative years in New England gave them not only an education in working the land but also a unique religious upbringing, one that would change the social and cultural landscape of New York State.

The emigrant New Englanders who made their way to western New York were the children of a turbulent religious culture. The old Congregational Church, heir of the Puritan founders of New England, had been rocked by the First Great Awakening of the mid-eighteenth century, a wave of fervent religious revival. The old-school religious establishment was increasingly allowing the children of church members to join the church without demonstrating their personal salvation, while a new wave of believers felt the church was lowering its standards. This upstart group, called "New Lights," placed emphasis on personal conversions—intense, emotional spiritual experiences that often took place at outdoor revival meetings—to qualify for church membership. These rustic gatherings were often called "camp meetings," a tradition that would continue through the nineteenth century and eventually be picked up much later by the founders of Lily Dale. This revivalism was also marked by a new fervor in worship as folks from miles around would flock to listen to a preacher, such as superstars like George Whitefield and Jonathan Edwards, deliver fire-and-brimstone sermons about sin and salvation.[19]

While this First Great Awakening lost some of its intensity after the middle of the eighteenth century, it continued to spark revivals through the Revolution in some places—specifically in Vermont. As the historian Whitney Cross notes, a young Vermonter "could hardly have escaped at least one such revival, whether he left his hillside home or valley hamlet as early as 1795 or as late as 1824."[20] This unique religiosity moved with the many Vermonters who migrated to central and western New

York. (From our experience with our resident Vermonter, Averill, we tend to agree that those folks are indeed unique.) Free from the social constraints about denomination and family churches that existed back home in New England, and influenced by the revivalism of their youth, western New Yorkers were willing to switch allegiances from one denomination or preacher to another on a whim. When a new preacher arrived in the region from back home, settlers might flock to him (or, in a few cases, her) only to move on when the next interesting camp meeting took place. The state was awash in waves of religious fervor. While we often think about revivalism starting sometime in the 1820s—during the "Second" Great Awakening—New York actually saw small but nearly continuous revivals for decades before that.

But it wasn't just mainline Christian denominations that found fertile ground in New York. This unique religious culture made the state ripe for radical religion. For example, when Mother Ann Lee, one of the founders of the Shaker faith, immigrated to America in 1774, she and a small number of followers eventually settled in Watervliet, just north of Albany. While the religion was first conceived in England, it was in New York that it took shape and grew.[21] Within a couple of years, Lee and her followers moved to New Lebanon, closer to the Massachusetts border, and offshoot settlements cropped up across the American frontier from New England to Kentucky. Only one settlement was established in western New York, on an inlet of Lake Ontario called Sodus Bay, just east of Rochester. Shakerism was centered on the belief that God was both male and female. As Jesus Christ was God's male embodiment, the Shakers believed, so Mother Ann was God's female manifestation. The Shakers believed in equality of the sexes, and adhered strictly to codes of celibacy, hard work, and perfectionism.[22] The Sodus Bay settlement did not last long before being folded into another utopian community. Despite its rules of celibacy for all members, the Shaker faith carries on, though just two Shakers are alive as I write this.[23]

The story of the Public Universal Friend is an even better example of the role of radical religion in New York. In 1788, followers of the Public Universal Friend, a prophet and spiritual leader whom adherents believed to be the embodiment of Jesus Christ, settled on a sliver of land in the Genesee River Valley. The Friend was born Jemima Wilkinson in 1756 in Cumberland, Rhode Island. In 1776, in the chaotic early days of the

American Revolution and just after three of their siblings were excommunicated from the Quaker church (two brothers were forced out for joining the Continental Army, and a sister for conceiving a child out of wedlock), Wilkinson became severely ill. Somewhat miraculously, Wilkinson recovered.[24] Wilkinson reported that "Jemima" had died and her soul had gone to heaven; what was left was a new spirit named the Public Universal Friend.[25] The Friend began to preach locally, gradually gathering followers throughout New England and Pennsylvania. The group established the township of Jerusalem, near Keuka Lake, one of the Finger Lakes. The inhabitants of Jerusalem had unconventional views on gender.[26] Many women were heads of household, and there were an unusual number of unmarried adult men, who lived with the Friend or in the homes of those female heads of household. Household and other labor was not divided along gender lines. The Friend is the best example of this: assigned female at birth, they later identified as genderless. Ultimately, the society's nonnormative gender conventions spelled the end of Jerusalem. The community was plagued with internal dissension, led by angry men who resented the Friend's landholdings, which fractured the society and contributed to already shrinking numbers.[27] After the Friend's death in 1819, the society dwindled, and by the eve of the Civil War had died out completely. The Friend's utopian Jerusalem was short-lived, but it still foreshadowed what was to come in upstate New York during the first half of the nineteenth century.

While the Shakers and the Society of Universal Friends were examples of how the New York frontier appealed to experimental religions, most western New Yorkers during the early 1800s were not drawn to the most radical sects. People were nominally Protestant and attended church, but they often were not members of a particular church or denomination. At the same time, canal construction created large populations of rowdy, often itinerant laborers. Even after the canal opened, travelers and boatmen filled taverns and indulged in decidedly un-genteel behavior. Between the low church membership and the drifting, hard-drinking population, the result was a perception—held mostly by outsiders—that the region was an uncivilized wasteland full of heathens in dire need of salvation. One report from 1827 declared that there were five towns in Niagara County that had no churches at all, but a closer look reveals two full-time pastors in the area and dozens of church services available. Nevertheless, the perception of a godless frontier fueled a campaign led by missionary groups, particularly the American Home Missionary Society, to funnel money and church planters to this wilderness. The result was an overabundance of churches and preachers in communities too small to support them. Ministers, desperate to keep their new churches afloat, turned to a combination of sectarian division and charismatic preaching to hold on to congregants. In turn, churchgoers learned to listen and be persuaded by a particularly effective preacher—yet another reason western New York was so receptive to the religious revival that began to intensify across the United States after 1820.[28]

The man who best exemplified the Protestant revivalism of the Second Great Awakening was Charles Grandison Finney. Finney, born in Connecticut, had moved with his family to Henderson, New York, as a child. In October 1821, in the midst of a spiritual crisis, Finney walked out into the woods north of Adams and, while praying, had a vision of bright light streaming out around excerpts from scripture. He felt God's presence. "I never can," he wrote in his memoirs, "in words, make any human being understand how precious and true those promises appeared to me."[29] That same year, Finney began studying to enter the Presbyterian ministry, and by 1824 he was traveling Jefferson County spreading the message of conversion. Sponsored by a women's missionary society headquartered in Utica, Finney and his proselytizing companion Daniel Nash journeyed around the North Country and the Mohawk Valley preaching. While we know that New York was already primed for revivalism, Finney and Nash's preaching during that decade seemed to have, at the very least, kicked things up a notch. The historian Whitney Cross estimated that around three thousand people were converted during this tour.[30] Word traveled quickly, and Finney became something of an evangelical celebrity. He was soon fielding requests to visit towns all across New York State and Pennsylvania, and spent time preaching in New York City.

In 1830 Finney relocated to Rochester. The city already had a religious presence, boasting two handsome stone churches in a downtown square and an ostensibly genteel middle class. But the arrival of the canal and recent economic prosperity had also spurred a boom in vice.[31] The growing blue-collar population flooded the city's new "dramshops, gambling dens, groceries, billiard rooms," and the canal brought in a transient population of "gamblers, pickpockets, prostitutes, confidence men, and a parade of show people."³² Finney was more than up to the task of bringing Rochester to Jesus. Indeed, Whitney Cross confidently declared that "no more impressive revival has occurred in American history."³³ Citizens from every denomination gathered to listen to him preach, mesmerized by his resonant voice and persuasive, lawyerly sermons. If Finney's first revival through the Mohawk Valley and North Country had raised his profile, Rochester made him the most famous preacher in the United States. More importantly, Finney helped to kick off the religious revivalism known as the Second Great Awakening, as preachers crisscrossed New York State spreading the good news, often following the canal but also venturing beyond it. Soon, revivals were taking place all over the young United States, in both rural and urban settings, and drawing crowds of white, Black, and Native American converts.³⁴ But it was the revivalism along the Erie Canal that inspired the nickname "the Burned Over District," suggesting that western New York was literally smoldering with the fires of religious fervor.³⁵

Protestant Christian revivalism spread all across the United States, but what was happening in New York State was different. New takes on Christianity, and even entirely new faiths, developed in the midst of the revivalist fervor that gripped the region—and many of them became major forces in the United States through the nineteenth century and remain significant today. Millerism, sparked by William Miller, is an illustrative example. Miller was yet another Yankee transplant to New York who came to espouse and preach radical new beliefs. Miller converted during a revival in 1816 and became obsessed with closely reading and interpreting the Bible. After much independent analysis, he concluded that the text indicated Jesus was returning, not at some unknowable time in the future, but very soon, on October 22, 1844. On the eve of Christ's return, Millerites shuttered their shops with signs indicating that they were closed "in honor of the King of Kings, who will appear about the 23rd of October." Some of Miller's disciples recommended that followers divest themselves of earthly possessions to prepare for the apocalypse.³⁶ But then the October date came and went with no Jesus appearance. Miller received scathing criticism, and the Millerite faith splintered; while some followers remained true to the faith, most left.³⁷

Even without a cameo from Jesus, Miller's "great disappointment" illustrates so much about this period of revival in New York State. First, it shows that there was a population that was ready and willing not just to listen to a new prophet, even one with fairly radical teachings, but to fling themselves wholeheartedly onto the bandwagon. And while the Millerites might have been disappointed in 1844, those who stuck around ended up founding a new wing of American Protestant Christianity known as Adventism, including the modern Seventh-day Adventist Church. It wasn't just the Millerites who rapidly gained adherents or who had sticking power. Another, maybe even more powerful example is Mormonism, which also emerged from the area. Like Millerism, Mormonism was grounded in the familiar precepts of Protestant Christianity but with new and exciting elements. And also, like Millerism, it grew quickly, and though it faced serious setbacks, found a permanent place in American religious culture.

The prophet of Mormonism, Joseph Smith, was born in Vermont to a religious family that had resettled in Palmyra, another small village east of Rochester. The town was home to several churches and hosted numerous revivals, but young Joseph Smith struggled to find a religion that called to him. According to the official story, Smith experienced a vision of God and Jesus in the woods, followed by several visitations from a heavenly being named Moroni several times over the 1820s. After a number of visits, Moroni shared a message that important revelations from God were recorded on golden tablets buried in a nearby hill.[38] This fit into Smith's worldview: it was a common belief in upstate New York that Spanish conquistadors and pirates had buried treasure all over America and it was only a matter of time before lucky searchers would find them. Smith and his father were well known for exploring the woods and hills around Palmyra using divining rods or seer stones to lead them to treasures.[39] Guided by faith, Smith later dug up a box containing the gold plates, along with other sacred objects, from the hill that would become known as Hill Cumorah.[40] While the Burned Over District may have been fertile ground for new and different belief systems to emerge, not all inhabitants were ready to accept all faiths equally. Within a few months, Smith's new faith had grown enough to attract both positive and negative attention.[41] Locals skeptical of Mormon teachings began to give the group a hard time.[42] While some Mormon missionaries joined the flocks of evangelists burning paths across New York State, by the summer of 1831, the majority of Mormons had picked up stakes and moved into Ohio.[43]

The region's atmosphere of religious experimentation also fostered other kinds of radicalism that foreshadowed elements of Lily Dale's culture. Much of the revivalism of the Second Great Awakening hinged on the Protestant belief in millennialism: a theological belief that human beings could help usher in the Second Coming of Christ and a thousand-year reign of peace by eradicating sin and perfecting humankind. Pumped up by revivals, many Christians now wanted to bring about that hoped-for millennium by cleaning up society. This helped transfer the energy of revivalism into the broader culture as Christians mobilized to combat sinfulness. Concerned that the canal was facilitating sin, residents of Palmyra founded a Society for the Suppression of Vice in 1823, for example, and citizens of Rochester and Utica started organizations dedicated to stopping all canal use on Sundays.[44] The effort for reform also went beyond individual vices toward rectifying structural sins within American society, such as slavery and injustice. Abolitionism, in particular, found a home in upstate New York. The Liberty Party, a minor political splinter group of the American Abolitionist Society, was founded in Warsaw, New York, and held its convention in Buffalo in 1843. That same year, Black abolitionists held the National Convention of Colored Citizens in Buffalo. Harriet Tubman and Frederick Douglass, who both escaped enslavement in southern states, found homes in the region—Douglass in Rochester and Tubman in Auburn. Abolitionism, in turn, helped to inspire other radical political movements: in 1848, frustrated with their treatment within the abolitionist movement, women gathered at Seneca Falls to hold the first women's rights convention.

New Yorkers also experimented with other ways to structurally reform American society. Not far from both the home places of Mormonism, two small intentional communities attempted to live out the teachings of Charles Fourier, a French philosopher who proposed a better way of organizing society using communal living and shared labor. One explicitly Fourierian society was founded (and very quickly folded) in Sodus Bay, occupying the farm complex built by the Shakers. Farther to the east, another Fourier-inspired society was founded in Skaneateles. The most well-known utopian community in upstate New York was Oneida, the communal society led by John Humphrey Noyes. Not only did the Oneidans live and work communally, but also they envisioned a radically different way of living that included gender equality, complex marriage, free love, proto-eugenic reproduction, and communal parenting.[45] The founding of the Cassadaga Lake Free Association in 1879 marked the tail end of these movements, but it proved to have much more staying power than most other nineteenth-century utopian communities.

Still smoking with the fires of revival and reeling from the rapid change of the canal days, this home of religious and political radicals, free lovers, and feminists brought forth one more radical faith: Spiritualism.[46] In 1848 two young girls, Maggie and Kate Fox, living in the tiny hamlet of Hydesville halfway between Syracuse and Rochester, were troubled by mysterious knocking in their modest rural home while they tried to sleep. Before long, they determined that the rappings were an attempt by ghostly spirits to communicate from beyond the grave—and the girls had the ability to understand them. We'll discuss the Fox sisters much more extensively in later chapters and explore the way their lives were shaped by their mediumship and later shattered by their fame, alcoholism, and accusations of fraud. But their experience at their tiny home in Hydesville started a broad and accessible religious movement. As the historian Robert Cox explains, in the Fox sisters' New York, "neither spirits nor specters were a rarity: there were Ichabod Cranes enough to populate any number of sleepy hamlets and seers and seekers like Jemima Wilkinson were just as familiar."[47] In New York's other radical religions, seers like Wilkinson, Smith, and Miller had been singular figures who gathered a faithful following. But the Fox sisters did not become the charismatic leaders of a religion. Instead, they inspired others to follow in their footsteps, setting off a faith practice in which each individual was equally able to communicate with Spirit. The people in Maggie and Kate's immediate circle, including their older sister Leah, soon began to interpret the knockings, then experiment with their own methods of spirit communication. "Discoveries of such latent psychic sensitivities became an important part of the lore of Spiritualists," Cox writes, "who maintained that while some might be more innately capable than others, mediumship was available to all who openly inquired."[48]

Thanks to the support of people like Isaac and Amy Post, the Hydesville rappings kicked off a national fascination with spirit communication as Maggie and Kate traveled, first to Rochester, then around New York State, then around the country, demonstrating their talent for speaking with the dead. Their success was facilitated by the conditions that made New York ripe for religious revivalism, but also by the disaffected Quakers of New York State. Quakers were at the core of numerous social reform movements in the nineteenth century. For several decades before the Hydesville raps, the Religious Society of Friends was rattled by the Second Great Awakening and by the preaching of Elias Hicks. Hicks emphasized Inner Light over scripture, rejecting the authority of ministers and elders, and attracted followers interested in liberal theology and social practices. In the 1820s, the Quakers split into the Hicksites and the "Orthodox" Friends. Nevertheless, the schism didn't stabilize the Religious Society of Friends, and Quakers formed smaller and smaller groups, often in conjunction with abolition efforts and other major social reform movements.[49]

The Posts were Quakers, but, as the historian Ann Braude notes, they were among the many who left the Society in search of "greater freedom of conscience on political issues."[50] They used their connections, which spanned Quaker communities all over New York and the mid-Atlantic states, to introduce the Fox girls and Spiritualism to a rapt audience. Many Quakers ultimately converted to Spiritualism. The beliefs that imbued the medium with religious authority resonated with Quaker theology. Quakers like the Posts believed that all humans have an "Inner Light," and Amy Post understood the Fox sisters' manifestations as an extension of that light.[51]

The Fox sisters were not unlike Charles Grandison Finney as evangelists for spirit communication. For instance, after they visited Cincinnati in 1851, some 1,200 people began advertising their services as mediums. Further, their mediumship quickly became linked to the radical politics of the mid-nineteenth century through their family friends the Posts. Isaac and Amy Post, the Fox sisters' first converts, were also prominent political activists in Rochester. They harbored fugitives escaping through the Underground Railroad, were friends of Frederick Douglass's, and were deeply involved in abolitionism. Amy Post was also an early feminist, and was present at the 1848 Seneca Falls women's rights convention.[52] Through their connections, the rappings that seemed to follow the Fox girls were elevated into something much more than an eccentric news story: an exciting new way of understanding the world in a time of activism, reform, and change.

The Hydesville rappings also touched off a grassroots movement that gathered up and welcomed all sorts of philosophies. The Fox sisters' experience, well publicized, demonstrated, and investigated around the United

States in the following months and years, made existing radical religious thinking both more popular and more accessible. For example, their communication with Spirit resonated for those already interested in the eighteenth-century philosopher Emanuel Swedenborg, who had argued that there were worlds beyond human sensory perception and ability to understand. By studying and expanding one's consciousness, Swedenborg suggested, humans could make contact with those other realms. The rappings also intersected with the work of Andrew Jackson Davis, a fellow New Yorker, prolific writer, and contemporary of the Fox sisters, a clairvoyant and spirit healer. But beyond simply talking to the dead, Davis also pioneered a grander theory of Spiritualism which suggested that the human consciousness had an inherent connection with the universe. This connection allowed for spirit communication as well as other forms of psychic work. Davis insisted, as did many in his footsteps, that Spiritualism was scientifically sound, encouraging Spiritualists to try out "the spirits against the rigors of scientific logic."[53] When a curious individual heard about the mysterious rappings or watched a compelling séance led by the Fox sisters, there was a wealth of literature to turn to in order to learn more about spirit worlds. "It cannot be questioned," wrote the English Spiritualist Emma Hardinge Britten in 1872, "that the rumor of the Rochester investigations, the visits of the mediums to its different towns, combined with the powerful effect which the phenomenal career of A. J. Davis produced, contributed to fill up the overflowing measure of spiritual life which has specially distinguished [New York] State."[54]

The Spiritualist movement didn't exactly coalesce into a formalized religion, but it did grow rapidly, particularly in the wake of the Civil War. The war, Britten argued, had been bitter, and the overwhelming scale of death drove heartsick Americans to Spiritualism. By the early 1870s, she saw the Fox sisters as the embattled prophets of an enormous groundswell:

> The rough and ragged path which the bleeding feet of the Hydesville mediums seemed doomed to tread . . . has now loomed out into the splendid proportions of the bridge which arches over the awful chasm of the grave, affording a transit for millions of aspiring souls into the glorious realities of eternity, and erecting a telegraph whereby legions of enfranchised spirits can transit their messages of undying affection or their glad tidings of immortal life and eternal progress.[55]

The closing chapters of Britten's history of Spiritualism, published in 1872, suggest a faith that, while still in its early decades, was thriving. Spiritualist newspapers such as *The Banner of Light* enjoyed huge readership, Sunday worship and spirit circles were well attended across the Northeast and Midwest, and new Spiritualist societies were established. "There is nothing more remarkable . . . in the whole spiritual movement," Britten reflected, "than the vast numbers which have joined the ranks of an army whose leaders are of the humblest and whose legion scarcely realize the meaning of discipline or the ordinary methods of essential action."[56] If people were flocking to the faith, as nebulous and half-formed as it might have been in its early days, she suggested, there had to be something real at its heart.

As the faith grew after the Civil War, Spiritualists began to find ways to gather. In cities, they held regular meetings and Sunday services, but they also turned to an old American religious tradition: the camp meeting. Camp meetings—temporary outdoor gatherings where people could listen to an itinerant preacher on a revival circuit—were a major part of the revivalism of the Second Great Awakening. The tradition was adapted from Protestant Christian "communion seasons" or "holy fairs," common in Scotland and England, typically a week-long celebration that culminated in a communion dinner.[57] As the nineteenth century wore on, camp meetings continued to be a major feature of American Protestantism—particularly for Methodists—but their nature shifted. Instead of temporary gatherings, they started to become real summer camps. According to the historian Samuel Avery-Quinn, "Associations or managing boards of Methodist ministers and pious laity acting as holy land companies purchased dozens to hundreds of forested acres, often along a railroad line, surveyed a few hundred lots on which Methodists could buy leases, build cottages, and thus help fund summer revivals."[58] American Second Great Awakening religious movements employed camp meetings to build community.

Within a decade of the Fox sisters' revelations at Hydesville, Spiritualists were able to draw two thousand attendees to a camp meeting in Waukegan, Illinois, and camp meetings became more common as Spiritualism gained in popularity after the Civil War.[59] By 1884 Britten could write that there were two features of American Spiritualism that could be considered "American Institutions": the Hydesville rappings and summer camp meetings.[60] Held in Massachusetts in 1866, Pierpont Grove, which many consider the first real Spiritualist camp meeting, was not incidentally planned by former Methodists who had converted to Spiritualism.[61] Pierpont Grove was small and makeshift, with a speaker's stage the only permanent structure. An official caterer set up a large tent to sell food and camping supplies. During three two-hour blocks, campers attended "volunteer speeches, experiences, narration of facts, singing and devotional exercises."[62] According to *The Banner of Light*, so many people attended one evening session that there weren't enough seats, and visitors had to stand around the speaker's dais.[63] Two Massachusetts camps founded in the early 1870s were most similar to the format Lily Dale would later use. Lake Pleasant, founded in western Massachusetts by the Fitchburg Railroad Company to create an attractive vacation and picnic destination accessible by rail, was used by a variety of groups. In August 1874, for instance, Spiritualists had their first two-week camp meeting at Lake Pleasant, which was followed by what was essentially a nineteenth-century music festival.[64] In 1876, Spiritualists at the Lake Pleasant meeting created the Onset Bay Grove Association to begin work on a permanent intentional community on Buzzards Bay near Cape Cod. During Onset's first season in the summer of 1877, Spiritualists had already constructed a dozen cottages so they could spend the summer rather than just a couple of weeks at the camp, as well as a dancing hall and restaurant.[65]

Unlike Protestant Christian camps, which emphasized worship, study, and moral entertainments, Spiritualist camps used popular entertainment specifically to draw in non-Spiritualist visitors. Island Grove, founded in 1869, offered visitors "Dancing, Swinging, Bowling, Boating, etc."[66] A camp in Connecticut built a dance hall that doubled as a roller-skating rink. In the summer of 1880, the Onset Bay Spiritualists held "gala days," including a regatta where attendees could take a boat ride on the bay while listening to a brass band, then enjoy a clambake.[67] Britten described what she considered a typical Spiritualist camp day this way:

> From the first peep of day, the campers are astir, lighting gipsy fires, preparing breakfast, and trading with the various hawkers who ply with their provisions regularly through the white-tented streets. After the morning meal, visits are exchanged, and the business of the day proceeds with as much energy and order as in the cities. Sailing parties, séances, amusements, and

business, all proceed in due course, until the hour for speaking arrives, when thousands assemble at the speaker's stand, to partake of the solid intellectual refinement of the day. Lectures, balls, parties, illuminations, public discussions, &tc, &tc, fill up the time until midnight, when the white tents enclose the slumbering hosts; the fires and lamps are extinguished, and the pale moonbeam shines over rocks, groves, and lakes, illuminating scenes as strange and picturesque as ever the eye of mortal gazed upon.[68]

Nettie Pease Fox, editor of the newspaper *Spiritual Offering*, reasoned that this was what made Spiritualist camps successful, in the pattern of Methodist camps: "Much of the success attending the spreading of Methodism, in its earlier and purer days, may be attributed to the effect of their camp meetings, held on almost every 'circuit.' The Spiritualists of Massachusetts years ago became convinced of their efficacy. . . . Through this instrumentality, our teachings may be scattered broadcast, thousands attend who would not otherwise hear the Gospel of Spiritualism."[69] Camps that combined fun entertainment with lectures and séances helped drive the popularity of the religion, bringing droves of visitors to camps each summer. Britten recalled speaking to a rapt audience of eighteen thousand at Lake Pleasant in 1880, and counted advertisements for twelve different camps happening during that same summer.[70]

Another major part of the appeal of Spiritualist camps was their naturally beautiful locales. Pierpont Grove was located in a private wood between Melrose and Malden, Massachusetts, an area so beautiful, according to the editors of *The Banner of Light*, that it caused visitors to gasp. "The grounds embrace about four acres of thickly studded woodland, composed of every species of forest trees," the newspaper reported, "from the smallest up to giants, reaching their arms more than a hundred feet into the open blue heavens, and glittering sunlight shimmering down through the luxuriant foliage like innumerable angel eyes." The location was integral to the success of the meeting. It was easily accessible by rail from Boston yet provided a "quiet, beautiful, secluded" place for Spiritualists to gather. The natural setting was a major part of how Pierpont Grove's speakers interpreted this first camp meeting experience, arguing that the wooded grove made for an ideal Spiritualist "church." Dr. J. N. Hodges argued that "out in the glorious church of Nature was just the place for a Spiritualist gathering," because "we believe in none but a natural religion. . . . We see God in all his works; and how appropriate that we should assemble here and mingle our voices with the song of birds and music of the rustling foliage."[71]

Time spent in rustic settings wasn't just lovely; late nineteenth-century Americans believed it was restorative to physical and spiritual health. Unsatisfied with posh hotels in pretty settings, and worried about the nervous exhaustion that came along with modernity, middle-class Americans increasingly sought out authentic experiences in the wilderness. In New York State, for instance, this resulted in a boom in travelers to the Adirondacks.[72] Camp meetings held in wilderness settings, then, provided the healing powers of nature along with spiritual sustenance, allowing "our wearied bodies rest by drawing nearer to Nature in her beautiful, leafy temple," according to Nettie Pease Fox.[73] A letter to the editor of *The Banner of Light* reflected that campers went to meetings to escape from the "heat and dust of city life . . . [and] to hold communion with nature and the spirit-world."[74] The healthful properties of the rustic setting were explicitly used in marketing materials for the Onset Bay camp: "Those who seek renewed health can find, regardless of creed, no better place than Onset for a summer vacation, for the air is lifegiving, being impregnated with the healing balm of the pine forests of Plymouth."[75]

It was within this context that the Cassadaga Lake Free Association, a group of Spiritualists from western New York, eastern Ohio, and northwestern Pennsylvania, held their first camp meeting in Chautauqua County, New York, in 1880. The Association had incorporated the year before and purchased twenty acres for the purpose of holding an annual camp on the shores of Cassadaga Lake, about an hour south of Buffalo. Chautauqua County was well known to Spiritualists of the region and had been home to a previous attempt at a Spiritualist intentional community. In 1852, two very early Spiritualists, Oliver Chase and William Brittingham, learned from Spirit that a local spring had healing powers. Further, they claimed that the tiny hamlet the spring was in, called Kiantone, had once been the home of an ancient race of "Celtic Indians"—undoubtedly code for mythical white Indigenous Americans—who practiced free love and lived free of any disease or evil until they were conquered by "semi-barbarians."[76] Just as Joseph Smith believed there was ancient treasure somewhere in the hills of central New York, Chautauqua County Spiritualists believed that these "Celtic Indians" had left behind buried treasure, though expensive and laborious digs to uncover it failed. In 1858, Spiritualists tried to establish an intentional community called Spiritual Springs, founded on free love and centered on the healing waters of the spring at Kiantone, and while some followers did live there for a while, the community ultimately failed. Instead, Spiritualists held small camp meetings, usually single-day affairs, around western New York until the 1870s, when New England's Spiritualist camp meetings like Pierpont Grove, Lake Pleasant, and Onset Bay started drawing huge crowds.

In 1873 Chautauqua County Spiritualists started holding their camp meetings at the rural property of Willard Alden in Laona, New York, but after Alden's death in 1878, a conflict with his heirs inspired the creation of the Cassadaga Lake Free Association to purchase new grounds for a permanent meeting place. In August 1879 the committee bought twenty acres on Upper Cassadaga Lake, and "men, women, and children worked" to clear the land that fall.[77] The camp would double in size within a few years. In early histories of the camp, such as the souvenir history published and sold there in 1889, the members of the Association emphasized the wild beauty of its surroundings.[78] The healing properties of the natural setting and pristine forest are still a major part of the village's identity, suggested by the name of the Forest Healing Temple. (I once had a lovely reiki healing there.)

Initially, Lily Dale was more or less like earlier camps, but it soon started to shift from the traditional camp meeting to something different. Camp meetings had traditionally lasted anywhere from one day to two weeks, but within a couple of summers, Lily Dale had extended the camp to the majority of the summer season. In 1887, Lily Dale held talks and events every day between July 30 and September 4, and by 1899 the season had been extended again, starting in mid-July. Lily Dale historians Ron Nagy and Joyce LaJudice suggest that the season was traditionally not opened in July out of respect for the camp, also called Lily Dale, that was still held on the old Alden grounds during June. With the exception of one- and two-day conferences and meetings, the programming of the camp season didn't begin in June until 1939. Eventually, in 1894 Theodore Alden sold his Lily Dale to Abby Louise Pettengill, including the Alden House tavern, which is now the Leolyn Inn, the only Lily Dale property outside the gates.[79] Tenting grounds remained available for campers—and still are, actually—but Lily Dale quickly transformed from something that

Figure 7. Cassadaga Lake Free Association entrance, 1888. "Places and Spaces" folder, Lily Dale Museum.

looked like a campground to something much more closely resembling a village. *The Banner of Light* reported that by the start of the 1888 season, thirty new cottages had been constructed during the off-season, as well as "a large hall, two stories, with lecture, Lyceum, Library, and reading room."[80] That same year, the Grand Hotel—now known as the Maplewood—installed modern water closets and the camp opened its own Post Office. By the camp's tenth anniversary in 1889, there were one hundred cottages on the grounds.[81]

Twenty years after Lily Dale was carved out of the forest on the shore of Cassadaga Lake, a resident named A. G. Smith wrote to the community's newspaper, *The Sunflower*, to suggest that Lily Dale residents more formally honor the legacy of its founding generation. A tablet placed near the entry gates would immediately draw visitors' attention to the names of the people of the Cassadaga Lake Free Association, who had created Lily Dale as a "labor of love." The camp—now officially a hamlet of Pomfret, New York—had changed so much in the twenty-four years since it was founded. "We well remember the small beginning over on the Alden grounds," he wrote, "where a rough temporary rostrum and a few rough seats constituted furnishings. . . . The few cloth tents that decorated the landscape at that time have long ago disappeared."[82] Over the decades, it evolved from a temporary camp meeting following the tradition of the religious revivalism of the Second Great Awakening to something more formalized, settled, and permanent.

It's true that today, the "camp" is more like a tiny village, but visitors are still immediately met with that sense of its history. The moment I first entered the gate, over a decade ago now, I could feel a deep connection not only to the history of Lily Dale that A. G. Smith wanted to honor but also to the long radical history of my home state. It felt as if all that wild history had culminated, manifesting itself as this little town out of time.

After we got settled and explored Lily Dale's narrow streets, my mom and I went to our first readings, held in the parlor of one of the Victorian houses near the Maplewood Hotel. Like countless seekers before us, as Averill explores in the next chapter, we entered into this private domestic space to try to make contact with the dead

2

Little Victorian Cottages

Averill

On our first visit to Lily Dale all together, we followed our GPS to the guesthouse we'd booked for our stay. Aurora's House of Light and Joy, also known as the Aurora Guest House, at 8 Melrose Park—the first house you see when you pull in through the gates of the town—promised us an entire floor to ourselves, air-conditioning units in all the rooms, and a butterfly garden. We were delighted to discover that the top floor included a little sitting room between the two large bedrooms. We'd have to share two beds among the four of us, but that was no big deal; we'd all shared a bed with one another at some point when we were grad students traveling to conferences on very tight budgets. Traveling cheap becomes a superpower when you're an academic.[1] It was in that sitting room that we stayed up late each night discussing archival finds and our experiences of the day. We spent hours with Ron Nagy at the museum and archive, but also had lunch and dinner at the Lily, walked to the former site of the Fox sisters' home, sat in on the daily messages at the Stump (though the gatherings that week were actually held in the auditorium, because it was too hot and buggy for folks to be out in the mosquito-infested woods), sat down with mediums for individual readings, and took the ghost/history walk. It was a formative first visit, rooted in the history that vibrated through the creaky floorboards of the Aurora Guest House, and in every building of this little town.

To me, Lily Dale is an echo of home, and that echo elicits both warm and uneasy feelings. I love rural areas with quaint, tiny old towns that just spring up in the middle of rolling hills or a forest. That's the kind of place I'm from, and that's the kind of place Lily Dale is. It's definitely a particular type of living. I could never persuade my partner, who also grew up in my small town, to move to a place like Lily Dale. He's too used to the amenities of near-city living after twelve years in the suburbs of Buffalo. As in our hometown in Vermont, in Lily Dale you have to drive thirty-plus minutes to find a decent grocery store, and there are stop signs only because the state mandated them. It's the kind of place where everyone knows everyone else's business, there are decades-old feuds over property lines and shared trees, and if there were children, their parents would feel safe letting them roam the town all day unsupervised. It's also—at least in part because of the gatekeeping—overwhelmingly white and relatively affluent. It shares the former characteristic with many sleepy towns in Vermont, though not the latter. When I was growing up in Vermont, over 50 percent of the kids were on free or reduced lunch, and hidden behind the quaint Victorian-lined main street were dilapidated trailer parks run by slumlords. You're less likely to find those visible signs of poverty in a place like Lily Dale, where house purchases are cash only, many houses are second homes, and the Lily Dale Assembly necessarily invests in appearances.

Staying in one of the homes of Lily Dale is essential to experiencing the town. This was as true in 1902 or 1982 as it is today. Every street of Lily Dale is lined with Victorian houses in various states of repair. Some are tiny two-bedroom cottages, like those you'd see in any lake community. Some are sprawling Victorian mansions, probably intended at their initial building to house visitors and host famous mediums every summer. Today, more than a century later, these houses are where mediums practice and meet clients, where visitors stay in rented rooms, and, of course, where seasonal and year-round residents live. The majority of the houses still standing were built between 1880 and 1920. There are communal public spaces too throughout Lily Dale: the Assembly Hall, the auditorium, the firehouse, the clearing in the forest known as the Stump, the Lily restaurant, and the Sunflower Café. But as one might *not* expect of a Victorian-era intentional community, the private homes of Lily Dale's residents have always played a central role in the public life and demonstration of Spiritualism.

Since the founding of the Spiritualist religious movement, mediums have made private homes into public spaces. Strangers were invited into the inner sanctum of the domestic sphere, the one place in the Victorian era where women were granted some modicum of authority, where women spoke and were heard. Lily Dale's cottages and houses, then, are more than quaint remnants of an architectural moment. They are the heart and soul of the town's religious character.

Situated on about ten acres, Lily Dale has five streets that run north–south, and eleven very short east–west streets. It's surrounded by woods or lakefront on all sides, including a little beach on Cassadaga Lake, and the houses can't be more than ten feet apart on any given street, because the entire town is only about five football fields in length and two football fields in width. And while some houses need a little love and repair—they are over one hundred years old, after all—many have clearly been taken care of. In the 1920s there was a plan drawn up to develop seventy-five acres of the Assembly's land to expand Lily Dale into a significantly larger community, but the Great Depression put the kibosh on that. In a lot of ways, the town hasn't changed all that much in a hundred years. If you look at photographs from the 1910s of Buffalo Avenue or the entrance gates, they appear remarkably similar to the town today. Though there's town water now and Wi-Fi, the streets are still just wide enough for carriages, and the aesthetics are Victorian gingerbread with touches of modern here and there.[2]

In 1895 the town was about half the size it would be by 1903. It started as just Lake Front Drive to the west, along (shockingly) the Cassadaga lakefront, East Street to the (you guessed it) east, with South Street and North Street framing it out, and just First through Fourth Streets in between. Library, Buffalo, and Marion Streets were added and lots meted out by 1902.[3] It is likely that the houses on those streets were completed in that time frame as well, or shortly thereafter.

Though some scholars have suggested that Spiritualism was on the decline at the end of the nineteenth century, the popularity of Lily Dale as a summer destination speaks to the contrary.[4] The earliest Lily Dale summer programs reveal an emphasis on the rejuvenating experience of time spent in the town.[5] In the first half of the twentieth century, the board of directors advertised Lily Dale as an exciting resort town rather than an exclusively religious retreat. It is likely that many of the earliest visitors made the journey for the spectacle more than for religious reasons—not that the two are mutually exclusive. Hereward Carrington, a British-born American psychic investigator, reported in the 1908 *Proceedings of the American Society of Psychical Research* that Lily Dale's summer visitors go "where they can see the most for their admission fee—the most extraordinary phenomena. They want, in fact, to 'get the biggest show for their money,' as one of the old visitors put it." Carrington also pointed out that Lily Dale's visitors were already convinced that the phenomena they were seeing were genuine, and few had any interest in testing or challenging the validity of those demonstrations.[6] Unsurprisingly, then, Lily Dale attracted believers who wanted to experience the phenomenon of the dead communicating with the living in tangible, exciting ways. Because, after 1906, the board often did not allow physical mediumship demonstrations to take place in the shared spaces of the town, the little cottages were regularly the sites of those kinds of séances and demonstrations.

"Physical mediumship" refers to a specific kind of spirit communication involving physical manifestations. At the time, a physical manifestation might have meant a materialization—taking the form of a substance called "ectoplasm" emanating from a medium's body—or a fully formed specter. Physical manifestations also included the use of instruments like the spirit trumpet, through which voices or music might emanate, apparently without the intervention of the medium herself; automatic or slate writing, in which a seemingly blank piece of paper was pressed between two slates and a message appeared via a spirit, or a medium who seemed to be asleep but whose hand was seized by a spirit, who wrote a message on a slate; table tipping, in which spirits might levitate or even spin a table; or any of a variety of nonverbal messages, like raps and knocks, which spirits used to communicate with the living, and for which the Fox sisters were most famous. These physical expressions of spirit communication were often presented by Spiritualists as proof of the afterlife and were also most likely to be scrutinized and tested by skeptics and psychic investigators. Trance mediums might produce physical phenomena, or might only fall into some degree of meditation or trance that would open them to the spirit world; it was in this state that they'd be able to channel messages, or sometimes channel a spirit directly. In other words, the spirit would take over their body and speak directly to the participants in a séance or sitting. There were also mediums who were neither physical nor trance mediums, but who were sensitive to the messages that the dead were trying to push into the world of the living. These mediums were clairaudient, which they described as a feeling or as actually hearing the voices of the dead.

During the camp season, the houses of Lily Dale play an essential role. The Aurora Guest House, where we stayed on that first group trip, built in 1872, is quintessentially Victorian, a white clapboard house with trim in shades of green and pink and a wraparound porch encircling its 2,400 square feet. We discovered later that the owner lived in a small apartment in the basement and rented out the rooms upstairs. In August the butterfly garden right across from the front porch was in full bloom, with monarchs fluttering from flower to flower. In the earliest pictures of Lily Dale, taken in the 1880s, you can see this house off to the right of the original gates. It seems likely that the upstairs balcony was added later, but all the other features—like the porch and grand turret in the southwest corner—are original to the house.

Lily Dale's little Victorian cottages are a mix of homes and businesses. Some folks summer in Lily Dale; others live there year-round. Those who run businesses out of their homes are either renting out rooms to visitors or providing medium services to visitors. Licensed mediums offering sessions for pay use their homes as the site for those transactions. Today, the mediums practicing in Lily Dale have to be approved by the Assembly. Many of the houses have been renovated to create small office-like settings for the purpose of sitting with a client for a reading.

The significance of the mediums of Lily Dale conducting séances in their homes cannot be overstated. Private domestic spaces were central to Spiritualism from its earliest iterations. Those who claimed to be gifted with the ability to contact the dead almost always conducted their sittings inside their homes or the homes of benefactors. It was immensely fashionable in the nineteenth century for high-society New Yorkers and Londoners to host séance parties in their homes. At the height of the Victorian

44   Chapter 2

Figure 8. Photo of what is now the Aurora Guest House taken in the 1910s. "Places and Spaces" folder, Lily Dale Museum.

Figure 9. Photo of Lily Dale gate with the present-day Aurora Guest House in the background, 1910s. "Places and Spaces" folder, Lily Dale Museum.

era, the middle- and upper-class home represented the private sphere and was the domain of women.[7] According to the historian Simone Natale, the very nature of the séance "symbolically reenacted typical leisure activities and had much in common with amateur prestidigitation tricks, music, parlor theaters, philosophical toys, and other forms of domestic entertainment that were popular in nineteenth-century households."[8] The Spiritualist séance as public spectacle and Victorian entertainment was both a manifestation and a corruption of domesticity in a way that empowered women mediums.

Home is a significant symbol and physical space in many religious traditions. Particularly in the Victorian era in the United States and the United Kingdom, the domestic sphere was the center of respectable middle-class Christian family life.[9] According to the Victorian ideal, there were separate spheres: domestic spaces were the sphere of women, and public spaces were the sphere of men. A good Christian woman might entertain guests for tea or at parties in specific areas of the home, but doors would keep the rest of the house private. The home was a sanctuary where a couple might show off their success and domestic bliss, but there were explicit expectations about what the home could and could not be used for. Business and politics, the realms of men, were outside. Of course, what was *expected* and what was *done* were not always the same, but the ladies' manuals and comportment pamphlets of the time were all clear on the matter of the domestic sphere, and one could face social consequences for straying outside what was acceptable.[10]

In early Spiritualism, the home became a space of connection rather than a "separate spheres" prison for women. Though séances took place in many different settings—parlors and lecture halls, but also fairs and cheaper public venues—and appealed to sitters across class, gender, and racial lines, the first and primary spaces allocated to séances were the homes of believers.[11] Spiritualism began in the modest Fox family home in Hydesville, New York, and believers continued to use those traditionally domestic spaces as public forums for connecting with the invisible world. Significantly, Spiritualism's founders were not divinely chosen men but two young girls sensitive to Spirit. In this origin story, and throughout the early unfettered years of the growth of Spiritualism, women were empowered in a world otherwise intent on keeping them in their place.

Ann Braude, the first historian to situate the rise of Spiritualism within the broader context of the women's rights movement in the nineteenth century, emphasizes that "mediumship was closely identified with femininity." While "not all mediums were women," Braude writes, "the association of mediumship [with women] was so strong that it was not dispelled by the contravening evidence of the existence of male mediums."[12] Elana Gomel affirms the association of femininity and mediumship, arguing that it was the early Spiritualists *themselves* who gendered mediumship. For example, in the early twentieth century, Sir Arthur Conan Doyle and the sociologist C. W. Soal both described mediumship as feminine. According to Gomel, "For Doyle, the female body is a passive filter for the masculine voice from the Great Beyond. For Soal, femininity involves wild, chaotic, unruly productivity, unconstrained by will or intellect."[13] So male mediums like Daniel Dunglas Home, who wowed the elite of Europe with his demonstrations in the 1850s, were problematic, but they were also accepted as mediums because they presented as effeminate. The historian Lisa Morton notes that Home most likely had sex with other men, and was described by his contemporaries as being delicate-featured and slender.[14] These physical attributes would have marked him as a man suited to the work of a medium—that is, a passive and open vessel, ready to receive Spirit.

Maggie and Kate Fox, heralded by early Spiritualists as the founders of the movement, made their first public appearance on the stage of Corinthian Hall in Rochester on November 14, 1849. The previous year, in March 1848, they had begun to experience spirit phenomena in their home in Hydesville, interacting with a spirit who revealed himself to be a peddler who had died and been buried in the Fox cottage basement years before the Fox family lived there. Before long, wherever the girls went, restless spirits seemed to plague the homes they stayed in. When Kate visited family friends Isaac and Amy Post in Rochester in the summer of 1848, the mysterious rappings that she and Maggie had heard at home followed her, and though the faithful Quakers were at first skeptical, the entire Post family was quickly converted to belief in spirit communication. In 1849, the spirits indicated that the power of spirit communication had to be shared and that the girls had a "duty to perform."[15] Contemporaries declared that when the girls were present, spirits were able to push through the veil just a little, making rapping sounds that the girls then translated into yes, no, and eventually an alphabet. The Fox family tried to keep the story under wraps, but the young sisters were already gathering a following. Sir Arthur Conan Doyle, in his *History of Spiritualism*, claims that "every effort was made to conceal these manifestations from the public, but they soon became known."[16] After that successful first appearance, the Fox sisters' stunning performance went on the road. The girls booked appearances all over the United States and Europe.

Though modern historians might point to the spectacle on that stage in Rochester in 1849 as the beginning of Spiritualism, the earliest historians of Spiritualism returned again and again to those March nights a year earlier in the Fox family cottage when the rappings first began.[17] Eliab Capron in *Singular Revelations* was the first to do so in 1850. Capron was one of the first skeptics to test and be convinced by the girls, in 1848. Robert Davis Owen's 1860 compendium of spirit communication across the United States and Europe, *Footfalls on the Boundary of Another World*, includes a succinct summary of the 1848 events in Hydesville, and was referenced widely by subsequent nineteenth-century scholars of Spiritualism. Uriah Smith, author of the 1896 *Modern Spiritualism*, notes, "Spiritualism, as the reader is doubtless aware, originated in the family home of Mr. John D. Fox, in Hydesville . . . in the spring of 1848."[18] Arthur Conan Doyle similarly dated the Fox girls' role in the founding of Spiritualism to the March 1848 evenings in Hydesville. In the self-imagination of Spiritualists, at least (and all of these men were believers as well as historians of the movement), *home* was the center of Spiritualism. So too did the homes of Lily Dale serve as both private domiciles and public spaces for communing with the dead.

There's only one recorded instance of a Fox sister visiting Lily Dale, in 1882, when Maggie spent some of the camp season performing séances for the crowds. Yet the Lily Dale Assembly ultimately integrated the Fox sisters into the town's history, not just telling the story of their founding of Spiritualism but establishing a physical connection to the Fox family home.[19] In 1916 Benjamin F. Bartlett purchased and transported the Fox family's cottage from Hydesville to Lily Dale and donated the building to the Assembly. The Fox home, "the Birthplace of Modern Spiritualism," was opened to the public as an attraction in 1916, and Flo Cottrell, "the most wonderful Rapping Medium in the ranks of Spiritualism," was onsite for many years to demonstrate the signature phenomenon in the cottage. For the first ten years that the Fox Cottage was open to visitors, it was listed among the attractions of the town, along with the Leolyn Inn, the Maplewood Hotel, the grocery store, and other popular Lily Dale amenities.[20] In 1927 the program committee decentered the "medium in charge" (though still Flo Cottrell) in the description of the Fox Cottage and expanded a little on the role of the physical space in the birth of

Spiritualism, noting that it "was in this home, three quarters of a century ago, that phenomena occurred which startled the world, attracted the attention of leading scientists and established the fact of communication between the two worlds."[21] In the 1936 program the Fox home was promoted from merely "The Fox Cottage" to the "Cradle of Spiritualism," and in 1939 it was titled the "Spiritualist Memorial" and described as "one of Lily Dale's outstanding Diamond Jubilee attractions . . . the most noted memorial of spiritualism."[22] Sometime in the 1930s, the Assembly started charging twenty-five cents' admission to the cottage. After a fire destroyed the Fox home in 1955, the programs stopped directing visitors there, but most programs offered a photo of the structure.

Like the rented cottages that were transformed into séance spaces each summer, the Fox home was transformed into a public space where the faithful could contemplate the origins of Spiritualism. All that remains today is a clearing, marked with a plaque, and the many photographs of the building in its final resting place that are held in the Lily Dale Museum. Lily Dale visitors are now encouraged to walk through the meditation garden there, although when Elizabeth and Marissa tried to enjoy the quietness of the area, they were swarmed by bugs and made a hasty retreat.

The Fox sisters weren't the first to deliver spiritual messages through séances. The historian Robert Cox traces the history of this kind of religiosity back to the phenomenon of "sleeping preachers" who seemed to deliver religious messages in a kind of trance.[23] But the Fox sisters touched off a widespread fascination with spirit communication in the second half of the nineteenth century, particularly in the United States and the United Kingdom. Spiritualism primarily attributed mediumship to young girls in the early decades of the movement, unlike previous movements, and counter to the dominant perceptions of girls' role in Victorian society.

Before Daniel Dunglas Home and other men entered the field, women and girls were at the center of the Spiritualist movement. Ann Braude notes that adolescent girls, in particular, were at the forefront of early successful communiqués with the dead. The Fox sisters, of course, were heralded as the first, but in the years following their interactions with the spirit of the peddler buried in their basement, dozens of other teenage girls took their place at the center of séance circles across New England, New York, and the Midwest. In families seeking a connection with spirits, girls and young women were most likely to be identified as "clairvoyant," and responses from spirits were most likely to emerge when a girl or young woman in the family joined the séance.[24]

In an era when middle- and upper-class women were pushing back against the restrictions of corsets and separate spheres, mediumship and Spiritualism offered both freedom and further bondage. On the one hand, the popularity of Spiritualism and séances helped to weaken the rigidity of the separate spheres. Séances opened the home to public audiences and gave women legitimate access to pulpits from which to speak and be heard. Victorian women were relegated to the home, excluded from public life. The séance undermined those boundaries and made the private space of the home a public forum, where philosophers and politicians and respected (though dead) members of society might pontificate and debate and deliver messages to the living. On the other hand, the presumption of passivity and lack of intellectuality associated with mediumship meant that mediums were seen as mere tools of Spirit. Many contemporaries understood mediumship to be feminine *because* the medium was passive and penetrated, submissive to Spirit and possession. While the feminine connotation was not grounds for dismissing the messages, legitimacy flowed from the masculine spirit that spoke through these mediums, not necessarily from the medium herself.

Like the Fox sisters before her, Cora L. V. Scott Richmond began her mediumship at a young age. According to one biography, Scott first manifested her mediumship at the age of eleven.[25] By the time she was fifteen, her parents were taking her on tour. She too was a native of western New York, born in Cuba, a small town one hundred miles southwest of Hydesville. Though more southerly than Hydesville, Cuba would have been well within the range of the Burned Over District's spillover. Although Scott's gifts were alleged to have manifested just a few years after the Fox girls', her emergence as a public medium coincided conveniently with the wave of other western New Yorkers who launched their mediumship careers at the same time: Lyman C. Howe, Amelia Colby, Elizabeth Lowe Watson, Mrs. R. S. Lillie, and the Davenport brothers, among others. And as with the Fox girls before her, Cora Scott's gifts manifested in her home. While she was asleep at her mother's feet in the sewing room one day, the girl's hand seemed to be moving as if writing, and so Scott's mother fetched the slate. The spirits visiting the house then etched out a message for the Scotts which promised they intended no harm. The Scotts invited friends and neighbors in to witness "Cora write in her sleep." Later, a recently deceased Spiritualist named Adin Ballou was said to have been led to Cuba to "control the daughter, Cora."[26] Thereafter Cora Scott, often the vessel through which the respected (and male) spirit of Ballou communicated, was deemed a great and powerful medium. She founded a group of Progressive Friends (Quakers) in 1857, which pulled her into the orbit of influential social reformers like Susan B. Anthony and Amy Post.[27]

Scott's first biographer was Harrison D. Barrett. Barrett became interested in Spiritualism in 1880, and his interests drew him to the Cassadaga Lake Free Association later in the decade. He was chairman of the Association from 1889 to 1895 and later published *The Banner of Light*, a popular Spiritualist newspaper, with his wife, Margarite M. Coffyn.[28] It is likely that he met Cora Scott in Lily Dale. By the time Barrett published her biography, Scott was already a well-established spirit medium. She was a regular on the Lily Dale program by 1887, coming for at least a week each season until 1910.[29] Together Scott and Barrett founded the National Spiritualist Association of Churches in 1893.

The significance of the feminine in mediumship was never lost on the Spiritualists of the nineteenth century. In his 1895 biography of Scott, Harrison Barrett opens with a firmly feminist position on the writing of history:

> Throughout all ages of the world, the lives of representative men have made up all there was and is in the history of nations. . . . We are struck, however, by the one-sidedness of historians as they write of the great personalities that make up the history of nations. Representative men are alone given prominence, and the names and works of representative women find but little place in the glowing tributes paid by the vast majority of writers to the eminent characters of history.[30]

What unfolds in the biography, then, is clearly intended to assert both that the thousands of history-making women deserve to be written about, and that Cora L. V. Scott belonged among those history makers. Barrett and Scott bemoaned the "clouds of bigotry and theological darkness" enveloping the globe, certain that "the pendulum of thought had oscillated far to one side and the mystic rap at Hydesville was the call to halt . . . to evenly balance between the male and female influence in life."[31] Barrett presents Spiritualism, and the lives of women like the Fox sisters and Cora Scott, as a revolution in gender equality. Like those before and those after who wrote about the founding of Spiritualism, he points again to the teenage Fox girls and their home in Hydesville. The grounding power of the Spiritualism movement always came back to those girls and their inversion of the symbolic home: a private space made public through female agency.

Though at the center of the Spiritualist movement, the medium—and her home—remained coded as feminine. In a short story titled "Playing with Fire," published in the *Strand Magazine* in March 1900, Arthur Conan Doyle wrote about a skeptic and his companions' encounter with a medium: "Our experience had shown us that to work on these [occult] subjects without a medium was as futile as for an astronomer to make observations without a telescope."[32] Reports from séances regularly confirmed the sublimation of the medium to the spirit that channeled through her. When spirits spoke through a medium, concerned audience members might ask where she was.[33] In Doyle's story, the spirit responds: "The medium is happy in another plane of existence. She has taken my place, as I have taken hers."[34] Fifty years later, in one of Scottish medium Helen Duncan's séances, her spirit guide Albert told the audience, rather crudely: "See her? There's the fat lady, Nellie Duncan, just sitting there in her trance. She can't see me. She can't hear me. She's out there in the Blessed Beyond. Gone. I am the man in control, and I love being in control."[35] So while mediumship gave women a literal stage on which to participate in public life, it also tended to remain a gendered role of passivity and subjecthood.

Celebrity Spiritualist mediums like Cora Scott, the Fox sisters, the Bangs sisters, D. D. Home, and the Davenport brothers performed regularly on public stages as well as in private parlors, but the vast majority of séances and physical phenomena took place in private domiciles.[36] Those who paid to sit in on séances in Lily Dale in the early twentieth century

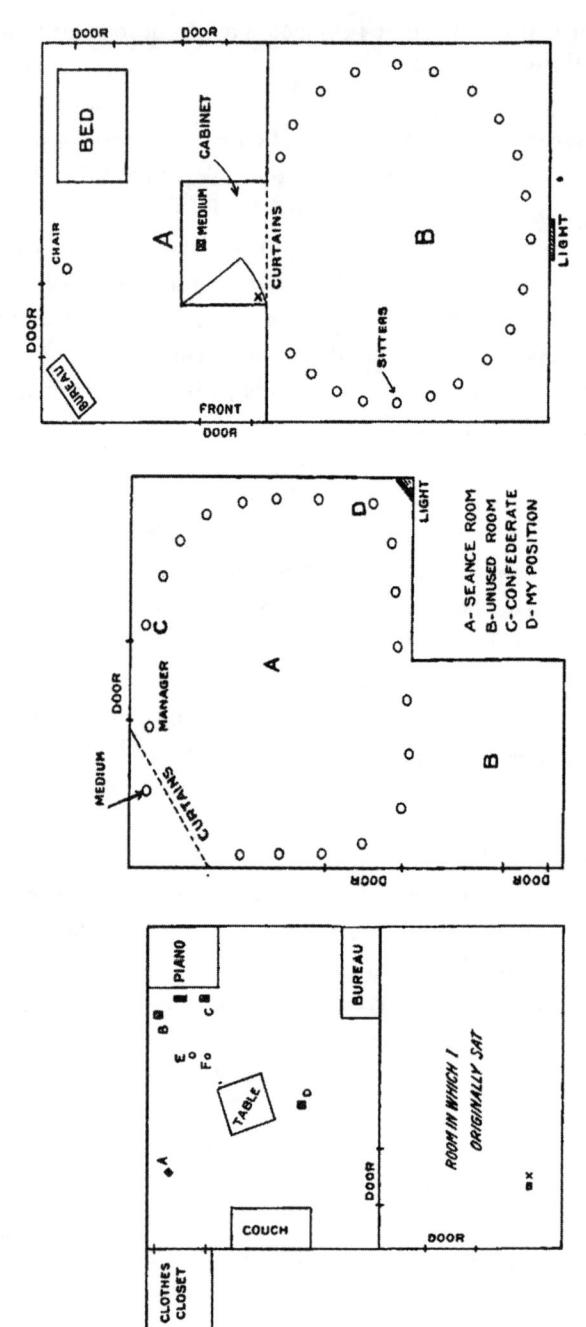

Figure 10. Images from Hereward Carrington's "Report of a Two-Weeks' Investigation into Alleged Spiritualistic Phenomena, Witnessed at Lily Dale, New York," published in *Proceedings of the American Society for Psychical Research* (1908). International Association for the Preservation of Spiritualist and Occult Periodicals materials, which include these diagrams, are licensed under a Creative Commons Attribution–NonCommercial 4.0 International License.

were likely not in the least surprised to learn that they had to enter the intimate space of the mediums' sitting rooms and kitchens to witness their demonstrations.

For much of Lily Dale's early history, the physical phenomena persisted in those quaint little Victorian houses lining the town's streets. Rooms were outfitted with trapdoors and curtains, windows were boarded up, lighting was hazy and mysterious. In this way the private domestic spaces of the Victorian period were made public venues for communing with the dead.

According to Hereward Carrington, who spent several weeks in 1907 investigating physical mediums in Lily Dale, the mixed use of the houses was standard practice from the beginning.[37] Traveling mediums and visitors alike rented cottages, and the mediums used those rented spaces to conduct their business. According to Carrington, the mediums at Lily Dale charged "fair prices for their sittings," from one to two dollars, and had up to fifteen sittings per day.[38] The nonresident mediums (in other words, those who rented, rather than those who were approved by the board to own a home) offered a range of services, from automatic writing and spirit photography to trance mediumship and séances. Assembly treasurer George B. Warne assured James Hyslop, secretary of the American Society for Psychical Research, that mediums officially hired by the Assembly for camp limited their services to the free readings at Inspiration Stump and the less ostentatious private readings in homes and on porches.[39]

In the early part of the twentieth century, the area surrounding Lily Dale was less built up than it is today.[40] Carrington observed that all there was around Lily Dale was the "[train] station, a couple of hotels, [and] a few farm houses."[41] Of course the Chautauqua Institution on Chautauqua Lake was only seventeen miles southwest of Lily Dale and accessible by train. Folks traveled from Buffalo, New York City, Erie, and even farther afield all summer long to visit both Lily Dale and Chautauqua, where popular speakers gave lectures in the large auditoriums twice daily. Inside the gates of Lily Dale in 1908, a visitor would find the Maplewood Hotel, the library, several small halls including the cafeteria, and a large auditorium, in addition to the houses and cottages.[42]

Mediums who spent their summers in rented cottages in Lily Dale had to make do with the available accommodations. Those who hosted séances quickly converted at least one room into a "séance room," with the windows boarded up to prevent unwanted natural light (or fresh air) from filtering into the space. They used lamps that they could dim or extinguish at the start of a séance, to ensure that they controlled how much the sitters could see. As renters, they were likely constrained in what changes they could make to their residences, but they typically constructed some kind of spirit cabinet using curtains and perhaps a simple wood frame. Mediums who used instruments like spirit trumpets or who were supposed to produce other physical manifestations typically sat enclosed in a spirit cabinet for the duration of a séance.

In each of his sittings, Carrington noted the temporary renovations the mediums made to serve their performances. Visiting a trumpet medium named Mrs. M. T. McCoy, Carrington was "ushered into a darkened room, and a lamp was lighted. Every crack and crevice was then carefully covered over, and I was requested to take a seat in the cabinet—a curtained triangular space in one corner of the room. The darkness here was intense, only at the top of the curtain a faint streak of light."[43] The houses of those performing physical mediumship were always modified in some significant way to facilitate their performances. For a materialization séance at her rented cottage, a medium named Mrs. Moss erected a spirit cabinet with a curtain in one corner of the room, right next to a door. She sat behind the curtain in the cabinet. The sitters sat in a circle in the room outside the cabinet. When the séance began, the light in the room was extinguished.[44] Carrington observed that "one would pass such cottages at night and hear issuing from them anything but melodious sounds—the house itself dark, shadowy, and closely boarded up."[45]

Although Lily Dale's cottages were spaces for public performances, they were also the private (if temporary) domiciles of the mediums. At a materialization séance with Joseph Jonson, Carrington described two rooms with a spirit cabinet between them. In one room—Jonson's bedroom—there were multiple doors. The sitters sat in the adjoining room; the spirit cabinet blocked the sitters' view of the bedroom. Carrington noted that the bed was pushed well away from one of the doors so as to allow access to it but did not otherwise comment on the fact that sitters were invited to tramp through and examine Jonson's sleeping quarters.

The use of the private as public space was well established according to Spiritualist norms by 1907.[46]

Our group trip in August 2021 was my and Elizabeth's first, and from the moment we passed through the gates, we were obsessing over the houses packed in neat little rows throughout town. Elizabeth mused that this was a place to which she could retire (although she's nowhere near retirement). She opened her phone and started looking to see which of the houses were for sale, and for how much. Because the Lily Dale community is aging—you won't see many children playing in the fields next to the old school, which was closed years ago—there are actually quite a few houses for sale at any given moment. If you visit the website, which is where all houses for sale must be listed, you'll see homes of all shapes, sizes, and states of repair, ranging in price from $57,000 to nearly $200,000. Buying one of those houses, however, is a little more complicated than your standard real estate deal.

When it comes to home ownership, Lily Dale is peculiar. No one in Lily Dale owns the land on which their house is built. The Lily Dale Assembly owns all the land of the town and leases it back to the people who own the houses. There are a total of 169 leaseholds in Lily Dale. People who want to buy a house have to be approved by the board of the Assembly before they can purchase it. The Lily Dale website warns potential home buyers that "purchasing a home in Lily Dale is not a typical real estate transaction. DO NOT make any agreements, verbal or in writing, before obtaining Lily Dale Assembly approval to purchase. Mortgages cannot be obtained to purchase Lily Dale property."[47] To even be considered for a home purchase in Lily Dale, you have to be an active member in good standing of the Lily Dale Assembly and (as it stands today) a member of the Spiritualist church. Your case goes before the board, and they vote on whether you can or cannot buy a house in their community.

It doesn't take much imagination to envision what strict parameters for membership and home ownership have meant for the growth and demographics of Lily Dale in its 150 years of history. Scholars estimate that, at its height in the late nineteenth century, there were anywhere between a few hundred thousand and 11 million Spiritualists in the United States.[48] As Ann Braude notes, the early movement was informed by and intertwined with major reform movements like abolition, temperance, and suffrage.[49] In its initial decades, Spiritualism was decentralized and attracted people from all walks of life and regions of the United States. There were no racial, class, or gender barriers to spirit mediumship; one needed only the inborn sensitivity to the spiritual plane. Yet while the disaggregated nature of Spiritualism in its first thirty years may have invited a greater diversity of practitioners, by the 1890s the formation of formal churches and national governing organizations with hierarchical structures facilitated Spiritualism's gradual shift toward white and male domination. As numerous scholars have demonstrated, Spiritualism was most popular among white progressive Protestants in the Northeast and mid-Atlantic regions of the United States.[50] And Lily Dale, as a community created during that formalizing moment in Spiritualism's history, ultimately reflected that narrower demographic in its residents. Similarly, after 1920, the leadership in Lily Dale gradually moved from greater gender parity to becoming male-dominated.

At its height of popularity in the United States, there was a robust community of Black Spiritualist practitioners, but the shift toward more formal church hierarchies left many Black practitioners dissatisfied with the white-dominated organizations like the National Spiritualist Association of Churches (NSAC).[51] The good intentions of early Spiritualism were frequently railroaded by the pressures of patriarchy and white supremacy. Some Black Spiritualist groups simply lost cohesion after their founding leaders passed away. In the South, the Cercle Harmonique was a group of Black Creole Spiritualists, including men and women, who, like most Spiritualists, performed séances in their private homes.[52] The Cercle Harmonique was active for only about twenty years, its membership dissolving after 1877 and the death of Reconstruction. Across the United States, Black men and women joined the larger NSAC organization after its formation in 1893, but the inequalities of de facto and legal segregation in the North and South, respectively, led the Black members of NSAC to break off and form the National Colored Spiritualist Association of Churches (NCSAC) in 1922.[53] The NCSAC had active affiliated churches in cities throughout the Midwest, the East Coast, and the South. By the 1970s, however, the NCSAC had broken into factions over organizational disagreements and effectively ceased functioning.[54] The structures of white supremacy that drove Black practitioners out of the NSAC diminished the potential pool of members and fractured an already fractious movement into smaller and smaller pieces.

Counterintuitively, as the popularity of Spiritualism declined after the 1940s, Lily Dale's gatekeeping increased. Over the course of the twentieth century, the leadership of the Lily Dale Assembly was dominated more firmly by the men of the town. After 1880, leadership trends in Lily Dale followed broader national trends, waffling between exciting liberationist feminism and conservative patriarchal norms. As Spiritualism faced the challenges of fracturing membership, the larger organizations operated more and more like traditional Christian and Christian-adjacent religious denominations in the United States, with mostly white men in positions of authority. Though women's political power declined in Lily Dale, women continued to dominate mediumship in both the white and Black circles of practitioners. All the same, with such a small pool of nonwhite practitioners to draw from, and the boundaries of membership and residency in Lily Dale growing more rigid with each passing decade, it is unsurprising that the demographics of Lily Dale closely resembled the demographics of the national religious movement as a whole. After 1970, the demographic possibilities shrank even further, as the Assembly board of directors started denying Assembly membership to people who were Spiritualists but not exclusively members of the Lily Dale Spiritualist Church (LDSC), under the umbrella of the National Spiritualist Association of Churches.[55] Significantly, the 2023 camp season was the first in recorded history that hosted a Black woman speaker as the headliner for a mainstage auditorium event: Dr. Lakara Foster spoke in the auditorium at Lily Dale on August 25, 26, and 27.

The original 1879 charter of the Lily Dale Assembly stated that, as a corporation, Lily Dale was "devoted to Benevolent, Charitable, Literary, and Scientific purposes and mutual improvement in religious knowledge."[56] In 1957, however, the board of directors changed the charter to specify the "mutual improvement in the *religious knowledge of Spiritualism.*"[57] This added language turned the charter from one broadly considering the religious and scientific questions about the afterlife and spirit communication into one dedicated specifically to Spiritualism as the official religion of the town. According to several lawsuits challenging the shift, the board also surreptitiously changed Lily Dale from a membership corporation to a religious corporation.[58] Lily Dale had already established a formal affiliation with the National Spiritualist Association of Churches in 1933, and the 1957 charter revision cemented that relationship.[59] This change in 1957 allowed the Lily Dale Assembly board of directors to prevent residents in violation of that rule from renewing their land leases and to bar non-NSAC applicants from buying houses in Lily Dale.

By 1957 there were a number of larger Spiritualist organizations in the United States. In addition to the NSAC, there was the National Spiritual Alliance (TNSA), the United Spiritualist Church Association (USCA), the Christian Order of Spiritual Scientists (COSS), and the National Colored Spiritualist Association of Churches, as well as numerous non-affiliated Spiritualist churches. These organizations disagreed on theological principles of Spiritualism, such as the role of scientific inquiry in the legitimization of the religion, the role of Christianity in the religion, and the belonging/exclusion of people of color. In the late 1970s there was a significant conflict in Lily Dale between the board of directors (who were LDSC/NSAC) and a group of townsfolk who were members of COSS and the Christian Order of Universal Spiritualists (COUS). When the board of directors established the NSAC as the official church of the Lily Dale Assembly, they established a precedent to deny Assembly membership, and thereby land lease holding, to any non-NSAC Spiritualists in the town, including members of COSS and COUS. The board effectively drew a boundary around what the town's theological identity would be and who would be welcome as permanent members of the town.[60]

We can't say how vehemently the board intended to uphold that change at the time they implemented it, or if they anticipated that the long history of theologically splintering Spiritualist groups could one day change the character of the town. Within two decades, those challenges came, and the board at the time responded firmly within the spirit of those changes. In 1974 Lily Dale resident Charles Cowen sued the Assembly, claiming that Lily Dale had been chartered as a membership organization, not a religious corporation. The court—citing the 1957 bylaws, unaware that those laws were not the original ones that had incorporated the town's association—determined that "Lily Dale Assembly is a religious institution as understood by the statutory exemption" and thus that it was permitted to deny Spiritualists who were not NSAC members the right to lease land in Lily Dale.[61] Cowen's challenge came on the heels of several disagreements that non-NSAC residents of the town had with the board. Building on the court's precedent, in 1976 the board voted to enact a 1932 charter of the NSAC which asserted that no member of the Assembly could hold active membership in another church. These changes seem to have been reactions to the growth of a small community of Christian Spiritualists in Lily Dale. This kind of gatekeeping (literally, in this case) is exactly what one might expect of a traditional religious organization responding to fractures. By firming up the line between canon and heresy, insider and outsider, the leadership of Lily Dale followed patterns set by religious hierarchies the world over.

The NSAC holds that God is "Infinite Intelligence." While the NSAC FAQs today note that belief in spirit communication does not conflict with the teachings of Jesus, "Spiritualism is not a branch of Christianity or other major religion. Spiritualism has been recognized by the US Congress as a separate and distinct religion."[62] The presence of Christian Spiritualists in Lily Dale was not new or even problematic, but throughout the 1970s, the theological—and ideological—differences between Christian Spiritualism and NSAC Spiritualism came to a head. The board of the Lily Dale Assembly utilized the 1957 bylaws change to reinforce their vision of what kind of intentional Spiritualist community Lily Dale could and would be.

Marguerite Hanny was the founder and a minister of the Buffalo-based Christian Order of Spiritualist Scientists, and had lived in Lily Dale since 1968. The board approved Hanny's 1969 application for membership in the Lily Dale Spiritualist Church, even though she noted on that membership application that she was also a member of COSS.[63] In the six years before Cowen's lawsuit, Hanny and her fellow Christian Spiritualists in the town started practicing their version of Spiritualism openly in Lily Dale. The board—staunch NSAC members—began enforcing the 1957 bylaws, attempting to push Christian Spiritualists out of Lily Dale.

For about nine years, Hanny, her son Gregory, and several other families were at loggerheads with the Assembly board and other residents of the community. According to Robert Sabol, president of the Lily Dale Assembly in the 1970s and 1980s, Hanny and the other self-identified Christian Spiritualists had violated Assembly bylaws "by setting up two Christian chapels on land owned by the assembly, by picketing within the grounds, and by disturbing the peace."[64] Gregory Hanny told the *New York Times* that he was being evicted because he believed Jesus was his savior.[65] In 1976 Marguerite Hanny's application for another ninety-nine-year land lease renewal was put on hold by the Assembly, which effectively prevented Hanny from putting her house on the market when she wanted to sell it. In 1977 Hanny and twelve other former members of the Lily Dale Assembly, including the Cockshott family, were then denied renewal of their Assembly memberships.[66] The Assembly attempted to force the Cockshotts, who owned an abandoned house in Lily Dale, to pay the daily gate fee for access to the village until a judge ordered the Assembly to allow the family free entry.[67] The board then tried to revoke their land leases on religious grounds.[68] Sabol attempted to initiate nine criminal cases against various members of the Christian Spiritualist faction in order to have them removed from the grounds, eight of which were dismissed.

The Hannys took the Lily Dale Assembly to court. In 1981 the New York State attorney general affirmed that the Assembly was originally chartered as a domestic business corporation—contrary to the 1957 bylaws—and it could not deny membership on the basis of religious discrimination.[69] But when Hanny attempted to build a case against Lily Dale and assert housing discrimination based on religious identity, the role of the Assembly (as an NSAC-affiliated church) and the Association (as a business corporation founded by the Assembly) complicated the issue. In August 1985 the New York State Supreme Court ruled that the Assembly had the right to evict Hanny and the other Christian Spiritualists.[70] Though Sabol maintained that the Christian Spiritualists were deemed problematic only because they had set up an unsanctioned chapel and protested the non–Christian Spiritualism practiced more broadly in Lily Dale, the parameters of membership—and home ownership—in Lily Dale were firmly rooted thereafter in NSAC membership.

In defining who could and who could not be a member of the community, and who could and could not buy a home in Lily Dale, the Assembly defined who belonged and who didn't. And the cottages of Lily Dale are, in many ways, the heart of the physical and symbolic intentional Spiritualist community. By defining in- and out-groups, those who belonged and those who didn't, the (white, male-dominated) board of the 1970s rewrote the intention of the intentional Spiritualist community.[71] Curiously, this shift coincided with firmer rules about what kind of mediumship was legitimized and permitted in Lily Dale. By 1949, for example, physical mediumship was banned there, as in other Spiritualist communities.[72] Though the Assembly members continued to rent their cottages out to visitors, what visitors could expect after 1949 from the mediums they visited in Lily Dale changed dramatically. Much of the radical, sensational nature of Spiritualism was culled from the late twentieth-century formal Spiritualist church.

In the first fifty years of Lily Dale history, physical phenomena were *the* draw for visitors. At the start of the twentieth century, Lily Dale averaged ten thousand visitors each camp season.[73] By 1985 it was drawing only a thousand visitors a season.[74] Under the more broadly conceived charter and bylaws, the Victorian houses of Lily Dale were once the site of a wide range of phenomena manifestations, séances, and one-on-one readings. The board was always cognizant of the problems that such a freewheeling approach to the lease of the cottages could produce, and in a 1903 report recommended ways that the Association could control when and where physical phenomena were manifested:

> We believe that through the different phenomenon of Spiritualism, a large number of seekers receive ocular proofs of the truths of spiritualism and we, therefore, desire to encourage and endorse honest mediumship, but as we have found by repeated experiences that a large number attending séances and having private sittings have received fraudulent manifestations . . . we would recommend . . . that all Physical and other manifestations of Mediumship shall be given under the auspices of the Trustees and in buildings as may be designated by them—that all manifestations be held under such conditions as may be agreed upon by the Mediums and the Trustees with a special view to guard against fraud.[75]

The authors of the report go on to assert that any and all events charging money should have to go through the board for approval, and any mediums in violation should be banned from Lily Dale. As we'll discuss in the next chapter, the Lily Dale board took accusations of fraud seriously. Certainly some hucksters were investigated and exiled from the community. Despite the misgivings and the persistent concern that Lily Dale leaders expressed about fraud, however, in those first decades there was little effort to curb the traditions of physical mediumship in Spiritualism. Spiritualist physical mediumship was, from its very first introduction to the world in the Hydesville cottage, regularly conducted in the private space of the domicile. Homes, and the process of making those private spaces public, were central to the practice of Spiritualism.

More than any of the religious movements of the nineteenth century, Spiritualism grappled with the separate spheres of Victorian society in controversial and subversive ways. The private domestic sphere—the domain of women—was at the very core of Spiritualism. While entertaining friends, family, and perhaps a few acquaintances would have been the norm for upper- and middle-class white women in the mid-nineteenth century, Spiritualist mediumship allowed those women to turn their private sanctums into public venues. Women dominated the limelight of mediumship, particularly in its earliest decades. Though some men made a robust living on the medium/séance circuit, mediumship was considered a feminine role for most of the nineteenth and twentieth centuries.[76] Today it is still a calling dominated by women. When the movement became a formal organization, however, the feminist identity of Spiritualism waned.

Spiritualism shifted from a decentralized, female-dominated religious movement to a hierarchical, male-dominated formal organization. As Ann Braude notes, female leadership in the American Association of Spiritualists (NSAC's predecessor) declined as the organization formalized its structure. Despite efforts to make its organizing committee equally representative of men and women, by 1866 there were twenty men and only eleven women.[77] Similarly, in 1893 Cora Scott was the sole woman identified as a co-founder of the National Spiritualist Association of Churches along with men like Harrison Barrett, William H. Bach, Luther V. Moulton, and James M. Peebles. The founding of the NSAC marked a break from the earlier movement. After Spiritualism became formally organized as a federally recognized religion, women were often represented among Spiritualist organizations' leadership positions, but only as figureheads. The majority of Lily Dale Assembly board seats, for example, were occupied by men, even though the president of the entire assembly in 1907 and 1908 was still a woman—Esther Humphrey. In 1906, the seven most powerful board members (officers and three trustees) were four women and three men. The executive staff, totaling twenty-two, were fourteen women and eight men. But in 1907, only two board members were female (president and secretary), and while seven out of ten executive staffers were women, they were now overseen by a male chairman, John T. Lillie. By 1908, only two board members were female (president and secretary); the rest were men. Four out of five of the executive staff (note their numbers are dwindling) were women, but they were still headed by a male chairman, Lillie. Unlike in earlier periods, the female board and staff members now tended to occupy traditionally feminine roles, such as secretary, teacher, librarian, pianist, or president of the Ladies' Auxiliary, with the female president serving as the one exception. This formula for the board and staff continued more or less unabated until 1918, when Abraham Rasner assumed the presidency and the two women on the board were confined to the roles of secretary and assistant treasurer (under the authority of a male treasurer, of course). By 1920, the entire board of the Lily Dale Assembly was male.[78] The revolutionary and feminist movement that Spiritualists insisted the Fox sisters launched from their home in 1848 changed dramatically over the first century of its momentum. Much of that change can be mapped onto Lily Dale.

In the town's early decades, Women's Day was a major event, attracting famous speakers like Susan B. Anthony, and the board was dominated by the women leaders who'd helped found Lily Dale. In the twentieth century, women were sidelined in their roles as leaders of the town (as in the larger organization). By 1920, the board of directors and program organizers were increasingly male-dominated. The ladies were relegated to the Lyceum and music organizing and had to form a Ladies' Auxiliary to regain power. Though the Women's Day tradition continued, its uniqueness was supplanted a bit by Children's Day, American Legion Day, Canadian Week-End, Firemen's Day, and a host of other themed days. As we'll discuss in the next few chapters, Spiritualism's empowerment—and constraint—of women is echoed in the women's rights movement, the temperance movement, and even the appropriation and celebration of Native American religious traditions. The waxing and waning of empowerment pulsated through the streets and buildings of late nineteenth- and early twentieth-century Lily Dale.

But as a place that still advertises its Victorian charm to visitors, the town retains some vestiges of the early Spiritualist movement. Women still make up the majority of working mediums in Lily Dale; at this writing, the president of the Assembly is a woman; and the little Victorian cottages remain the center of mediumship and connection to Spiritualism. Shared public spaces—the Stump, Forest Temple, the auditorium, the picnic pavilions by the firehouse, the cafeteria and the café—serve particular needs of the community as well, but the intimate spaces of mediums' homes have always been and will always be the foundation of Spiritualism. And though you can't visit the Fox Cottage anymore, the story of the rappings in that little house has been central to Lily Dale's self-identity since 1916.

3

The Fox Cottage

Averill, Sarah, Marissa, and Elizabeth

After hours bent over the wooden desk in the museum, scanning every scrapbook and pamphlet and program Ron Nagy brought to us, we often needed to stretch our legs. Not far from the little old schoolhouse that houses the museum is a road that takes you away from the center of town and out toward its northernmost edge. Unlike the streets in the rest of the village, the roads and pathways up here curve and meander, making it a perfect area for aimless walking. On the eastern side of the path tucked just inside the woods is a small garden with a gravel pathway through it, almost like a labyrinth. At the entrance to the garden is a rock monument topped with a plaque. It reads: "Memorial to the Fox Family, who lived in this cottage at the time Margaret and Kate Fox aged 9 and 11 years received the first proof of the continuity of life, which was the beginning of modern Spiritualism, March 31, 1848. This cottage was bought and moved from Hydesville, NY, its original site, to Lily Dale, NY, in May 1916, by Benjamin F. Bartlett." But there's no cottage in the clearing. Just ferns, overgrown vinca vine, hostas, a cement urn, and the worn gravel path.

Once, this little grove held the famous Fox Cottage itself, moved from Hydesville to Lily Dale at the (probably enormous) expense of prominent resident Benjamin Bartlett. Unbelievably, the small two-story home—the birthplace of the Spiritualist religion—burned down in 1955. The *Rochester Democrat and Chronicle* reported that "flames raced through the two-story frame structure despite a spirited battle by two fire companies to save the building."[1] No cause was ever determined for the fire, but it left a hole in Lily Dale and added another layer of mystery to the history of Spiritualism. Without the tangible presence of the little cottage, the tale of two young girls and spirit rappings seems more mythical than ever.

It was easy for us, standing in this little clearing looking at nothing but a slightly overgrown shade garden, to start to wonder whether any of it was real. If there's no cottage, was there really a ghost trying to communicate through knocking noises? Were the rappings anything more than tricks played by children? Is *any* of this real? Or is it all just a story, one repeated over and over in the town to create a sense of history for quirky beliefs and alternate lifestyles? Except for true believers, most visitors to Lily Dale (including us) probably spend at least some time wondering whether their readings and workshops are real or just an unusual way to spend a couple of hundred bucks. For its entire history, Spiritualism has been dogged by these same questions. As the Fox sisters and other mediums became increasingly famous for their work, skeptics sought out ways to test their faith, their abilities, and their honesty.

In 1882 Maggie Fox (by then calling herself Maggie Fox Kane, in honor of her dead fiancé, the aristocratic Arctic explorer Elisha Kent Kane) spent the camp season in Lily Dale. *The Banner of Light* declared that her arrival had "caused a ripple of pleasure throughout the entire camp."[2] She was one of eight physical mediums at the Cassadaga Lake Camp that summer, giving séances, likely several times each day, for paying customers. According to one prominent resident, Thomas Lees, reporting at the end of the season, all the physical mediums were kept busy by the camp visitors, despite rainy August weather that thinned the crowds a bit.[3] By 1882, Maggie and her sister Kate Fox had long been accepted by the Spiritualist community as the founders of the movement, and their experiences in Hydesville some thirty years prior propelled them to fame on both sides of the Atlantic. The year after she visited Lily Dale, Maggie was the guest of honor at a Michigan Spiritualist camp, entertaining gathered crowds

Figure 11. The Fox Cottage, after being relocated to Lily Dale. This is a reproduction of a photocopy of the original picture. Fox Sisters binder, Lily Dale Museum.

with the "sacred" story of the Hydesville rappings.[4] Kate was warmly welcomed by Spiritualists in London, where she lived for nearly a decade with her English husband, the Spiritualist lawyer Henry Jencken. But within a few years of Maggie Fox's visit to Lily Dale, the sisters' reputation completely fell apart. While the "little girls" who founded the religion were treated as prophets, the adult Fox women became more of a liability than an asset, between the substance abuse, insolvency, and fraud accusations. Maggie Fox's 1888 disavowal of her mediumship was a dramatic and unique moment, but charges of fraud and grift were not limited to the famous Fox sisters. For the most successful Spiritualist mediums, public spectacle and accusations of fraud became just another part of their notoriety.

According to the historian Simone Natale, it wasn't the first instance of the Hydesville rappings that was the foundational moment for Spiritualism; that came over a year later, when Maggie and Kate Fox took the stage at Corinthian Hall in Rochester. Rochester, the boom city of the old canal days, was home to curious thinkers and radicals eager to hear about the Hydesville phenomena. The announcement for the event read: "Let the citizens of Rochester embrace this opportunity of investigating the whole matter, and see if those engaged in laying it before the public are deceived, or are deceiving others, and, if neither [let them] account for these truly wonderful manifestations. . . . Come and investigate."[5] From the very beginning, mediums like the Fox sisters invited speculation, skepticism, and controversy—and so, like the other popular entertainments of the day (scientific lectures, freak shows, theatrical productions, magic acts, and the like), the physical medium had to dazzle her séance sitters, whether she was performing on a huge lecture stage or in a private parlor. At that Rochester reading, four hundred paying "sitters" witnessed the adolescent Fox girls' first major public appearance as physical mediums, where they demonstrated their ability to communicate with the dead.[6]

Spiritualism emerged at a pivotal moment between the religious fervor of the Second Great Awakening and the professionalization of scientific investigation and discovery. As science threatened to usurp faith, there were a lot of questions that needed new answers. Where does the afterlife fit into the human experience? Can it be tested or measured? Can the people claiming to have a special connection to the other side be proven wrong? Spiritualism ended up in the middle of a lot of debates and scandals. As the grand combination of "science, philosophy, and religion," Spiritualism gave people who had lost their faith in the invisible the opportunity to "test" the existence of an afterlife.[7] As the historian Janet Oppenheim notes, "[Spiritualists] were absolutely convinced that theirs was the faith that united all faiths, that reconciled religion and science, and gave man the facts to prove his immortality."[8] Men and women from all walks of life sought answers and comfort from spirit mediums. In the early decades of the movement, spectacle in the form of physical mediumship was common, almost expected. Sitters didn't just want to believe; they wanted *proof*. James Hyslop, founder of the American Institute for Scientific Research, captured the conundrum when he wrote that "Spiritualism has, of course, been a concession to the scientific spirit, in so far as it claims to give *evidence* of life after death. . . . The result was and is that, in order to sustain its allegations, it has thought it a duty to give 'demonstrations' of its doctrine as a part of its regular work."[9]

Insisting that Spiritualism was as much science as religion, and that there was proof of spirit communication, however, invited the application of the scientific process: observation, testing, and analysis. For those true believers, the ethereal phantasms, precipitated paintings, ghostly noises, and channeled voices were in themselves proof of the reality of spirit communication. Take, for instance, Amy and Isaac Post, friends of the Fox family, skeptics who quickly converted to believers after their first encounter with the spirit rappings in their Rochester home in the summer of 1848. Or Sir Arthur Conan Doyle, who proclaimed that "there is no physical sense which I possess which has not been separately assured, and that there is no conceivable method by which a spirit could show its presence which I have not on many occasions experienced," from ectoplasm to spirit photography to ghostly touch.[10] For others, though, unless it could be tested and proven or disproven, the performance was just that: a performance.

From the very beginning, skeptics and scientists were invested in testing the claims made by Spiritualists. Maggie and her sister Leah were investigated first by curious individuals from the area, like Eliab W. Capron, who devised a test in the fall of 1848 in which he asked the spirit to tell how many tiny seashells he had in his hand. Both times the spirit was correct.[11] In 1851 a group of medical professors from the new Buffalo Medical College—Austin Flint, Charles Lee, and C. B. Coventry—visited Leah and Kate at their lodgings at the Phelps Hotel.[12] Medicine as a profession was in a moment of proving itself. "Regular" doctors—that is to say, scientific doctors—like Flint, Lee, and Coventry were constantly at odds with "irregulars" like mesmerists and homeopaths. With no standardization of medical education or licensing, "regulars" were eager to further cement their professionalism by quashing any claims that bore a whiff of the unscientific.[13] After watching Leah and Maggie perform, the doctors quickly concluded that Maggie was creating the "rappings" by popping her knees imperceptibly. They just so happened to have encountered a "highly respectable lady" in Buffalo who could make the same sound. (Their respectful reference to this woman was a far cry from how they referred to the Fox sisters, deemed "females.")[14] Maggie and Leah felt insulted and invited the doctors back for an extended observation. This time the doctors put the sisters through a series of experiments to determine whether their knees were creating the rapping sounds. Their conclusion was the same: that Maggie was creating the rapping using her knees. In their report to the *Buffalo Medical Journal*, the doctors expounded on superstition versus science, education versus ignorance.

A person interested in the knockings, the doctors reported, had told them that people who had faith in spirit communication usually got responses from the spirits, while those who had doubts didn't. "We do not doubt the correctness of this observation," the doctors wrote derisively, stating that "it is fully explained by reference to the consideration just stated."[15]

A few years later the sisters were tested again, this time by a team of Harvard professors—and again, the investigators had an ax to grind, albeit this time a more personal one. While Maggie was grieving the death of her fiancé Elisha Kent Kane, his friends and family remained mortified by his relationship with a medium. One of Kane's friends, the geologist Louis Agassiz, sat on the investigation board. The professors were again unconvinced by the rappings and declared that "any connection with spiritualist circles, so called, corrupts the morals and degrades the intellect." As noted by the historian Barbara Weisberg, this may have been a particular jab at Maggie. Many in Kane's elite circles believed she had tainted their otherwise brilliant friend.[16]

Throughout the nineteenth century, leaders and members of the Spiritualist community were all too aware of both the challenges frauds created for Spiritualism and the inevitability of hucksters seeking to profit off the believers.[17] After all, in both Buffalo and Boston, the Fox sisters had volunteered to be investigated, aware that such accusations were a stain on their reputation which had to be faced directly. Real fraud had to be eliminated if Spiritualism was to be taken seriously. In 1898 the Spiritualist newspaper *The Liberator* noted that "commercial mediumship is at the bottom of the whole swindling business, and the sooner it is done away with, the better for Spiritualism." Above an article titled "The Present Condition of Spiritualism," an editorial cartoon depicts a young woman, the embodiment of Spiritualism, chained to a chariot labeled "Fraud," on which stand a spirit trumpeter and a woman wearing a crown that reads "Divine X Ray," while people in "etherealization" sheets stand behind her, one holding up a magnetized slate. The characters in the chariot represent the various manifestations of physical phenomena produced by Spiritualist mediums of the era, and the entire thing is pulled along by "state convention" and the "spiritualist press." *The Liberator,* personified as an angel swooping down to free Spiritualism from her chains, whispers, "The Truth Shall Make You Free." (This reference to William Lloyd Garrison's earlier antislavery newspaper *The Liberator* would have been immediately

Figure 12. Cartoon from "The Present Condition of Spiritualism," *The Liberator* 1, no. 2 (September 15, 1898): 1. International Association for the Preservation of Spiritualist and Occult Periodicals materials are licensed under a Creative Commons Attribution–NonCommercial 4.0 International License.

recognizable to nineteenth-century Americans.) In the background, a line of "Honest Mediums" is headed toward the "Poor House" as the fraud chariot rolls along in sparkling jewels and velvet crowns.[18]

Science and spirituality clashed at the end of the nineteenth century as parapsychology, the study of psychic phenomena, became increasingly popular. The Seybert Commission, made up of faculty from the University of Pennsylvania, investigated a number of respected Spiritualist mediums between 1884 and 1887, including the Fox sisters. The commission was established in 1883 on the death of the avowed Spiritualist Henry Seybert. Seybert had left money to the University of Pennsylvania for an endowed chair in philosophy, but as part of the bequest, he required the university to establish a commission to investigate "all systems of Morals, Religion, or Philosophy which assume to represent the Truth, and particularly of Modern Spiritualism."[19] Far from being a group of debunkers, the Seybert Commission was composed of one devoted Spiritualist and several self-proclaimed "impartials," including physicians, scientists, and a Shakespeare scholar. Seybert's interests were represented by his friend Thomas R. Hazard (described in the commission's preliminary report as "an uncompromising Spiritualist"), who agreed to oversee the conduct of the investigators and prevent abuse of mediums. The commission performed dozens of tests before publishing a preliminary report in 1887. It cited a few incidents of proven fraud as well as many more inconclusive results implying suspected but unproven fraud, and entirely debunked certain practices—such as slate writing, which the report described as nothing more than a magician's sleight of hand. Though the investigators repeatedly claimed they represented pure logic and objectivity, the overall tone of the report was snarky and dismissive.[20] The commission members, for instance, reported hearing the Fox sisters' rapping as "very light but very distinct," and while they couldn't detect Maggie's foot moving, commission chair Horace Howard Furness noted "pulsations" when he grasped her foot, gleefully telling her, "The most wonderful thing of all, Mrs. Kane, I distinctly feel them in your foot."[21] After two séances and with tentative plans for another meeting, Furness told Maggie that a third session "would necessarily be of the most searching description." Maggie declined to meet again. No matter—despite having found nothing definitive in Maggie's case, Furness wrote that the commission was already "satisfied in their own minds" as to the nature of her mediumship.[22] Their dismissiveness in Maggie's case was mild. As their investigations entered their third year, though, some of the commission members lost their scholarly filter. Chemist George Koenig, clearly exasperated, wrote in his notes about one séance in 1887: "Wants to cure my skepticism and so on, *ad nauseam*. Me is tired. Me wants go. . . . Stifling atmosphere breathing for 1-½ h, for what? *Quelle bêtise*! [What stupidity!]."[23]

Spiritualists were livid. Even before the report was completed, Hazard expressed his discontent with the commission's process. He claimed that he had protested the investigators' methods, believing they were not in line with Seybert's standards, but that his complaints were ignored. In 1885 Hazard requested that three members of the commission be removed and their conclusions be left out of the report, citing their bad faith experiments. The provost of the University of Pennsylvania and commission chair Furness ignored his protests.[24] Spiritualist media also decried the report well before it was released. "It is a huge mistake to leave a legacy to non-Spiritualists," declared *The Medium and Daybreak*, "on the expectation that they will use it to the advantage of Spiritualism."[25] After the report was released in 1887, the Spiritualist newspaper *Light* tore into the commission's investigation of Maggie Fox Kane, and while the editors admitted that it was probably correct in some "elementary matters," it was "to the last degree crude and misleading."[26] *The Banner of Light* declared that the commission members must "descend from their stilts and become imbued with clearer ideas concerning the naturally possible and impossible" before they could understand what they were seeing—and reported that "if what we get from Mr. Seybert at present time is correct," he must be disappointed in his commission from beyond the grave.[27]

Spiritualists argued that they themselves were committed to exposing fraud and encouraged one another to ostracize bad faith actors. Editor and Spiritualist John C. Bundy used the pages of the *Religio-Philosophical Journal* to root out fraud, even employing the legal system to stop mediums who refused to give up practice after he'd exposed them. He implored camps like Lily Dale to do more to guard against abuse.[28] The Seybert Commission never investigated any Lily Dale Assembly members or permanent residents but some of the mediums they suspected of fraud practiced temporarily on Lily Dale grounds as independent contractors who rented space. In 1887 A. B. Richmond, a Pennsylvania lawyer, critic of the commission, and, importantly, a Spiritualist, conducted an investigation in Lily Dale. In one respect he wished to better carry out Henry Seybert's imperative to evaluate spiritual claims, but in another he sought to repudiate the commission's sarcastic report. His investigations resulted in two books centered on his experiences at Lily Dale.[29] Ever lawyerly, Richmond compared his investigative work to presenting a case before a grand jury. Jurors (the public) with a "candid, thinking mind will most willing concede," he wrote, while "from the bigot who can see no truth outside the logic and teachings of his creed, I expect nothing but the contumely of ignorance and the condemnation of intolerance." Further, Richmond assured the commission that Spiritualists themselves *wanted* to be investigated: "Remember that Spiritualists ask no special favors at your hands; they desire that fraud may be exposed as sincerely as you do."[30]

An investigation could damage a medium's reputation. The Seybert Commission, for instance, had a devastating effect on some of the slate writers they so thoroughly and bitingly debunked. But for other mediums, even credible accusations of fraud could be parlayed into celebrity. Lizzie and Mary (also called May) Bangs, raised by Spiritualist parents in Kansas, had been active in mediumship their entire lives. Their powers had been covered by the Spiritualist media since at least 1872, when Stevens Sanborn Jones, the founding editor of the *Religio-Philosophical Journal*, visited the family and witnessed the girls perform slate readings. (Jones also caressed the "spirit kitten" the girls produced.)[31] The sisters maintained a residence in Lily Dale but traveled extensively giving séances. In 1888 A. B. Richmond investigated Lizzie Bangs at Lily Dale with what became known as his "hanging slates" test. He placed a pencil between two clean slates, screwed them together, covered the slates with a tablecloth, and held it down. Lizzie Bangs then placed her fingertips on the slates, and Richmond heard the pencil inside the two slates scrawl a message. When they opened the slates, there was a written message to Richmond from the spirit of George Seybert. Lizzie Bangs had passed his test with flying colors, and Richmond presented the experience as conclusive evidence that the Seybert Commission had committed malpractice.[32]

But Richmond's effusive praise for Lizzie and May Bangs looked a little silly two years later when the sisters faced much more serious criticism. In 1872 the *Religio-Philosophical Journal* had lauded them in childhood; by 1890, under the direction of a new editor, the *Journal* called the Bangs sisters out as frauds. After reminding readers of Richmond's praise of Lizzie Bangs, editor John Bundy ran an exposé featuring the testimony of H. H. Graham, the ex-husband of May Bangs, who admitted that he had helped Lizzie trick Richmond at Lily Dale:

> I was at the camp [Lily Dale] with May Bangs. I was drinking heavily, and under the influence of liquor. It was generally understood that Mr. Richmond was to publish a book, and he was then seeking experiences in "independent slate-writing" the records of which would be incorporated in his volume. May Bangs wanted to go into the book as the star medium for slate-writing. She wanted to utilize my skill and versatility in drawing and composition to further her trick. I refused. . . . But at a time when I was more intoxicated than usual I prepared a slate such as described by Mr. Richmond.[33]

Richmond did not take this lying down. He managed to get Graham to issue a formal retraction of his testimony (complete with a notary's signature!), which he then published along with a very snide rebuttal in a rival newspaper, *The Progressive Thinker*. He and Bundy continued to argue about the Bangs sisters for years in the pages of various national Spiritualist newspapers.[34]

In spite of—or perhaps *because of*—this scandal, the Bangs sisters persisted in their mediumship and became Spiritualist celebrities. Between their encounter with Richmond and the Graham scandal, the Bangs family built a mediumship firm called the Bangs Sisters with several locations around the Chicago area. In April 1888 May and Lizzie Bangs were arrested for fraud during a materialization séance. According to the media, a complaint was made to the police by a Chicago Spiritualist, D. P. Trefny, who believed the Bangs sisters to be committing fraud. This was the Bangs sisters' second run-in with the Chicago police. Just months before, the family of a prominent photographer, Henry Jestram, had filed a complaint that Lizzie and May Bangs had defrauded him and driven him into a mental institution because he felt "afflicted by constant brooding over 'spirit manifestations.'"[35] The police dispatched Trefny and a plainclothes detective, armed with a warrant for the sisters' arrest, to investigate the accusations. The result was dramatic. When a "spirit" appeared in the séance room, Trefny raced to grab it:

> The two detectives rushed to his aid and someone else lit the gas. The spook made a furious resistance, striking out right and left and tried to throw off its shroud and wig. "I have a warrant for you, May Bangs," said Detective Tyrrall, and just then the light mask she wore fell off disclosing her well known features. . . So threatening did the sisters and several male attendants of the séance become that the officers were compelled to draw their revolvers to clear the room. . . . A search revealed a satchel filled with white muslin shrouds, and the like, three sets of whiskers of different hues, five wigs, mustaches and a great variety of make up material such as is used by actors. They also found that in the cabinet was a curtain that ran up, the center of it making two compartments and also a side entrance which admitted the first operator behind the curtain, whereby all changes of costume were made. The cabinet[,] satchel [and] sisters were then loaded into a patrol wagon and taken to the station and locked up.[36]

Unabashed, the sisters took to the *Chicago Tribune* to plead their innocence, claiming that the court had cleared them of all charges and hoping their clients might return:

> The grand jury of Cook County, after having heard the statement of the witnesses for the State, has discharged us, although not a single one of our witnesses was or could be heard by them, thus deciding after hearing the testimony of our persecutors, and without a single word of defence, that the charges were baseless. The object of this card, which we ask a generous Press to circulate as freely as it did the articles to our injury, is to inform the public of the final result of this effort to degrade and humiliate us.[37]

But, according to the *Religio-Philosophical Journal*, this was another sleight of hand. The grand jury had actually found that the sisters were running a show to "amuse and entertain," and that their claims of spirit production were unbelievable. According to John Bundy's interpretation of the jury's findings, "they were not guilty of obtaining money by deceit, because everybody ought to know the pretences were false."[38]

It was the Bangs sisters' showmanship—not their mediumship—that protected them from legal trouble. Still undeterred, the sisters continued to work in various forms of mediumship, including the one they became most famous for at Lily Dale: producing precipitated "spirit paintings," in which an image would appear on a blank canvas.[39] In 1909 May Bangs, again in hot water on fraud charges, testified in court that she was not actually a medium. Nevertheless, many faithful Spiritualists continued to believe in the sisters' power, maintaining instead that she had lied for legal reasons. If May Bangs was guilty of anything, a believer wrote in *Light* in 1909, it was of "false and cowardly denial of the mediumistic gifts bestowed on her by Nature."[40]

For true believers, no amount of evidence of fraud impacted their faith. Indeed, several of the spirit paintings rendered by the Bangs sisters still hang in the Lily Dale Museum today, where they are admired by visitors in spite of the sisters' complicated legacy. As suggested by the way Spiritualists rejected H. H. Graham's admission of fraud, even confessions were ignored.

In 1888 American Spiritualism was rocked by the confession of one of its founders: Maggie Fox Kane. By the late 1880s, Maggie and Kate were both struggling to make ends meet and with their alcohol addictions. In the spring of 1888 Kate was arrested—drunk—for child neglect. At the same time, oldest sister Leah Fox Underhill was still reaping the benefits of her scandalous book *The Missing Link in Modern Spiritualism*, which offered "sparkling effects, intimate confidence, false family histories, startling facts, and a shiver of the erotic," according to the historian Barbara Weisberg. Maggie and Kate also suspected Leah of plotting to have Kate's children taken from her.[41] Angry with Leah, publicly humiliated, and somewhat desperate for money, both Maggie and Kate went to the press in the summer and fall of 1888. In September, Maggie gave an extensive interview to the *New York Herald* in which she savaged Spiritualism, defended Kate, and blamed everything on Leah and their mother, who used the girls to make money. In October she went one step further, publishing a lengthy personal statement in the *New York World*. "I think it is about time that the truth of this miserable subject 'Spiritualism' should be brought out," Maggie snarled. "It is now widespread all over the world, and unless it is put down soon it will do great evil." She went on to explain how she had created the rapping noises and accused Leah of exploiting her younger sisters for money.[42] That very night, Maggie took the stage at the New York Academy of Music to demonstrate to the gathered crowds how she and her sister had cracked the joints in their toes to make the rapping sounds that had first dazzled the audience of the Corinthian. The exposé was quickly turned into a book by journalist Reuben Briggs Davenport, titled *The Death-Blow to Spiritualism*. Only five years before, Maggie had spent the camp season at Lily Dale as an honored guest. Now she was calling for the destruction of Spiritualism itself.

Maggie and Kate's confessions, while hugely scandalous, were rationalized by the faithful. In December, Elizabeth Cottell wrote to *Light* in their defense, attaching a letter that Kate had written to her in November, suggesting that Kate had never betrayed Spiritualism, and assuring the paper's readers that "not withstanding a grave and painful fault," she was a "good and true medium." (The "fault," no doubt, was Kate's drinking.) Kate had written to Cottell that the organizer of Maggie's performance in New York had made $1,500 from it. Likely thinking of that princely sum in contrast to their constant struggle to make ends meet, Kate wrote to Cottell: "I think now I could make money in proving that the knockings are not made with the toes. . . . They are hard at work to expose the whole thing, if they can, but they certainly cannot."[43] A year later, Maggie was interviewed again and, moved by Spirit, recanted her previous recantation. "Their first and paramount idea," Maggie said of the journalists and managers who had orchestrated the events the previous fall, "was to crush Spiritualism, to make money for themselves, and to get up a great excitement."[44] She followed up that interview with a signed statement in November 1889 attesting to its veracity. After their deaths—Leah in 1890, Kate in 1892, and Maggie in 1893—it became even easier for Spiritualists to shape the women's memory in ways that were useful for the religion. Love Willis wrote to *The Banner of Light* to say that Maggie and Kate had indeed struggled, but that it was because society neglected to care properly for its mediums, judging them harshly and failing to support them. "Who of us," she asked in their defense, "would have done better, when the exhausted nerve-power failed to give energy for action, and the forces of soul, spirit, and body were depleted by unnatural demands upon them?"[45] Isaac Funk, a Spiritualist who wrote extensively on his own investigations of mediums, insisted that Maggie did have the power to communicate with Spirit. Her confession was essentially meaningless, Funk wrote: "I . . . know that so low had this unfortunate woman sunk that for five dollars she would have denied her mother, sworn anything. At that time, her affidavit for or against anything should not be given the slightest weight."[46] Even the most vocal apologist for Spiritualism, Arthur Conan Doyle, got involved, trying to resurrect Maggie and Kate's reputation over twenty years after their deaths in an essay analyzing their life in mediumship called "The Mystery of the Three Fox Sisters."

Physical manifestations made spirit communication more legible to the public, and of course made for an exciting show, but also invited both increased fraud and increased skepticism. High-profile scandals, such as those involving the Bangs and Fox sisters, heightened tensions in Spiritualist communities and kept patrons on high alert for scams. As the century turned, visitors to Lily Dale, and indeed, the mediums who resided there, were hypersensitive to potential fraud in the village. In 1907 Hereward Carrington visited Lily Dale on a mission to investigate physical mediumship. Carrington was a member of and investigator for the American Society of Psychical Research (ASPR), founded that year. Though that relationship lasted only a year, Carrington went on to write dozens of books on parapsychology (and also many on fruititarianism, of which he was an obsessive proponent). Carrington investigated several of Lily Dale's physical mediums. First was spirit photographer A. Norman. Norman refused to let Carrington watch as he developed his photography plates. In the resulting photograph,

Carrington's youthful frame is surrounded by the faces of strangers. The faces were, Carrington wrote, clearly "copied from some newspaper, or from some magazines, reproducing [the image] from the paper in which it originally appeared." He didn't even take more time to investigate Norman: "I think we need have no hesitation in attributing all that transpired through this individual's mediumship, at least on the occasion of my own sitting, to perfectly ordinary methods of deception and the resort to spirits is absurd."[47] Carrington also visited several other physical mediums. During one séance, the "drapery" of a ghostly apparition became hooked on a lady's hat. Instead of simply dematerializing, the "ghost" had to stand and wait to be disentangled.[48] In another, Carrington had a reading with two mediums who used a spirit trumpet, a large cone intended to serve as a kind of megaphone for ghostly voices. The mediums brought forth the voice of his father, speaking in an American accent. Carrington noted in his report, "My [English] father had never been to America in his life."[49]

When he visited the trumpet medium Mrs. McCoy at her house near the auditorium, he elected to be accommodating to the medium's efforts. McCoy kept Carrington chatting while they waited for the spirits to arrive—to cover the sound of preparations, Carrington decided—then he felt the spirit trumpet near his head. He decided to "help" the medium, that is, offer bits of information to lead her into traps: "I intended to help the medium as much as possible, at first, so as to get her started. Later, I intended asking for tests." When a spirit voice came, Carrington asked if it was his father:

> The reply was "yes," and the message continued,—giving about the usual messages for mediums of this class, such as:—"I am glad to see you are investigating this grand truth"; "so glad to see you here and talk to you"; etc., etc. The messages and the language were absolutely inappropriate to my father; they could not be more so. For instance, in answering a question of mine, my father replied, "yes, sir!" with a very American accent. I may say that my father was a very conservative Englishman, almost classical in his speech, and disliked most things American—particularly the manner of speaking and the slang. . . . The voice also said that my father had been ill "many months" before he died; while the truth is that he died as suddenly as the snuffing out of a candle, and was dead before any of us could reach him by train, in reply to telegrams.[50]

Carrington's approach was to observe rather than to actually test mediums; in other words, he did not ask for or create conditions that would prevent fraud in order to test a medium's powers, as had the Seybert Commission. In the case of slate writer Pierre L. O. A Keeler, Carrington noted that when such conditions were agreed upon, it was curious that mediums weren't able to perform. Keeler had been investigated in 1885 by the Seybert Commission at Horace Furness's home, but while the commission had theories about how he produced his results, they weren't certain. Carrington's experience was similar, and he considered Keeler a "clever trickster."[51] But a story Carrington heard secondhand made him wonder why mediums never seemed to be able to perform when the conditions weren't quite right. When a large party of twenty skeptical men came to Keeler for a reading, they asked if they could sit all around the room—meaning that there was no angle from which Keeler could not be seen at all times. Keeler agreed in exchange for a hefty fee—and then was unable to produce any spirit writing. "While I can quite see why it is that a sceptical temper of mind might offset the occurrence of many psychical phenomena," Carrington wrote, "I could never see why it is that the conditions invariably demanded at a slate-writing séance are just such as to render fraud possible—unless it is to practice fraud."[52] In all, Carrington reported on eight mediums who he'd determined, on the basis of his observations, were defrauding their customers. Dozens of mediums lived and worked at Lily Dale during the summer camp season, so this number may represent only a small percentage; it's hard to know, as Carrington neglected to report on anything except those individuals he suspected of fraud.

Carrington's criticism of physical mediumship is unflinching, but he was also respectful of the other mediums who lived and worked at Lily Dale. Physical mediumship, he suggested, produced a problematic cycle at places like Lily Dale: physical mediums created the dramatic moments that paying visitors craved, which in turn made it difficult for leadership to effectively drive them out. "Of course, all spiritualists are not of this type," Carrington wrote in his report to the ASPR. "There are some who attend the camp meetings and go away disgusted, and I spoke to many such. The officers of the Camp are of this more or less sceptical mind, so far as I could judge, but knew that phenomena of the sort craved must be supplied, or the camp would languish and finally cease to exist."[53] Before publishing Carrington's investigation, ASPR secretary James

Hyslop began a correspondence with Lily Dale Assembly treasurer George B. Warne, who admitted that combating frauds was a challenge for the Assembly. Warne informed Carrington and Hyslop that "the Directors [of the Lily Dale Assembly] engage the talent for the summer programme and never employ mediums for physical phenomena," though he conceded that physical mediums did "visit the camp like any other class of individuals, knowing they will have more patronage because of the crowds there, than if they stayed at home."[54]

While the Assembly may have been on the watch for fraud, they were reluctant to ban physical mediumship outright from the grounds. Rejecting popular practices like spirit photography and slate writing very likely would have meant losing visitors and their spending money. In his report, Carrington noted that the Spiritualist camp in Onset, Massachusetts, had banned physical mediumship after an exposé, *The Vampires of Onset*, had trashed the camp's reputation. The result of the ban was "that spiritualists ceased to visit the camp, which is now virtually a summer camp," Carrington wrote, adding, "It would be the same at Lily Dale."[55] It's unsurprising, then, that the Assembly was slow to ban physical mediumship. In 1903 board president Abby Louise Pettengill recommended to the board that some central space, like the Octagon building, be "furnished by the Association for physical manifestations, whenever practical, and that any one practicing fraud or admitting sitters without a ticket purchased from the Association, accepting money instead, shall forfeit their permit for that season."[56] While this would have limited physical mediumship and perhaps kept it under the Association's watchful eye, it also didn't entirely repudiate physical mediumship or exclude it from the grounds. It also makes clear that although the board members were concerned about fraud, they were equally concerned about mediums taking money from sitters without giving the Association its cut. In any case, Warne assured Hyslop that "whenever visitors submit charges of trickery, the [Lily Dale] board investigates, and if they are sustained in the evidence, after hearing both sides, the offending medium is compelled to leave the camp."[57]

Carrington confirmed that an "Investigating Committee" existed at Lily Dale, and that such expulsions did happen. In 1907 Hugh Moore, a physical medium who performed materializations, was renting a house in the village, where he performed up to five séances a day for paying customers. The Assembly grew suspicious of Moore's intense work schedule and appointed a committee to investigate him. They asked Moore to perform a séance on neutral ground in the Maplewood Hotel, but he refused, saying that the house he rented was properly "magnetized" for his work. Eventually, the committee attended a séance at his rented house. Carrington described the event:

> A strict examination of the house was made, and nothing was found out of place—no trap doors were discovered, and the Committee pronounced everything secure, and the séance given under test conditions. . . . A successful séance was held, until one of the [spirit] forms was "grabbed" by one of the investigators, when the whole trick was discovered. A trap was brought to light, which had not been detected, and the "spirit" turned out to be one of the young women, living upon the grounds. I was informed that at least three of the waitresses of the hotel were in the habit of "spooking" for him.

Moore escaped into the woods and was never heard from again.[58]

When Carrington's report on his investigations during the summer of 1907 was published, the officers of Lily Dale were, unsurprisingly, displeased. George Warne wrote to the ASPR in response to the report with carefully maintained civility: he had "only words of appreciation for the motives which prompted Mr. Carrington's investigation of Physical Phenomena at that center during August of 1907, while the spirit which dominates his report thereon is certainly commendable."[59] His forced politeness barely veils the frustration that the officers of the Lily Dale Assembly felt after the publication of Carrington's exposé. Despite Carrington's understated investigations and tone of general respect, Warne wrote, "the Report has caused no little misunderstanding and serious misrepresentation of the real character of Lily Dale."[60] He, and presumably the board, was frustrated that the report had garnered the interest of the media around the Northeast, so that, to the reading public—including readers of the *Toronto Mail and Empire* and the *New York Times*—it appeared that Lily Dale was nothing *but* "ingenious frauds" and "swindles."[61] Carrington's report, which focused only on physical phenomena at Lily Dale and ignored other forms of mediumship and spirituality, had generated a bad reputation.[62] What's more, Carrington's report had missed something quintessential about the tiny camp. As Warne tried to explain:

Lily Dale is above all things else a place for summer outings and education opportunities, instead of merely a financial harvesting time for fakirs. The large majority of people are drawn there for renewal of old and the formation of new friendships; to enjoy both in and out-of-door amusements; for the instruction of Special Classes conducted by those of acknowledged competency on Psychic questions; to profit by the daily platform lectures; to strengthen conviction and find comfort in listening to messages given in the auditorium by worthy mediums.[63]

While physical mediums worked at Lily Dale, Warne argued, they didn't represent everything that Lily Dale truly was—and to judge the community based on the trickery of a craven few was to miss the larger point of its existence.

Warne had a point: Carrington's report would leave a reader thinking that all there was to be found in Lily Dale were individuals running cons out of rented cottages. As Warne noted in 1908, and as evidenced by decades of annual camp programs, Lily Dale was as much a summer resort as it was a "religious colony" for Spiritualists.[64] For several summers a floating dance floor was pulled gently around Cassadaga Lake by a little boat, and concerts featuring local bands and visiting groups like the Boston Ladies Schubert Quartette entertained guests and residents.[65] People played baseball, billiards, tennis, quoits, and croquet. The 1916 program implores potential visitors to "Come to Lily Dale and be Happy," a caption placed above a peaceful scene of boats on the lake.[66] While physical phenomena, including those proven to be fraudulent, were part of Lily Dale's unofficial (and sometimes official) summer programming in its first sixty years of camp seasons, the Assembly endeavored to cultivate an experience that was more than spirit trumpets and automatic writing. Whether a visitor was seeking a peaceful retreat in the woods, the opportunity to speak to dead celebrities or loved ones, or a chance to listen to riveting traveling public speakers, Lily Dale had something for everyone. The specificity of Lily Dale as the "world's largest Spiritualist camp" was always at the forefront of publicity, including the negative publicity of Carrington's report, but as demonstrated in the programs that the Assembly used to market the summer camp, it had to be *more* to stave off the challenges of fraud and irrelevance.

Though today physical mediumship is banned in Lily Dale, that decree wasn't handed down until 1949. Banning physical mediumship could be bad for business; after all, as Carrington noted in his report, the camp at Onset had been permanently altered after it instituted a ban.[67] Keeping Lily Dale going was always a balancing act. On average, throughout the years prior to the ban on physical mediumship, visitors paid twenty cents to pass through the gates of Lily Dale, and anywhere between 2,500 and 10,000 people might visit in a single season. In the 1900s and 1910s, the Association typically had around $4,000 in available funds by the end of the fiscal year, barely enough to address any major issues that might emerge (as in 1910, for example, when it became obvious that the Assembly needed to build a new auditorium).[68] The Association simply couldn't afford to ban the physical mediums who brought in cash. As the historian Peter Lamont notes, "Séance phenomena were, after all, the primary reason given by spiritualists for their initial conversion to spiritualism and for their continuing beliefs."[69] Physical mediumship may have been prone to fraud, but it also drove the flow of income and brought new believers to the faith.

Although there is very little documentation about how the decline of physical mediumship may have changed Lily Dale mediums' practices, we do know something about how the decline inspired innovation in the practice of other Spiritualist mediums outside the camp. Far from suggesting purposeful fraud, Spiritualists' responses to physical mediumship scandals suggest that most mediums were less concerned with covering up fraud and more with elevating their practice and instituting their own test conditions to ensure, to themselves as much as to the public, that they were achieving "true mediumship."

One such medium, Elizabeth Hope Reed—known in England as Madame d'Espérance—is a good example of this. Following a spirit-grabbing scandal in 1888, d'Espérance was constantly worried that she was unknowingly perpetrating fraud. Like many mediums caught impersonating conjured materializations, d'Espérance and her allies claimed she was in a trancelike state, unaware of her body's movements. Rather than materializing out of nowhere, the spirit merely used her body to visit the world of the living with the medium caught entirely unawares.[70] To be fair, her exposer was later found to have been a spurned love interest who exhibited behaviors we would now consider stalking.[71] Skeptics regarded

Madame d'Espérance's trance story as an excuse by a medium caught red-handed, but there is plenty of evidence that she believed her own mediumship to be authentic; perhaps she was not knowingly complicit in any dishonesty.

D'Espérance continued to practice mediumship, but in her autobiography she described a nagging uncertainty about the veracity of her own manifestations: "I had begun to have a feeling of dissatisfaction with respect to these materialised forms. I could not analyze my own feelings with respect to them, but a vague sense of doubt that had not yet grown into a thought, began to puzzle me. I hardly knew how it arose or where it came from, but I could not get away from it—it haunted me constantly."[72] At the same time, d'Espérance was aware that physical mediumship was on the decline. "Materialization," she wrote in 1903, "has fallen into the greatest disrepute with the world at large."[73]

The obvious choice, and one that many mediums made, was to move away from physical mediumship. That did not feel like an authentic choice for d'Espérance, who earnestly believed in Spiritualist principles and was committed to improving her mediumship with the spirit world. Instead, d'Espérance made intentional innovations to her practice so she could continue to manifest spirits that many (even she herself) considered to be genuine. First, she abstained from all intoxicants and insisted that her sitters also abstain for six months prior to a reading. To d'Espérance, intoxicants clouded the mind and could, theoretically, result in unintentionally fraudulent practice.[74] In that same vein, she eliminated all passive mediumship. D'Espérance believed that fraudulent mediums relied on either mind-altering substances or ambiguous "trance states" to mitigate accusations of fraud: if a medium was truly only a vessel through which messages arrived, then they could argue they were not aware of or responsible for any funny business. D'Espérance rejected this approach, insisting on remaining conscious during all of her readings. She also remained in full view of sitters at all times. According to reports of her sittings, materialized spirits continued to make appearances, with d'Espérance still completely in view.

Perhaps the most important aspect of d'Espérance's innovation is that she decentered herself as the subject of the mediumship. The circle—the sitters, their beliefs, desires, their togetherness—was the medium, not d'Espérance. "When she shifted the responsibility to the room," the scholar Marlene Tromp writes, "the individual medium could no longer be the focus of the charge or the experience."[75] As Averill and Elizabeth discuss in their chapters on Spiritualism in the Victorian home and in the women's rights movement, the authority that women asserted in mediumship was often perceived as passive, channeling the spirits of men or, in d'Espérance's case, diffusing their power to the mixed circle of sitters. But to d'Espérance, turning the mediumship over to the circle was also a way of avoiding the appearance of fraud.

Spiritualists were committed not only to removing the appearance of fraud, like d'Espérance, but also to preventing any unintentional or associated fraud. True believers, which most Spiritualists were, had an interest in eliminating fraud, not perpetrating it. Take, for example, Julia's Bureau, a nonprofit automatic writing organization created by the famed British journalist W. T. Stead. The bureau conducted readings through an elaborate process designed to demonstrate their veracity while also eliminating the possibility of fraud. While Stead set the bureau in motion, it was said to be overseen by the spirit of the dead American temperance activist and journalist Julia Ames. Stead instituted extensive test controls on the process, refusing to take any money from sitters. According to Estelle Stead, W. T. Stead's daughter, having Julia Ames's spirit oversee the operation helped reduce both the opportunities for fraud as well as inaccuracies: "To minimize the risks and diminish the dangers attaching to this attempt to bridge the grave, Julia undertook the personal direction of the Bureau, and herself defined the rules and conditions which had to be observed by all those who wished to avail themselves of its advantages."[76] Therefore, all decisions about the organization came from the dead Julia. People who desired a reading had to file an application. These would be judged by "Julia." In order to determine her ghostly decision, the applications were given in triplicate to two automatic writers and a psychic medium who channeled Julia. If their messages agreed—and Estelle Stead says they almost always did—then her decision was honored. Accepted applicants then filled out another form which requested various kinds of information the mediums might offer as proof (for example, a loved one's cause of death, incidents in the deceased's life, or the loved one's personal appearance or mannerisms). At the bottom of the list, the applicant had to agree that if the reading hit on any of that information, they would "be satisfied" that, in the words of the application, "I have been put in communication with my dead."⁷⁷ The applicant kept that form, sealed safely in an envelope.

Once all the forms were filled out, the service could take place. Many applicants attended the séances in person, but some received readings from afar. Whether the reading was to be in person or remote, the mediums who had considered the individual's application—with their loved one's information on it—were excluded from attending the séance. All sessions were attended by a stenographer who recorded the messages. These reports were sent to the sitters, who only then forwarded the secret form with their loved one's information to the bureau, where it was, for the first time, unsealed and compared with the medium's report. In its first four months, the bureau performed readings for 150 applications. It remained active for three years, during which time its mediums performed six hundred readings, most of which produced satisfied customers convinced they had made contact with their loved ones. Doubters might remain skeptical, but careful organization and deliberate processes protected Julia's Bureau from accusations of fraud while providing clients with added confidence in their readings.

When the Fox Cottage burned to the ground in 1955, it marked something like the end of an era. This direct link to the earliest days of the religion was gone, leaving behind a history fading into myth and an empty shade garden. From that point on, Lily Dale had to rely on itself to create and protect its own legitimacy. As they had faced Carrington's investigations at the turn of the twentieth century, Lily Dale's leaders continued to face skepticism head-on. The Center for Inquiry (CFI), first conceived of by the philosophy professor Paul Kurtz in 1976, is a national nonprofit organization headquartered in Buffalo and dedicated to advancing critical thinking and scientific reasoning. For decades the CFI has investigated and researched paranormal claims around the United States, even offering a $250,000 prize to anyone who has a claim of paranormal powers that the organization isn't able to disprove.⁷⁸ Lily Dale, no doubt because of its proximity to the Buffalo headquarters, has had a long relationship with CFI investigators from its Committee for Skeptical Inquiry. Joe Nickell, a longtime investigator and senior research fellow for the committee, was even profiled by *The New Yorker* during one of his many visits to Lily Dale. Nickell wore dark sunglasses and a straw hat during that visit, telling the journalist that he'd changed his appearance in the car to avoid detection, but he also made real connections with the folks who live and work at Lily Dale, including Ron Nagy, whom he now considers a friend. Nickell's approach is one of true open-mindedness rather than the motivation to disprove. In the profile, he described his own experience with hardline skepticism by telling a story about the time he fell down the stairs while at a skeptics' conference. When he told his colleagues he thought he'd broken his leg, they didn't believe him until he showed them his dangling foot. "What we need is a kinder, gentler skepticism," he told the journalist. "I'm tired of these debunkers coming by my office and saying, 'Hey, Nickell, seen any ghosts lately? Har har har. . . . I'm not saying there's a fifty-fifty chance that there is a ghost in that haunted house. I think the chances are closer to 99.9 per cent that there isn't. But let's go look. We might learn something interesting as hell."[79] In our conversations, Ron recalled his relationship with Joe fondly, demonstrating what we already suspected: that skepticism and Spiritualism can—and do—coexist. Lily Dale is a place that, as it always has, invites faithful and skeptic alike to come, listen, think, and perhaps learn something interesting as hell.

In 1897 May Wright Sewall, a leader in the national women's rights movement, was invited to speak at the yearly Woman's Day celebration at Lily Dale. Though she was no Spiritualist when she arrived, her life changed during that visit. Persuaded by fellow suffragist Elnora Babcock to consult a medium while at the camp, Sewall was stunned when her deceased husband came to her during a reading. Sewall spent the rest of her life in constant conversation with her husband's spirit, and only months before her death published *Neither Dead nor Sleeping*, a memoir of her journey into Spiritualism.[80] Brought to the shores of Cassadaga because of her feminist politics rather than her faith, Sewall captures another facet of Lily Dale's history: its role as a Spiritualist hub for women activists seeking equal rights.

4

The Auditorium

Elizabeth

The Lily Dale auditorium sits on the side of a rolling hill, nestled among the Victorian-era cottages that line the roads on either side. The wooden building is starkly white against the lush greens and purples of the hostas and cone flowers lovingly planted along its edges and sidewalks. During one of our summer research trips, the weather was unseasonably warm and humid and the mosquitoes were running rampant. Apparently the heavy rains of the weeks before had left countless hidden pools of standing water, where the mosquitoes bred with impunity. They kept us away from Inspiration Stump, instead forcing the messages from Spirit to seek shelter inside the auditorium for the daily spectacles of truth. As we stepped into the dim light of the auditorium, a spry white-haired woman handed us each a paper fan. The fans were emblazoned with the black-and-white image of Susan B. Anthony, who visited Lily Dale many times during the struggle for women's suffrage. Anthony has become the face of the women's movement in Lily Dale. Ask any resident or frequent visitor and they will gladly point you to the museum, where the walls are covered with evidence of Anthony's visits to this sleepy town.

Seated in the auditorium's folding chairs, we lazily flapped our fans back and forth over our faces, and me over my legs. I seemed to be the only one who continued to attract mosquitoes, even inside the auditorium. We waited, checking our phones and scratching our ankles, as a motley crew of Lily Dale visitors meandered into the building to find a seat and wait for inspiration to take hold. That day, we learned, acolytes would be reading the spirit messages. One was visiting from South Africa, another from New Jersey. The medium from New Jersey walked to the front of the room, introduced herself, and began. Taking a deep breath, she said that a spirit by the name of Gino was coming through. Her eyes searched the room, waiting for someone to claim him. After a long silence, and plenty of audience members nervously glancing at their neighbors, a woman in the back tentatively raised her hand. "My uncle's best friend was named Gino?" she said, more as a question than a statement. Maybe it was him?

As the acolyte and the women went back and forth, attempting to pinpoint Gino's tentative spiritual connection, my eyes wandered around the room. I took in the stage and the empty chairs lined up in a row, ready for a more orchestrated event than the free-flowing public message service we were attending. My eyes drifted up the walls, then to the ceiling, where I was struck by the inoperable gas lamps that hung from the rafters. Thin iron tubes trailed from the ceiling and split to form two arms, on which frosted glass domes sat. Interspersed between these antique light fixtures were modern-day fixtures, their bulbs sitting gray and unsparked as the sunlight through the open walls warmed the cool inner room.

Returning my gaze to the stage, I continued to fan myself as I thought about the thousands of people who have come and gone from this room. Lily Dale was an important stop on the suffrage circuit in the late nineteenth and early twentieth centuries—not only because of its close proximity to the famous Chautauqua Institution, but also because Lily Dale was a destination in itself, a place where forward-minded individuals came to commune with others who were focused on changing the world. The Lily Dale auditorium was built in 1883 and represents the spirit of communal action, of gathering together to enact change. That is the purpose it served at the turn of the century, and to an extent, that is still its purpose today.[1]

The auditorium has changed over the years yet still feels intimately connected to its nineteenth-century roots. The earliest building was a simple barn of about four thousand square feet, covered by a shingled roof supported by poles. It was not enclosed, which allowed the cool summer breeze to waft through as patrons quietly listened to speakers. Heavy curtains were added that could be lowered from the roof supports, protecting listeners from wind and rain. Soon, with the addition of eleven rows of seats, the space comfortably held up to 1,500 people at once.[2] Lily Dale's popularity required a further addition to the auditorium in 1910, which made the space much larger. The official program for the 1911 camp season boasted that the auditorium had "6,000 square feet of floor without obstruction and one of the finest structures of its kind in the State." Patrons could listen to lectures during the day and dance there every Wednesday and Saturday evening.[3]

Over the past century and a half, countless Lily Dale visitors have sat within the auditorium to hear the truth spoken, whether the truth of the spiritual presence among the living, the truth that men and women are created equal, the truth that one can bend spoons with one's mind, or some combination of those truths and others. The auditorium—whether the building itself or the land it sits upon—is infused with the energies of truths both apparent and not.

Although it is Susan B. Anthony who garners the most attention for her visits to Lily Dale in the late nineteenth and early twentieth centuries, other suffrage luminaries such as the doctor and minister Anna Howard Shaw, Charlotte Perkins Gilman, Isabella Beecher Hooker, and a host of other well-known speakers spread the message of women's rights in Lily Dale. But it wasn't just these acclaimed leaders of the national suffrage movement who nurtured the ties between Spiritualism and women's rights. The work by lesser-known grassroots reformers and Spiritualists such as Marion Skidmore, Abigail Louise Pettengill, and Elizabeth Lowe Watson ensured that Lily Dale was a garden that nurtured the progressive fruit of women's rights. These reformers and Spiritualists connected to Lily Dale weren't fringe radicals working at the tail end of a waning nineteenth-century Spiritualist movement but rather a group of cosmopolitan activists who were well traveled, well connected, and at the vanguard of some of the late nineteenth and early twentieth century's most pressing questions. The network of women reformers who lived, worked, and passed through Lily Dale were part of a national movement, connected through Spiritualism as a religion, Spiritualism as a science, or Spiritualism as a vehicle of reform.

As we have shown in previous chapters, Lily Dale is a vestige of the Second Great Awakening and the radical reform culture that burned through western New York in the early to mid-nineteenth century. The year 1848 was momentous in the Burned Over District. That was the year Margaret and Kate Fox first heard the rappings at their cottage in Hydesville. It was also the year that the Seneca Falls Convention, recognized by many as the first women's rights convention, was held in nearby Seneca Falls, and where Elizabeth Cady Stanton's manifesto "The Declaration of Sentiments" proclaimed the self-evident truth that "all men *and* women are created equal."[4] Thus in 1848, western New York gave birth both to Spiritualism and to the organized women's rights movement, and it comes as no surprise, then, that many of their central tenets overlapped.

Reformers at the Seneca Falls Convention insisted that women deserved equal rights not only in civil and political affairs but also in religious matters. Women, for the most part, were denied positions of authority in organized religions. This included ministry. When men excluded women from the clergy and from religious office, reformers argued that men were stepping into the place of God.[5] This was not unlike abolitionists' reasoning (and most early women's rights advocates were also abolitionists) that slaveholders usurped the power of God because only God could rule over another man. Many white women saw a connection between their own subservient condition and that of the enslaved. The formal call at Seneca Falls to dismantle American patriarchal hierarchy kindled a nationwide demand for social, civil, political, *and* religious equality for women.[6]

Like other religions sprouting in the Burned Over District that usurped traditional church authority, such as the Shakers and the Mormons, Spiritualism offered women frustrated by the strictures of traditional religion a measure of independence.[7] Spiritualism alleged that truth came directly to the individual, through Spirit, without mediation by a church-appointed authority. This lack of male or "superior" intercession (by means of a minister) meant that women could receive divine messages themselves. It presented a very different possibility of religious *authority*. The appeal of a form of religion that could forgo religious authority through mediumship was intriguing and opened up possibilities for usurping all forms of gendered control. Thus Spiritualists argued that women needed to be freed from societal structures and restrictions such as those that limited their education; denied them control of their property, their children, even their own bodies; and forced them into economic dependency on men. Spiritualists saw the innate inequality in marriage, which granted a husband sexual access to his wife's body which she had no legal right to refuse. Spiritualists sometimes likened marriage to prostitution or rape. *The Banner of Light* proclaimed in 1864 that "rape is punished out of wedlock but *in* it paid no attention to."[8] These were very radical ideas at the time and were very attractive to many men and women who were looking to cast off the shackles of hierarchy. Thus, it's not really surprising that numerous participants in the Seneca Falls Convention eventually became Spiritualists.

Ann Braude's groundbreaking work showed how the women's rights movement, particularly during the antebellum period, was closely linked with Spiritualism. A more recent study by the historian Nancy Hewitt reveals how people like the radical Quaker Amy Post were at the center of developments in reform and radical religion. Post attended the Seneca Falls Convention and orchestrated the follow-up convention held in Rochester. Post was also a mentor to the Fox sisters. Her support for and belief in the Fox sisters' abilities lent the early Spiritualist movement credibility. Once the news of the Hydesville rappings was taken seriously by the Posts, people respected and known for their religious piety, then other respected people became interested in hearing spirit communication from sources—like teenage girls—that they might not previously have considered credible. Amy and her husband, Isaac, were at the center of a large and active network of abolitionists, radical reformers, and radical Quakers in the Rochester region and aided in the spread of these movements.[9]

Spiritualism became *the* main vehicle for spreading the message of women's rights before 1861. Every Spiritualist newspaper, pamphlet, and lecturer sang the merits of women's rights, and many of the movement's leaders became Spiritualists themselves. Susan B. Anthony commented in her diary that "Spiritualism as usual [was] the principle [sic] topic" at a dinner party among a group of Quaker abolitionists in the early 1850s.[10] Although neither Anthony nor Stanton was a Spiritualist herself, they did participate in séances. Nevertheless, many leaders in the movement were Spiritualists, and this trend continued into the twentieth century. With

Lily Dale as a hub, it is possible to see how Spiritualism and women's rights were *still* intimately connected in the period after the Civil War.

Long before Susan B. Anthony became the face of suffrage at Lily Dale, and indeed before Lily Dale was founded, Elizabeth Lowe Watson, trance medium and women's suffrage leader in California, spoke of the merits of Spiritualism on the shores of Cassadaga Lake. Born Elizabeth Lowe in Solon, Ohio, in 1842, Watson experienced trance mediumship at an early age. In 1849, when she was only seven years old, a series of rappings permeated her one-room schoolhouse. Elizabeth, or Libbie as she was known to her friends, was the one student whom the raps seemed to answer to. At first, her mother fretted over Libbie's mysterious power. Sometimes the raps indicated that they were the spirit of Libbie's departed baby sister; at other times they were expired neighbors or friends. Libbie's spirit communication developed during the same period when the Fox sisters first communicated with the spirit realm and many western New Yorkers were becoming interested in séances and spirit rappings. As her mother became more accustomed to Libbie's apparent mediumship, she slowly converted to Spiritualism.[11]

After several years, Libbie began to experiment with other forms of spirit manifestation, such as trance mediumship. Whenever Libbie fell into a trancelike state, her family would gather and listen as Spirit spoke through her, reciting abstruse scripture and waxing poetic on science and philosophy. Soon, neighbors and passersby were gathering regularly to hear Libbie speak. As she was just thirteen, it was easier to accept that a spirit spoke through her than that a young girl could discuss science and scripture so eloquently.[12]

When Libbie turned fourteen, she set out on the lecture circuit, displaying her mediumship abilities to the curious and converted alike. Libbie's father retired from farm life in order to travel as her guardian and chaperone full-time.[13] Apparently the money reaped on the circuit was enough to support the entire Lowe family. During these years Libbie was surrounded by other mediums such as the Fox sisters and another young rising star, Cora L. V. Scott.[14] Libbie developed deep lifelong friendships with these other Spiritualists, as well as with Progressive Quakers like the Posts. These connections put her within the orbit of the radical reform networks pushing at the boundaries of family, religion, and citizenship.[15]

Libbie's connection to Lily Dale also began during these early days. Like Cora, Libbie was one of the young Spiritualists who traveled the lecture circuit during the mid-nineteenth century. Another young woman on the Spiritualist circuit, Harriet Doolittle of Laona, a tiny hamlet in Chautauqua County, had also been called to mediumship during this period. Doolittle's gifts became well known enough to draw other mediums, including Libbie and Cora, to congregate on the shores of Cassadaga Lake during the summers. The group of intellectuals and early Spiritualists who gathered there formed the Laona Free Association in the 1850s. These camp meetings continued to attract truth seekers, and by the 1870s, meetings drew anywhere from one hundred to four hundred people.[16] This group would eventually form the Cassadaga Lake Free Association (CLFA).

In 1861 Libbie married Spiritualist and oil tycoon Jonathan Watson. From that time forward, she was professionally known as E. L. Watson. Jonathan made his fortune relying on guidance he received from Spirit when deciding where to place his oil wells.[17] During their marriage, Libbie traveled frequently back to Rochester and to camp meetings in Lily Dale to speak and attend lectures.[18] All was not well in the Watson household, however. Jonathan's spirit guides were increasingly leading him astray from lucrative oil wells. Some of his wells were productive, but more frequently they came up dry. By 1878 his millions were all but gone. Soon thereafter the couple divorced and Libbie Watson moved to California.[19]

Almost immediately upon her arrival, Watson became the pastor of the First Spiritual Union of San Francisco, which later grew into the Religious and Philosophical Society of San Francisco. She led regular Sunday services at the ornate Metropolitan Temple. Hundreds of people from all Christian denominations would come to hear Watson speak on the philosophy of Spiritualism as well as pressing political issues of the day, particularly women's rights.[20] She also returned frequently to western New York and the network of friends and co-religionists building a Spiritualist community on the shores of Cassadaga Lake. In the summer of 1880 Libbie gave the dedicatory address for the newly formed CLFA, which would in time change its name to the Lily Dale Assembly. Standing on the rustic speaker's stand, surrounded by nature and evergreen boughs, she lectured on the "Ideal Home," tying Spiritualism to the equality inherent between men and women.[21] Her inaugural address would forever establish E. L. Watson as one of the founders of Lily Dale.

Figure 13. The Grand Hotel, now called the Maplewood, in the 1890s. The woman in white, second row from the top near the middle, is Elizabeth Lowe Watson. "Lily Dale Assembly History," three-ring binder, Lily Dale Museum.

Watson's ministry and travel schedule increased over the following years. In 1882 she went on a four-month lecture tour throughout Australia, speaking to large audiences wherever she went. She also traveled extensively across the United States, preaching the truths of both Spiritualism and human equality, but made it back frequently to Lily Dale.[22] Watson also turned her California ranch, Sunny Brae, into a working orchard, a beautiful oasis known for "lovely lawns, noble trees, rare shrubbery, wooded ravine and nearby mountains." She delivered sermons from underneath a large oak tree at Sunny Brae, with Susan B. Anthony, Anna Howard Shaw, and other suffrage luminaries in attendance.[23]

Another woman present at the founding of the CLFA, and a key player in making Lily Dale a hub of women's rights, was Marion Skidmore. It is because of Skidmore that Lily Dale established an annual Women's Day and hosted numerous famous women reformers. Skidmore was a regular attendant at state and national suffrage conventions. She was also an ardent Spiritualist. Skidmore brought her reformist zeal and penchant for organization to bear in Lily Dale, ensuring that it would be a home for spiritual seekers and early feminists alike.

Marion Johnson was born in 1826 in Butternuts, a town in central New York State. She and her father, William Johnson, were integral to the beginnings of Lily Dale. Her father had witnessed mesmerism in Laona as early as 1845 and joined the Spiritualist movement early. He was one of the organizers of meetings in Laona before the formation of the Laona Free Association.[24] Marion married Thomas J. Skidmore, another eager seeker at the summer meetings in Laona, in 1854. The Skidmores' faith in Spiritualism was cemented after the deaths of their children. They lost an infant girl shortly after they were married, and then another daughter, who died in young adulthood just a few days after her wedding in 1875. Marion and Thomas were both founders of the CLFA. Thomas first served as treasurer, then president, and Marion as a trustee. Marion made creating and building the future Lily Dale the "all-absorbing theme of her life."[25] According to many, Marion Skidmore was single-handedly responsible for making Lily Dale an idyllic camp and was affectionately known as the "mother of Cassadaga." Throughout the 1880s, she orchestrated the landscaping of Lily Dale, planting trees and flowers with her own hands and laying out parks and promenades. Soon the hamlet was a picturesque retreat. One of Skidmore's many lasting legacies was the creation of the library, now named in her honor, which began as a lending collection in a tent; its present iteration is housed in a grand neoclassical building dedicated after her death in 1923. By the late 1880s, the CLFA had added eighteen more acres to the grounds and attracted enough year-round residents that Skidmore guided the community in establishing a public school. Skidmore was also the impetus behind the foundation of the Children's Lyceum, a day school for the children of visitors to the camp. On Fridays the children would parade through the grounds, which became a special weekly event for many years.[26]

Marion Skidmore exemplifies how Spiritualism and the women's rights movement interconnected at Lily Dale. Her earnest belief in equality, affirmed by her inherent faith in Spiritualism, led her to make Lily Dale one of the preeminent stops on the suffrage lecture circuit at the turn of the twentieth century, and her presence in the village attracted those fighting for women's suffrage, temperance, and economic reforms. She was an important member of the network of women reformers fighting for these causes, and in turn was instrumental in bringing those speakers to Lily Dale. Because of the influence of reformers like Skidmore and Watson, Lily Dale became a place where many national reform movements overlapped.

At the urging of Lillie Devereux Blake, the leader of the New York State Women Suffrage Association, men and women in Jamestown, New York—only twenty miles from Lily Dale—organized a Political Equality Club in 1887, which championed equal rights for women. That same year, Marion Skidmore created the first Women's Day event during the Lily Dale camp season. She invited local suffragists, many already members of the Jamestown group, to lecture. She also established a women's tent by the lakeshore to be the hub of suffrage activities.[27] The following year Skidmore founded the Political Equality Club of Lily Dale, which met regularly in the Octagon Building to champion women's suffrage and other reforms. Also in 1888 suffragists organized a countywide Chautauqua Political Equality Club, electing the suffragist and Spiritualist Elnora Babcock as their president. The Lily Dale Political Equality Club was part of this organization and regularly hosted countywide events on the Lily Dale grounds.[28]

Grassroots organizing such as this was happening across the country in the 1880s. The mainstream national suffrage movement, composed mostly of middle-class white women, was in the process of reconciling after a decades-long split that stemmed from disagreements over the passage of the Reconstruction Amendments. The early feminist and abolitionist movements had been closely tied since the early nineteenth century. After the Civil War, women's suffrage supporters organized the American Equal Rights Association in 1866 "to secure Equal Rights to all American citizens, especially the right of suffrage, irrespective of race, color or sex."[29] Nevertheless, debates over the Fourteenth and Fifteenth Amendments caused a major split in the movement. First, the Fourteenth Amendment marked the first time that the word "male" was inserted into the US Constitution. Then the Fifteenth Amendment declared that states could not deny the right to vote on the basis of "race, color, or previous condition of servitude," omitting any mention of sex. This deliberate exclusion led to fierce debates among advocates for women's suffrage. Anthony and Stanton were privately asked to suspend their work for universal suffrage and to concentrate on getting the vote for Black men only. Anthony responded that "she would sooner cut off her right arm before she would ever work for or demand the ballot for the black man and not the woman." She considered it a betrayal to be asked to compromise on universal suffrage. "It is not a question of precedence between women & black men," she continued. "Neither has a claim to precedence upon an Equal Rights platform. But the business of this association is to demand for every man black or white, and for every woman, black or white, that they shall be this instant enfranchised and admitted into the body politic with equal rights and privileges."[30]

Though many suffragists had been part of the abolitionist movement, they were not immune to racial prejudice. Stanton claimed that "it's better to be the slave of an educated white man than of a degraded black one," arguing that Black men would be "despotic" if granted the vote ahead of white women.[31] Stanton and Anthony split with others in the women's rights movement over this issue, forming the National Woman Suffrage Association (NWSA) with the sole focus of securing immediate voting rights for women. Other suffragists, led by Lucy Stone and Julia Ward Howe, formed the American Woman Suffrage Association (AWSA), which continued to support suffrage for Black men with the understanding that the vote for women would come next. By the late 1880s, reconciliation seemed to be in the works, although this also meant that the two major suffrage associations had all but abandoned working with African American women, with minor exceptions.

A rising luminary in this reconciliation was the physician and minister Anna Howard Shaw, who had been lecturing for suffrage since 1881 as a representative of the Massachusetts Woman Suffrage Association (MWSA). By all accounts Shaw was an amazing speaker, rarely writing speeches out. Instead, she read her audiences and spoke *to* them, not above them. In 1883 the Women's Christian Temperance Union (WCTU) adopted an equal suffrage plank as part of its "do everything" campaign, and its president, Frances Willard, recruited Shaw to be its spokeswoman. The late 1880s were a whirlwind of activity for Shaw. She continued working for the MWSA, was named one of two national lecturers for the AWSA, and continued working as the associate superintendent and lecturer of the Franchise Department for the national WCTU. This put her into contact with Anthony when they spoke on the same platform in Newton, Kansas, in October 1887. Soon, Anthony recruited Shaw to the NWSA. Shaw wrote of Anthony's persuasive argument:

> I was very happy in my connection with the Woman's Christian Temperance Union. . . . But Miss Anthony's arguments were always irrefutable. . . . "You

can't win two causes at once," she reminded me. "You're merely scattering your energies. Begin at the beginning. Win suffrage for women, and the rest will follow." . . . From then until her death, eighteen years later, Miss Anthony and I worked shoulder to shoulder.[32]

When the NWSA hired Shaw in 1889, she became a link between the AWSA and the NWSA, helping to negotiate the joining of the two organizations into the National American Woman Suffrage Association (NAWSA) in 1890.

As important as the creation of NAWSA was, it was local organizers across the country who gave the movement its backbone. Suffragists in Chautauqua County, and Lily Dale specifically, were no less organized and important to the national movement. The CLFA wasn't the only major meeting place for late nineteenth-century truth seekers in the county. The Chautauqua Institution, founded in 1874 as a summer camp to train Methodist Sunday school teachers, later expanded to become a lecture center for social issues and the arts and sciences. In 1890, the Chautauqua Institution created a platform for women's suffrage, which brought many suffrage leaders, including Shaw, to promote women's rights. The following year, women's suffrage clubs from across the country met at the Chautauqua Institution for a political equality event, with over fifty people from Lily Dale in attendance.[33] That fall, the Chautauqua County organization voted to become an auxiliary of the New York Woman Suffrage Association, creating the largest women's suffrage club in the United States.[34]

Marion Skidmore, ever the organizer, was integral to the suffrage work in Chautauqua County. Her friendliness and energy made her a major force in the movement, leading groups of reformers from Lily Dale over the hills to the Chautauqua Institution to participate in meetings and attend lectures.[35] In 1891 Skidmore invited Anthony and Shaw to stay with her at her cottage in Lily Dale and speak at that year's annual Women's Day. That invitation created a link between the leaders of the national suffrage movement and the Spiritualist camp.[36]

Lily Dale residents joined in on the celebration of "Spiritual Truth, Freedom and Progress" by decorating tents and cottages with evergreen boughs and cut flowers. The streets were lined with star-spangled bunting, flowing in the breeze off the gingerbread verandas and balustrades. Men, women, and children trotted the grounds wearing golden suffrage badges on their breasts. Thousands swarmed the campgrounds, arriving in trains and private carriages. They entered the campgrounds under a banner proclaiming "Lily Dale, Greetings to Political Equality." Other banners declared "Equality Is Justice" and "Eternal Justice Knows No Sex." One banner simply stated "WYOMING," highlighting the sole state that allowed equal suffrage for white men and women, although Native Americans were barred from voting in that state. That afternoon, speakers lectured from the Assembly Hall stage, decorated with images of suffrage leaders such as Elizabeth Cady Stanton and Lucretia Mott, interlaced with golden bunting.[37] Anthony wrote fondly about the event:

> People came from far and near. Fully 3,000 were assembled in that beautiful amphitheater decorated with the yellow and the red, white and blue. . . . There hanging by itself was our national suffrage flag, ten by fourteen feet, with its regulation red and white stripes, and in the center of its blue corner just one great golden star, Wyoming, blazing out all alone. Every cottage in the camp was festooned with yellow, and when at night the Chinese lanterns on the piazzas were lighted, Lily Dale was as gorgeous as any Fourth of July, all in honor of Woman's Day and her coming freedom and equality. Our hosts, Mr. and Mrs. Thomas Skidmore, are the center of things at Lily Dale, and right royal are they in their hospitality as well as their love of liberty for all.[38]

Marion Skidmore's connections were also instrumental to the arrival of another suffrage leader and ardent Spiritualist, Abby Louise Pettengill. Pettengill met Marion Skidmore on a train as she was traveling to the eastern seashore. The two immediately bonded over their shared passions for women's suffrage and Spiritualism. In fact, Pettengill was so taken with Skidmore's descriptions of Lily Dale that she abandoned her travel plans and instead went with Skidmore to Lily Dale, where she stayed all summer. From then on, Pettengill was a Lily Dale booster, returning every summer for the next two decades. In 1902 she was elected Lily Dale's president, and in 1903 she oversaw the name change from Cassadaga Lake Free Association to the City of Light Assembly. She served as president until

Figure 14. Gathering of suffragists at Lily Dale, outside the Maplewood Hotel. Anna Howard Shaw is in the second row, third from right. Schlesinger Library, Radcliffe Institute, Harvard University.

1906, the same year that the camp's name was changed again, this time to its final form: Lily Dale Assembly.[39]

Abby Louise Burnham (Pettengill) was born in 1843 in Cleveland, the seventh of nine children. The Burnhams were one of the "founding" families of Cleveland, and Abby grew up there in a stately home.[40] Her father, who died when Abby was nine, was said to have "awakened a consciousness in her to the Great Unseen Power that governs all things."[41] Her mother, Matilda, did not remarry, raising the children on her own with love and care.

Abby attended Hillsdale College, a school opened by reformist Baptists that welcomed both African Americans and women. In 1864 Abby married Charles Pettengill. Like most Spiritualists, the Pettengills were intimately connected to reform movements espousing equality and justice. Charles Pettengill was a founding member of Cleveland's Society for the Prevention of Cruelty to Animals in the 1870s, which evolved into one of the first humane societies in the country. The Pettengills were very wealthy; Charles even financed the city's first professional baseball association in 1871.[42] By the time Pettengill met Skidmore, the couple had four grown children. Abby's eldest daughter, Josephine, was married to Henry Everett, a street railway developer who owned and controlled railways in Cleveland and other growing cities. The Everetts often joined Pettengill for long Lily Dale summers.[43]

The same year Abby Pettengill joined Marion Skidmore on the board of trustees, New York State suffragists were gearing up for a constitutional convention, to be held in 1894, where they hoped to add an amendment to the state constitution allowing full women's suffrage in New York. Serious planning for the event had begun as early as 1887, and fundraising and marketing were in full swing by the summer of 1892. Suffragists devised a massive campaign in the state, and Lily Dale played a vital role. That August, thousands of women's rights advocates swarmed the town, causing visitors to describe the scene as a "mass of Humanity." Tents and houses were again decorated with evergreen boughs, flowers, and star-spangled and yellow bunting, proclaiming the town's support for women's equality. There was a decidedly larger number of women than men out for the weekend, but all sexes were accounted for in record numbers.[44]

The auditorium was again festooned with bunting and portraits. Banners emblazoned with phrases like "Government Derive Their Just Powers from Consent of the Governed" and "Woman's Ballots Mean Enlarged Opportunities for Doing Good" framed the stage. Hours before the day's lectures were to start, it was standing room only. Lily Dale chairman H. D. Barrett invited suffragist and Spiritualist Isabella Beecher Hooker to the dais. Hooker was the Skidmores' personal guest for the week and was joined by Anthony and Shaw in the day's festivities.[45]

Isabella Beecher Hooker, half sister of Catharine Beecher and Harriet Beecher Stowe, and the daughter of clergyman Lyman Beecher, was an early abolitionist and had worked hard in the NWSA for women's suffrage. By 1892 Hooker was a close friend of Skidmore, a regular guest at Lily Dale, and a seasoned suffrage advocate. She was also a Spiritualist, having worked closely with devoted Spiritualists since the 1850s and having received messages from Spirit herself since at least 1875.[46] Earlier that year Hooker had joined Anthony, Stanton, and Lucy Stone in front of the US Senate Committee on Woman Suffrage. When it was Hooker's turn to speak, she had asked the gentlemen of the committee to consider that "if we want to help the republic . . . we must honor the mothers equally with the fathers in the Government." She stressed that the law made sons their mother's rulers, teaching men to disrespect women from an early age. The women closed with an appeal to the committee to recommend a Sixteenth Amendment to the US Constitution granting women full suffrage, but to no avail.[47]

On Women's Day in the warm August air of Lily Dale, Hooker asked her audience, "If women are not citizens, what are they?"[48] Although not adhering to the New Departure of the 1870s any longer (the argument that the Fourteenth Amendment gave full citizenship and thus voting rights to women), Hooker still maintained that citizenship *should* inherently equal suffrage.[49] She also spoke of the need for women to play a greater role in civil society by participating in policing and serving as jurors in a court of law. She then turned her sights on the upcoming New York State constitutional convention, asking her audience if "the women of New York [are] less free to be trusted than those in Wyoming?," which was still the only state that allowed full suffrage for all citizens.[50]

The year 1893 began auspiciously for Spiritualism and women's suffrage. Both Marion and Thomas Skidmore were delegates to the NAWSA annual meeting, held in January in Washington, DC.[51] New York suffrage supporters, led by the indomitable Lillie Devereux Blake and helped along by Spiritualists like the Skidmores and Elnora Babcock, were gearing up for the 1894 state convention, where they hoped to present a suffrage amendment for negotiation. Women's Day at Lily Dale in 1893 was no less a success than in previous years, boasting standing room only in the auditorium. The celebrations were opened by Cora L. V. Scott, who offered an "impressive invocation" to the large audience. H. D. Barrett then introduced Babcock, a rising star in state suffrage circles. As a Spiritualist, and as the wife of James Babcock, superintendent of schools in Dunkirk, New York, she had familial and spiritual roots in the area. She thanked her audience for the warm welcome, drawing "a sharp contrast between the 'tolerance' of Chautauqua and the cordial support of Cassadaga."[52] There was certainly support for women's suffrage outside the town—the Chautauqua County arm of NAWSA was the largest in the country after all—but the *zeal* for women's rights and suffrage was on fire in the Spiritualist camp of Lily Dale. This was in no small part due to Marion Skidmore, Abigail Pettengill, and the cadre of early feminists intimately connected to the camp.

By 1893 people were putting down roots in Lily Dale, making it no longer just a summer camp but a year-round residence. The first sewer pipes were laid that year, and 215 cottages had already been built, with approximately forty families in residence year-round. Well-off families like the Skidmores and the Pettengills put their money to use in the grounds, investing in beautifying the landscape. Pettengill's daughter Josephine donated a "very powerful and melodious organ" to the town, which filled the Octagon House with a range of music.[53]

Throughout the spring and summer, suffragists raised funds and met in their political equality clubs in preparation for the upcoming constitutional convention. New York suffragists spent the majority of 1893 fundraising and collecting petitions in anticipation of the Convention. Susan B. Anthony, at the age of seventy-four, traveled around the state to rally support for a state women's suffrage amendment. Anna Howard Shaw also traveled tirelessly, though visiting only forty counties to Anthony's sixty. Spiritualist and suffragist Mary Seymour Howell traveled to nearly that many counties as well.[54] Even during the 1893 depression, one of the worst in years, New York's suffragists were able to raise $10,000 for the cause. And of course the stars of Lily Dale were integral to funding the movement. Marion Skidmore donated $100 to the cause, and Pettengill donated $220 (roughly $7,200 in 2023 dollars, about three times what it cost to build a three-bedroom colonial cottage in any major city).[55] By the spring and summer of 1894, New York suffragists had circulated five thousand petitions throughout the state and collected 332,148 signatures. The WCTU, labor organizations and unions, and various granges gathered more signatures, bringing the total to around 600,000.[56] Despite the enormous support by suffragists around the state, the convention voted again not to support a suffrage amendment.[57] Surprisingly, neither the national nor the local Spiritualist press reported on the Spiritualists involved with the New York State convention, perhaps because it was so commonplace that it needed no special attention. *The Banner of Light,* however, did comment on the absence of Lucy Stone, who had passed away the previous year, quipping that she was not "ignorant of the occasion," as her spirit was surely present.[58]

Despite the setback, zeal for suffrage in Lily Dale did not wane. In fact, the suffrage movement in New York gained adherents across the state and taught more women how to organize a grassroots movement. Just a week after the defeat at the constitutional convention, leading suffragists again congregated in Lily Dale. On the morning of August 22, 1894, Anthony acknowledged their defeat but offered praise and gratitude for the hard work that Spiritualists at Lily Dale had done. She thanked the assembled crowd, telling them, "The suffragists of America have been also afraid to give voice to the 'Thank you' which has always been in their hearts for Spiritualism."[59] Later, Anna Howard Shaw joked that "she would not weary her Lily Dale audience with a lecture on the right of women to the ballot, for there was no one within the sound of her voice who doubted the same." She insisted she "could say nothing new, for there was no argument in favor of suffrage that they had not already heard dozens of times, and she would merely entertain them for a short time with a little homey talk which might serve as a kind of light dessert after Miss Anthony's substantial feast."[60] Both Shaw and Anthony were again the guests of "dear Mr. and Mrs. Skidmore."[61]

The zeal for suffrage is clear in a photograph taken in front of the "Women's Tent" on the Lily Dale grounds. Marion Skidmore stands proudly in the middle, holding aloft a banner on a pole with two stars emblazoned upon it. The stars represent Wyoming, the first state to allow women's suffrage, and Colorado, which had recently amended its state constitution to grant women full and equal suffrage across the state. Seated to Skidmore's left are Anthony and Abby Pettengill, surrounded by Lily Dale residents and visitors who were there to support Spiritualists' devotion to women's suffrage.

The 1894 camp season was an overall success, again bringing thousands of visitors to the CLFA. That summer Abby's son-in-law Henry Everett donated funds and materials for a bowling alley to be built on the grounds. It housed three bowling lanes plus an area for billiard tables and was in use well into the mid-twentieth century.[62] That fall, the Chautauqua County Political Equality Club held their annual convention at Lily Dale, Skidmore having opened the grounds and the Maplewood Hotel to the group. And later in October, Skidmore traveled to Washington, DC, as a delegate to the National Spiritualist Association Meeting.[63]

Figure 15. Suffrage Tent, erected for Women's Day, 1894. Marion Skidmore, founder of Lily Dale's first library, is holding a banner with the words "Wyoming" and "Colorado" on it, celebrating the first two US states to extend suffrage to women. Susan B. Anthony is in the middle row, third from the right. Marion Skidmore binder, Skidmore Library, Lily Dale.

Auspiciously, on New Year's Eve, Abby Louise Pettengill purchased the old "Alden Grounds" and house, twenty-three acres of mostly native woods "left as nearly as possible in a state of nature." Most of the woods was passable by only a few paths and carriage roads, the rest impenetrable with dense underbrush filling the space between gigantic mature trees. Carefully placed benches offered rest for Lily Dale patrons in the cool shade.[64] Abby renamed everything after her beloved granddaughter, six-year-old Leolyn, daughter of Josephine and Henry Everett, who were also intimately tied to Lily Dale. Today the woods are still known as Leolyn Woods, and the Leolyn Inn bears her name as well. A spirit painting of Leolyn still hangs in the Maplewood Hotel, painted by one of the Bangs sisters. Although rumor had it that Leolyn died young, in fact she lived a long and full life, passing away in 1971 at the age of eighty-three.[65]

For those who believe in fate, it must seem as if Abby's chance encounter with Marion Skidmore was more than just luck. Their meeting allowed the torch to be passed, so to speak, between the "mother of Lily Dale," Marion Skidmore, to the new protectress of the camp, Abby Louise Pettengill. As was her practice, Skidmore had spent the winter of 1894–95 traveling. A typical middle-class woman of her time, she traveled for leisure and to attend conferences for her chosen passions, Spiritualism and women's rights. She also occasionally traveled for her health, as when, a few years earlier, she made a trip to Mount Clemens, Michigan, to take the "cure." At fifty-two, Marion was far from old age, yet she was periodically plagued by minor colds as well as aches and pains.[66]

In the early spring of 1895, Marion became violently ill on her way home to Lily Dale following an extended stay in the warmer climate of Florida. She and Thomas made an impromptu stop in Cincinnati, at the home of her friends and fellow Spiritualists R. S. and J. T. Lillie, where she hoped to recuperate. The Lillies were part of the core group of people from the CLFA's early days. R. S. Lillie was a staple on the Spiritualist circuit, often lecturing in Lily Dale as well as traveling to California to preach with her friend E. L. Watson, and she functioned as another linchpin in the network of women reformers associated with Lily Dale. Unfortunately, Marion Skidmore succumbed to her illness while at the Lillies' and passed away on the morning of February 2, 1895, with the words "all is well" on her lips. R. S. Lillie traveled with Marion's body back to Lily Dale, where she conducted funeral services for the beloved Skidmore. A special train ran from Dunkirk, New York, to Lily Dale to carry Skidmore's friends and relatives who wished to attend her funeral service. Instead of finding black crepe and ribbons, funeral attendees entered a parlor decorated with white ribbon, evergreen boughs, and a profusion of flowers. Marion's body was robed in white in her open casket, and she held white flowers. She was buried in Forest Hill Cemetery in Fredonia, New York, in a family plot.[67]

Lily Dale lost a true leader when Marion Skidmore died. She had been integral to making Lily Dale a permanent settlement, seeing to the necessities of building enduring establishments to make the camp a home. She was instrumental in bringing the suffrage movement to Lily Dale—not that it was foreign, but her connections to the women's rights movement made Lily Dale an important stop on the suffrage lecture circuit.

Suffrage leaders lamented Skidmore's passing. Susan B. Anthony wrote in a letter to *The Cassadagan*:

> It seems impossible that dear Mrs. Skidmore has gone from our mortal sight forever. I loved her. She was the light and life of Lily Dale. How we all who impartially shared in her kind thoughts, will miss her! And on Woman Suffrage Days—can it be possible that the noble, motherly woman will be no more there to preside over it? And yet, when I think of the belief or knowledge, as she would say, of so many of her dear friends, that she is not gone, but with them in fuller sense than ever, I am led to exclaim, "Verily Spiritualists eat the bread the world knows not of.[68]

Spiritualist and suffragist Isabella Beecher Hooker knew that Skidmore was not truly gone but just transitioned to the other side. Nevertheless, her sorrow over Skidmore's passing is palpable in the obituary she wrote:

> I cannot understand why my friend Marion Skidmore, has been called from her post of usefulness. This problem is too heavy for me. At the time I enjoyed delightful hospitality I looked upon her as a woman who would work for Lily Dale and its spiritual growth for years to come and never grow weary over her task. All I can say is that we who are left, must strive to be like her and to do what we may to supplement her glorious work of saving souls through the ministry of love.

She signed it "Yours in the bonds of faith, hope and charity." [69]

No doubt the summer festivities at Lily Dale were not the same without Marion Skidmore in attendance. Nevertheless, Women's Day and suffrage support at the camp went on. Mary Anthony, Susan's sister, visited that summer, as did one of NAWSA's most conservative leaders, Carrie Chapman Catt, who headlined that summer's Women's Day festivities. NAWSA eulogized Skidmore at its annual meeting in Washington, DC, the following year.[70] Skidmore had truly been a grassroots organizer and was severely missed, not just by those in Lily Dale who loved her but by those who relied on her organizing acumen across the country. Although Lily Dale had lost a true leader, however, it was also because of Skidmore that an indomitable new leader became a pillar of Lily Dale: Abby Louise Pettengill, who continued Skidmore's legacy in building Lily Dale into a stable community.

Time marches on, and Lily Dale regulars turned toward celebrating the twentieth anniversary of their founding, holding a "Pioneer Meeting" celebration in July 1896.[71] That summer, Lily Dale welcomed back many of the founders of the movement, including E. L. Watson. In the sixteen years since she had first dedicated Lily Dale's grounds, Watson had been preaching, lecturing around the world, and building Sunny Brae into a spiritual center. She was also involved in politics, weighing in on issues of women's rights, immigration, assimilation, and world peace.[72] At Lily Dale, she "baptized" the place once again "with her heavenly messages and rare oratory." She delivered a sermon titled "One World at a Time," and closed with a comment on the equality between women and men.[73]

That summer Anna Howard Shaw also made her annual pilgrimage to Lily Dale but would soon be traveling to California to stump for women's suffrage in that state's constitutional amendment campaign, speaking before California's constitutional convention. As in New York, California legislators did not choose to put a suffrage amendment before the state's male voters. Nevertheless, Anthony and Shaw crossed paths with E. L. Watson on this trip and others, joining her under Temple Oak, a large tree at Sunny Brae where Libbie gave sermons, for rest and camaraderie while in California.[74]

In February 1898, though still without a vote, suffragists celebrated the anniversary of Seneca Falls at that year's NAWSA annual meeting in Washington, DC. Displayed reverently on the convention stage was a small table covered in patriotic bunting—the exact table where Elizabeth Cady Stanton and Lucretia Mott had drafted the Declaration of Sentiments fifty years earlier.[75] What was not mentioned, however, was that that very table had been used for séances at Thomas and Mary Ann M'Clintock's house in Waterloo, New York. Their neighbor Stanton had experienced the same spiritual knockings in her own house. This mundane material object, a little table, epitomizes how the things we use on a daily basis can also link seemingly unrelated movements and events in fascinating ways. The fact that the Declaration of Sentiments table was also a séance table puts it squarely at the intersection between the nineteenth-century women's rights movement and Spiritualism.[76]

A month later, Spiritualists traveled to Rochester to celebrate the fiftieth anniversary of the famous "Rochester rappings," likening the occasion to "holy pilgrimages to Mecca." And for the faithful, the "opportunity of visiting the birthplace and home of the Fox sisters" was the main event. Prominent Spiritualist speakers attended, and undoubtedly Lily Dale residents made the four-hour train ride to participate in the festivities. Libbie, always listed as E. L. Watson, was one of the many speakers who addressed the thousands of Spiritualists who joined the week-long celebrations.[77]

Anthony attended as well, listening to speeches by her friends and fellow suffragists Cora Scott and E. L. Watson.[78] While there, she was confronted by a Spiritualist who chastised her for not more publicly associating Spiritualism with women's suffrage, as they had been one and the same since their inception. Anthony wrote about the experience: "I was at the Spiritualistic jubilee meeting here yesterday evening, and at its close one woman upbraided me for not declaring that I was a Spiritualist and giving to that cause the weight of my influence, saying that Spiritualism and woman suffrage both had their birth here in Rochester the same year, and that they were twins and ought always to be associated together." True to form, Anthony replied with an answer she had given many other reformers before, saying, "While I rejoiced in every good work and word for women by any and every society, yet I could not feel that the objects of the different societies were questions to be discussed on our platform." This was an answer in the spirit of her earlier effort to persuade Shaw to abandon lecturing for the WCTU and to focus solely on suffrage. Anthony was singularly focused on her cause and feared that any attention to other issues would divert energy that ought to be expended on suffrage. She nevertheless accepted that not everyone was as singularly minded as she was, acknowledging, "It is very difficult for people to understand this position."[79]

Anthony, her sister Mary, Shaw, and Lucy Anthony, Susan B. Anthony's niece and Shaw's life partner, continued to make almost yearly trips to Lily Dale. One gets the sense they came not only to speak for women's suffrage but also to relax and enjoy their "sojourn in this pleasant place," as Ida Husted Harper, Anthony's biographer, commented.[80] They were often the guests of "the president," Abby Pettengill, and stayed at her cottage, although they would occasionally check in to one of the hotels on the grounds, usually for a suffrage brunch or dinner. Other suffrage celebrities visited Lily Dale throughout the early 1900s including the lawyer and suffragist Gail Laughlin in 1901, reformer and author Charlotte Perkins Gilman in 1903 and 1904, investigative journalist and reformer Helen

Campbell in 1904, and leading women's rights reformer and Spiritualist Mary Seymour Howell in 1907.[81]

Shaw and Anthony were back in 1905. This was the last time Anthony traveled to Lily Dale. A picture taken of Pettengill and Anthony during this trip shows a clearly aging Anthony. She did not lecture but made only brief remarks, Harper writing, "But the audience were satisfied if she would sit on the platform and let them look into her face."[82] As always, Shaw and Anthony appeared in front of a packed audience; extra chairs had to be brought in to accommodate the overflowing crowd.[83] Susan B. Anthony died only a few months later, in March 1906. She was eighty-six years old.

Nearly three thousand miles away from Lily Dale, events in California had an impact on the Spiritualist community. On April 18, 1906, San Francisco experienced a devastating earthquake that caused massive damage. Although Pettengill was from Cleveland, most of her investments were in San Francisco. Because of this devastating blow to their finances, the Pettengills left Lily Dale and moved to Pasadena, joined by Josephine and Henry Everett. Abby did retain ownership of her cottage on Melrose Park and the Leolyn Inn until 1910, when she sold the hotel to the Assembly.[84]

But looking westward was part and parcel of the suffrage movement. As loud as fights for suffrage were in the East, it was in the West that the suffrage movement was gaining ground. First Wyoming and then Colorado had started the state-by-state westward trend. The battle for women's suffrage in California was especially important to the larger suffrage movement. It was a large and highly populous state with a diverse economy. E. L. Watson was at the vanguard of the battle there, and in 1909 she was voted in as president of the California Equal Suffrage Association, the state affiliate of NAWSA.[85] She was a leader in the campaign, which used modern technology such as moving pictures, posters, and automobiles to champion suffrage. Finally, in 1911 the men of California voted to change their state constitution to allow women the right to vote. Watson was quoted as saying that the momentous event "has sounded the death knell to sex aristocracy."[86]

Throughout the 1910s, Lily Dale still carried the torch for women suffrage. Speakers such as Charlotte Perkins Gilman and Harriot Stanton Blatch spoke regularly, and in the summer of 1914 Anna Howard Shaw told her Lily Dale audience that "she always felt like she was coming home, when she appeared at Lily Dale."[87] Shaw and Lucy Anthony continued their almost annual sojourns to Lily Dale until Shaw turned her full attention to moving the Nineteenth Amendment through Congress. She died in July 1919, just a few weeks after the amendment passed the Senate and was submitted to the states for ratification. E. L. Watson gave a stirring tribute to her soon after at the WCTU annual convention in Berkeley, California.[88] That same year, Abby Louise Pettengill also crossed over. Her friend the author Harriet Bartnett wrote a booklet about Pettengill's life and devotion to Lily Dale and suffrage. Bartnett highlighted Pettengill and Shaw's long friendship. In one of her last letters to Pettengill,

> [Shaw] dwelt upon her loneliness and hunger for those dear friends who in earlier years had passed through so many vicissitudes with her and who had preceded her across the Border. Strong with the belief in Immortality, yet she wrote Mrs. Pettengill asking her to assure her that these loved ones still lived and waited for her there; inquiring eagerly for those proofs which made Mrs. Pettengill such an ardent believer in Spirit existence.[89]

In some ways Shaw's and Pettengill's deaths were indicative of a shift in the suffrage movement. After the passage of the Nineteenth Amendment, NAWSA disbanded, becoming the League of Women Voters, which focused on teaching women how to exercise the vote. Unfortunately the racism that was rampant during the nadir of American race relations overwhelmingly curtailed the ability of Black women to vote. Alice Paul's National Woman's Party continued working for women's equality and the Equal Rights Amendment but decidedly did not consider the fight for Black women's right to vote as important to the movement. In many organizations that fought for suffrage, once white women were able to vote, major suffrage organizing halted, and the issue wasn't picked up again until the civil rights era and the Voting Rights Act of 1965, which finally helped Black women gain the right to vote en masse.[90]

After the ratification of the Nineteenth Amendment, Women's Day at Lily Dale faltered. Only a few major speakers spoke on Women's Day after 1920, including Ida Husted Harper in 1930 and Margaret Sanger in 1931.[91] The highlight of Women's Day throughout the 1920s seems to have been the "Fancy Ball," as opposed to the airing of radical ideas. Nevertheless, Women's Day is still an annual event in Lily Dale, and in more recent years, as the town's connection to the suffrage movement has come to light, there is more celebration surrounding Lily Dale's suffrage history.

The close ties between Lily Dale, Spiritualism, and the women's rights movement are apparent once you begin pulling the threads. But overwhelmingly, this close relationship doesn't appear in the standard histories of the suffrage movement. The four-volume *History of Woman Suffrage*, edited by Susan B. Anthony and Ida Husted Harper, contains few references to Spiritualism, and only in passing to Lily Dale. The historian Lisa Tetrault, in her gasp-inducing epilogue to *The Myth of Seneca Falls*, shows us how Anthony shaped the history of the mainstream suffrage movement by burning the paraphernalia that didn't fit her narrative.[92] Perhaps Anthony and her cohorts intentionally wrote Spiritualism out of the story. Though she was friendly with Spiritualists, Anthony would occasionally make fun of them. In 1896, when Isabella Beecher Hooker lost her sister Harriet Beecher Stowe, Anthony jested that she'd sent Hooker a letter "with the nicest word I could say—on mundane—not etherial [sic] affairs—Well—we must take our fate—being so of 'the earth-earthy.'"[93] Not too harsh, but definitely a slight against Hooker's perceived etherealness (and her Spiritualism).

To her credit, Anthony did not let her lack of faith in Spiritualism get in the way of the suffrage mission or her friendships with Spiritualists. She maintained long and fruitful relationships with Lily Dale Spiritualists like Skidmore and Pettengill, and periodically participated in séances and private readings. Pettengill joked that "Aunt Susan used to say 'We love you but we don't care anything about your religion!'" Once, when Anthony was accompanying Pettengill to a séance in Lily Dale, the first spirit voice to break through

> gave the name of a long-deceased and evidently not very popular Aunt of Miss Anthony. No sooner had she announced her identity than Susan B. flashed back with her usual directness, I don't want to hear you. I didn't like you when you lived and I don't care to talk to you now. Why doesn't Elizabeth Cady or someone else come? But as the Aunt insisted on being heard, the sitting came to an early end.[94]

(Frankly, as someone who's been desperate to hear from departed family during readings with a medium, I can totally relate!) Yet despite Anthony's skepticism, she and Pettengill maintained a long friendship.

Anthony was famously against focusing on religion in the movement. But she was also quick to use religion to her advantage when needed, having no hesitancy to send speakers to congregations where they would be appreciated. When organizing suffrage speakers for various faiths, she noted, "Mrs. Hooker and Mrs. Howell are such strong spiritualists that they cannot help talking their particular faith."[95]

Unearthing the history of Spiritualism and suffrage is an evolving story. Historians are still discovering connections, sometimes hiding in plain sight. Even as people like Skidmore and Pettengill passed from Lily Dale, their legacies live on. For Skidmore, it's in the library bearing her name and the landscaped grounds. For Pettengill, it is in the Leolyn Woods and hotel, but also farther abroad. When Abby's daughter Josephine passed away, she left her vast library of suffrage books to the Huntington Library in San Marino, California, forming a core collection of its important women's history holdings. Yet little do most researchers know about the connection to the Pettengill legacy in western New York.[96]

Like the plants and flowers that Skidmore orchestrated on the grounds, Lily Dale was a fertile garden, nurturing the individuality of self and Spirit and promoting radical reforms such as women's rights. Reformers like Skidmore, Pettengill, and Watson were key actors in connecting earlier movements born of the Second Great Awakening and cultivating them into the twentieth century. Their collective organizing was often on display in Lily Dale's central auditorium, a space where radical ideas were nurtured and explored. Today, visitors to Lily Dale undoubtedly become aware of the connection between Susan B. Anthony and the tiny town. The place and the people who inhabited its spaces, however, are what united to create something truly special. Lily Dale's auditorium is a place where the past and the present intersect. I was reminded of this by the sound of a deep, hiccupping sob that jarred me from my thoughts during the inspiration meeting we were attending that hot summer. Spirit had come through one of the mediums running the meeting. A woman sitting a few rows away shook with happy tears as her father spoke through the medium, telling her that he loved her and watched over her daily. Perhaps Lily Dale is a place where the past really is alive.

5

The Maplewood Hotel

Marissa

It was July 2016, and I was part of a bevy of young moms who had escaped our hellions for a day trip to Lily Dale for our friend Laura's dry bachelorette party. Laura, an alcoholic, had been sober for only one year. It didn't help that our group of friends was scattered along the spectrum from teetotalers to social or binge drinkers to alcoholics in denial. What better solution for a sober bachelorette than a day trip to a dry town for psychic readings, picturesque strolls, and sober galivanting at historic Cassadaga Lake? I wasn't too bothered by the lack of alcohol. I had a love affair with pinot noir but was happy to put it on hold for the day. We enjoyed a scenic drive with loads of giggles, though we hushed one another and feigned seriousness while we purchased our entry at the gates. We spied the sign notifying visitors that alcohol was prohibited on the grounds. After driving around a bit, we parked near a quaint white building in the center of town—the Maplewood Hotel. We made plans to come back to the Maplewood to sit on the rocking chairs that decorated its cute little wraparound porch.

Figure 16. The Maplewood Hotel, 1907. Maplewood Hotel website, https://www.lilydaleassembly.org/maplewood-hotel. The Maplewood continues to be the only hotel on Lily Dale grounds, though the Leolyn is just outside the gates of the village.

Then we descended on the house of one of Lily Dale's mediums for a group reading. I was first—and I was not prepared. With alarming assuredness, the medium looked at me and asked if I was missing a late-middle-aged man, perhaps my father. I nodded and let out a great sob, shocking my friends, who had rarely seen me cry. The ninth anniversary of my father's passing had been two months earlier. The medium said my father's spirit was telling her that I was a special gift to him, born late in his life, unexpected but so welcome. I nodded my agreement. "He had something wrong with his lungs?" she ventured softly, assuming this had been his cause of death. I heaved another great sob. He had been chronically ill with pulmonary fibrosis for half my life. As the medium articulated the contours of my relationship with my father, I turned inward, thinking about the irony of this moment. My father had died from stomach cancer, no doubt a result of his many decades of heavy drinking. By the time it was discovered, it was so far gone that it had eaten through his stomach lining, hydrochloric acid burning his guts from the inside out. There should be no better deterrent to alcoholism than watching a parent die that way. How fitting that it came out during this dry bachelorette.

I was twenty when my father died. I had not entirely abstained, but several of my closest friends prided themselves on their ability to have a good time without alcohol, and I bought into that ethos as well. When I met the man who would become my husband, he was the opposite of my father in many ways: introverted, even-tempered, and a self-identified straight edge hardcore kid.[1] In the 1980s, the heyday of cocaine parties and Greek life binge drinking, being straight edge was radical. He got along well with my friends, and alcohol was unimportant to us. After my father's death, I became consumed with cultivating the parts of my personality that were similar to his. I had always been just like my father: a quick-tempered know-it-all, a socially gifted workaholic, belligerently agnostic, politically independent, and intellectually curious. To me, my father's penchant for vodka was inseparable from his essence. After his death, high-functioning alcoholism became interesting and artistic to me. Sobriety was boring, something for the simple-minded, not for someone stimulating and smart like me.

Becoming a mother only accentuated this behavior. I had friends who also drowned their parenting sorrows in glasses of red and white. My reading, among my lovely mom friends, brought all of this to the fore. I couldn't help but think that the experience would have been more cathartic if I had been wine-drunk. The philosopher William James wrote in 1902: "The sway of alcohol over mankind is unquestionably due to its power to stimulate the mystical faculties of human nature, usually crushed to earth by the cold facts and dry criticisms of the sober hour. Sobriety diminishes, discriminates, and says no; drunkenness expands, unites, and says yes."[2] I wanted to expand, unite, and always say "yes."

As I sat with my friends on the porch of the Maplewood Hotel, in comfy rocking chairs, discussing our group reading, more than one of us was fiending for a drink. It felt weird to be at a hotel without a bar. While Laura sat for a second reading on her own, we chatted about how strange it was that Lily Dale prohibited alcohol since Spiritualism seemed to be aimed at achieving higher planes of understanding. During our visit to the museum, we had learned that Lily Dale was founded by women's rights activists who labored for temperance (moderation or prohibition of alcohol) as well as suffrage and other progressive values. I had already learned about nineteenth-century feminism and the temperance movement in grad school. I was even appalled, but not surprised, that nineteenth-century "progressives" were often nativist, racist, and supportive of eugenic policies. My reaction to Frances Willard, Carrie Nation, and the rest of the temperance women was "Wow . . . they sound like a total bummer." I was glad I had fun, smart, feminist, wine-loving, pluralism-appreciating, sex-positive women for friends. It was nearly impossible for me to identify these temperance women as our forebears.

To our untrained eyes in 2016, it seemed like Lily Dale had its own historical identity crisis. The town has Woodstock vibes: rural upstate New York, pacifism, radical performances, unorthodox thought, populated by hippies. And hippies were not known for their sobriety. There seemed to be a disconnect. Were these crystal healers, spoon-benders, reiki practitioners, and psychics really the heirs of the buttoned-up temperance women I'd learned about? We didn't know it at the time, but this conversation looked an awful lot like (a slightly less learned version of) the conversations I would have with my grad school besties about Spiritualist and temperance histories we encountered as we produced our feminist history podcast. Under the tutelage of our resident nineteenth-century experts, I came to understand that Lily Dale's commitment to sobriety was not a contradiction after all.

Though it remains a big part of its identity, Lily Dale wasn't destined to become a dry town. The townships sandwiching the Lily Dale hamlet, Pomfret and Stockton, were themselves dry municipalities at various points in history. One historic building near the grounds, 55 East Main Street, built in 1852, was a tavern that served alcoholic beverages. The building had to be physically moved back and forth between Pomfret and Stockton townships in response to the towns' changing alcohol laws: whenever one township outlawed alcohol sales, the tavern would seek refuge in the neighboring township and then back again when the laws changed.[3] There was a tradition of alcohol prohibition in the Lily Dale area long before the Cassadaga Lake Free Association was incorporated in 1879. But as demonstrated by this traveling tavern, there were always ways to circumvent the rules, and folks took advantage of them.

Lily Dale's alcohol prohibition is not a municipal statute. Rather, it stems from the bylaws of the two organizations with the most authority over the community: the Lily Dale Assembly, formerly the Cassadaga Lake Free Association, and the National Spiritualist Association of Churches (NSAC). As noted in earlier chapters, the Cassadaga Lake Free Association was incorporated in 1879, though the place that is now Lily Dale had been home to Spiritualist picnics and camp gatherings for years. A rail line from Buffalo to Dunkirk opened a station in Cassadaga in 1851. In June 1873, Willard Alden hosted a Spiritualist picnic at Alden House, the building now known as the Leolyn Inn, across the road from the Lily Date gates. Only months after that first picnic at Alden House, the Fredonia chapter of the largest women's organization in the United States, the Women's Christian Temperance Union (WCTU), was established a few miles away in December 1873.

There's no record of whether alcohol was prohibited at Alden House, but Alden's grandfather was a preacher and early temperance pamphleteer, so the events it hosted were likely dry, or at least very temperate, affairs.[4] It's also unclear how dry the CLFA was in the early years. Though the timing is significant, there's no known overlap between the Spiritualists who incorporated the CLFA and Chautauqua County temperance activists. In fact, there was a liquor salesman, Albert S. Cobb, among the ranks of the CLFA. Only one known copy of the 1879 bylaws exists, and it is inaccessible, so we can't be certain of the language. Nevertheless, every accessible copy of the CLFA's bylaws prohibits the sale, purchase, or use of intoxicating substances on CLFA grounds.[5] The founding documents of Lily Dale's sister Spiritualist camp at Cassadaga, Florida, drafted in 1894, contain the same article 12 that appears in later versions of the CLFA bylaws, so all evidence suggests the prohibition was an original bylaw.[6]

Rules, however, are meant to be broken—or at least bent. The Iroquois Hotel, one of the primary lodging options for visitors to Lily Dale prior to 1967, is a case in point. The Iroquois was built in 1895 on the plot where the first Lily Dale railroad station stood in the 1880s. In 1898 hotel owner Jacob Scheu obtained a liquor tax certificate.[7] After his death, his widow, Louisa, obtained liquor tax certificates in 1908 and 1910.[8] Thus, despite being located on the Lily Dale grounds (albeit outside the gate), the Iroquois was licensed to sell intoxicating liquors. The hotel served as a restaurant, inn, and saloon adjacent to the railroad line running from Buffalo to Dunkirk. Perhaps visitors to Lily Dale were not its only customers; surely rail service would have brought other folks to the area for other reasons. The railroad, however, discontinued passenger service in 1937, but the hotel remained. The Iroquois underwent many renovations and rebrandings before it burned down in 1967.

You could be forgiven for thinking that perhaps the Iroquois Hotel sat on land owned by the railroad, since it served the station. Then its connection to Lily Dale might have been one of convenience, and nothing to do with Spiritualism. Indeed, the area where the Iroquois sat is outside the Lily Dale postal code, on the other side of the channel connecting Upper and Middle Cassadaga Lakes. The Assembly never advertised the Iroquois Hotel in its official programs, but *The Cassadagan* and *The Sunflower* newspapers, both published for Lily Dale residents and visitors, ran advertisements for the Scheus' establishment quite often.[9] And the Scheus were not just the owners of the Iroquois; they were also members of the Assembly.[10] This seems like a contradiction: the Scheus were members of the teetotaling Assembly closely aligned with temperance, but they also ran an institution that served liquor to folks visiting Lily Dale. When I asked Ron Nagy about this curious situation, he replied that the Scheus must have been part of the "wild bunch." His remark suggests that the moral, theological, and philosophical pluralism that characterizes Lily Dale today was also an important part of its past. Spiritualism (generally) and Lily Dale (specifically) are not a monolith.

Whatever the details, we know that the Iroquois, under ownership of the Scheus, served alcohol and that it had a close relationship to Lily Dale. This suggests that the Assembly's commitment to alcohol prohibition was not absolute but rather negotiable. The Iroquois's location outside the gates and near the railroad station may have created enough distance between the Assembly and the Iroquois's bar. Perhaps this was an early and tacit acknowledgment by the Assembly that, despite all of their lectures, pamphlets, and bylaws, some Spiritualists were always going to consume alcohol. This attitude toward the Scheus closely resembles a later, caveat-riddled bylaw from 1995: "It shall be the policy of the Board of Directors to recognize the internationally accepted standards for the moderate use of distilled and fermented spirits as part of individual and family dining customs while at the same time standing opposed to public display and/or abuse of alcohol upon the Assembly Grounds regardless of location."[11]

If the prohibition against alcohol is not, and never was, absolute, then why has the bylaw persisted for nearly 150 years? While Spiritualism and temperance are deeply connected movements, there is, and always has been, a practical element to Lily Dale's alcohol-free customs. As a result, the rule has survived for generations, but it has served different purposes for the many Assembly boards over the years. These purposes range from devoutly held beliefs, to symbolic solidarity with related movements, to public relations strategies and everything in between.

Nineteenth-century Spiritualists were generally committed to health reform and clean living. More than just a lifestyle, this preference had a practical purpose. Many Spiritualists believed that abstaining from alcohol and/or meat put the body in a condition that allowed people to better achieve their spiritual goals.[12] Spirit healers were especially encouraged to avoid alcohol and nicotine in order to bolster the effectiveness of their healing. Popular logic held that "a drunken medium mostly likely would control drunken . . . spirits and religious mediums would most likely control good spirits."[13]

Most importantly, at precisely the time when Lily Dale was founded, Spiritualists were working to rehabilitate the religion's image. Spiritualism had weathered a series of public relations crises in America and Britain in the late nineteenth century, as discussed in chapter 3. The realities of Spiritualism's tarnished reputation during the camp's early years help explain the connection between temperance and Lily Dale. Long after the zealousness of temperance has subsided, and even after Prohibition failed miserably, public sobriety continued to protect Lily Dale's reputation and shore up Spiritualism's legitimacy in an increasingly hostile world.

Religious radicals have always faced accusations of impropriety with alcohol, going hand in hand with allegations of immorality, sexuality, and madness. For example, in 1659 Englishman John Fox, the founder of Quakerism, composed a religious tract with a ludicrously long title, some of which read "Anabaptists, Independents, Presbyters, Ranters, and many others; who out of their own Mouths have manifested themselves not to be of a true descent from the true Christian Churches: But it's discovered that they have been all made drunk with the Wine of Fornication received from the Whore which hath sitten upon the Beast, after whom the World hath wondred."[14] Nearly two centuries later, in 1817 William Hazlitt published a compilation of essays, one of which had similar things to say about Methodists: "[Methodists] may be considered as a collection of religious invalids: the refuse of all that is Weak and unsound in body and mind. . . . One of [Methodism's] favorite places of Worship combines the turbulence and noise of a drunken brawl at an ale-house with the indecencies of a bagnio [i.e., brothel]." Methodism was founded during the First Great Awakening in the 1730s and 1740s, and its growth can be attributed to the popularity of itinerant preachers who delivered impassioned speeches at camp meetings. The 1874 Chautauqua Institution was an iteration of these Methodist circuits, and as Sarah discusses in chapter 1, Lily Dale's camp season also followed the Methodist model. By the time of the advent of Spiritualism, Methodism had left behind accusations of insobriety and was regarded as an orthodox, well-respected religious sect.

Spiritualism, like the other radical religions formed during the Second Great Awakening, was transgressive from the beginning but experienced increased acceptance over time, though certainly never to the extent of Methodism. Moreover, there are several aspects of Spiritualism that amplified its transgressive nature. First, it was a religion launched by girls, and young women continued to play a central role in mediumship as Spiritualism thrived. Women mediums enjoyed an authority that was hard to find elsewhere in this resolutely patriarchal Victorian context. But their activities also flew in the face of increasingly conservative Victorian norms and, consequently, required great sacrifice.

Second, Spiritualism relied on physical mediumship during its first phase. Indeed, Lily Dale was founded at the height of the materialization craze, as Averill and Sarah described in previous chapters. Materializations could appear as ghostly matter like ectoplasm, partial ghostly apparitions, or even full-fledged materialized dead people. Women's central role, combined with the tactile and performative aspects of their physical mediumship, highlighted the sexual vulnerability of Spiritualist mediums. For example, the rappings that began the Fox sisters' mediumship occurred in the teenage girls' bedroom when they were in their nightgowns. Their teenage forms, in a state of undress, and their private moments were opened up to public scrutiny in a way that violated nineteenth-century gender norms. Skeptics inspected their bodies and observed them while they were scantily clad under test conditions. Their bedroom became a revered site of Spiritualism's origin but also the object of male fantasies.[15]

One experience of the Fox sisters suggests that American mediums often found themselves in contexts that were soaked in alcohol. In a letter to her older sister Leah, Kate wrote about a show she and Maggie had performed in Washington, DC:

> I am sick of this life! Only think of it! Last evening a party of twelve fine-looking gentlemen visited our rooms. All but two were as drunk as they

could well be. They made mean, low remarks. Only imagine Maggie and me, and dear mother, before a crowd of drunken senators! One very fine-looking man stood up before the crowd and addressed them thus: "I wish to be heard, gentlemen. This is all a humbug, but it is worth a dollar to sit in the sunlight of Miss Kate's eyes." . . . Maggie had left in disgust. At this sudden announcement all was as still as death. My face was red as fire. A friend walked up to me . . . and said, "Don't mind him, he is drunk; I would not pay the least attention to him."[16]

Most scholars argue that the mistreatment the Fox sisters suffered at the hands of skeptics and the public lives they led as teenagers and young adults contributed to their later struggles with substance abuse.

This was complicated by Spiritualism's overlap with the free love movement after the 1860s, exemplified by Victoria Woodhull. Woodhull was a stockbroker, newspaper editor, socialist, free lover, and feminist juggernaut who was elected president of the American Association of Spiritualists (AAS) in 1871. She grew up impoverished with abusive parents who enlisted Victoria and her sister into their professional scams, which included spirit healing or mediumship. As an adult, Woodhull was endlessly controversial, not least because she had a flair for publicity mongering. For example, she used her platform at the 1872 Spiritualist convention to expose the extramarital affair of the respected clergyman, abolitionist, and reformer Henry Ward Beecher, son of temperance giant Lyman Beecher. Herself a divorcée, Woodhull faced constant accusations that she was a prostitute.[17] Woodhull's very public transgressions scandalized respectable American Spiritualists. Her election to the presidency of the AAS had a ripple effect, and ultimately her radicalism tore the association apart. In 1873 Woodhull delivered a speech advocating free love and suggesting that disease was caused by bad (that is, passionless or nonconsensual) sex and that eliminating bad sex would eliminate disease and deaths.[18] Furious at Woodhull's radicalism, conservative Spiritualists broke off to form the barely renamed American Spiritualist Association. The *Religio-Philosophical Journal* quickly endorsed the new organization, but *The Banner of Light* angrily declined to recognize its legitimacy.[19]

After the exodus of the conservatives, Woodhull and the other free lovers rebranded themselves as the Universal Association of Spiritualists

(UAS). The *Religio-Philosophical Journal* printed the proceedings of their October 1874 meeting in Boston under the mocking headline "Free-loveism—The Universal Association of Spiritualists Assembled at the Hub—Victoria C. Woodhull and E. V. Wilson both Absent, and yet the Quintessence of Nastiness Prevailed in the Superlative Degree." One of the organization's resolutions declared, "We demand the repeal of all laws enacted for the purpose of restricting the individual in any sense from the full exercise of both social and sexual rights."[20] Free lovers generally regarded the institution of marriage as a form of enslavement or forced prostitution, but many Spiritualists felt Woodhull and friends were going too far and they worried that her antics would delegitimize the Spiritualist movement.

Spiritualists had not always felt this way. In the religion's early years, there were plenty of ordinary Spiritualists and free lovers whose philosophies and social circles overlapped. In 1856 the physician, Spiritualist, and free lover Thomas Low Nichols wrote that "the truth is, and it is well known to those who know anything, that the Free Love Doctrine, rightly understood, is the Great Central Doctrine of Spiritualism."[21] Early Spiritualist tracts demonstrate this to be true. Spiritualist Joel Tiffany, for example, included a piece on free love in his 1856 collection of essays published as *Spiritualism Explained*.[22] English traveler and author William Hepworth Dixon observed in 1868 that "though it cannot be said with truth that all Spiritualists are Free Lovers, yet it may be said that all Free Lovers, with rare exceptions, are Spiritualists."[23]

Lily Dale also had its fair share of free lovers. Free-loving George A. Fuller and Cephas B. Lynn often appeared on the program during the 1880s and 1890s.[24] Moses Hull was among the core group of Spiritualists who signed the CLFA's articles of incorporation in 1879. Hull was a Seventh-day Adventist who shocked his co-religionists by converting to Spiritualism and adopting the doctrine of free love around 1870. In 1873 he divorced his first wife and took up with a fellow free lover and UAS member, Mattie Brown Sawyer. Hull was deeply involved in Spiritualist educational centers during the 1890s, and his educational model was funded by the Spiritualist Morris Pratt in 1901, though Pratt died before his first center opened. Hull became the director of the Morris Pratt Institute after Pratt's death. The institute is now the educational arm of the

National Spiritualist Association of Churches, and Lily Dale is still home to a Morris Pratt Institute today.

Despite the long, intertwined history of free lovers and Spiritualism, by the 1870s Woodhull's politics had the larger Spiritualist organizations clutching their pearls. The early years of Spiritualism coincided with the declining years of the Second Great Awakening as well as a host of moral panics and a national crackdown on immorality. The radical religions and reform societies that enjoyed the most success after 1870 were those that worked to appeal to a conservative public and distanced themselves from their scandalous pasts. For Spiritualism, this scandalous past revolved around female sexuality, alcohol use, madness, and the interplay among the three. High-profile psychic researchers seized on all three of these perceived weaknesses in Spiritualist spaces as they set out to discredit the movement and expose mediums as frauds.

Celebrated mediums, especially women, faced well-publicized battles with substance abuse that injured the legitimacy of the movement early on. Maggie Fox's drinking problem was publicly acknowledged, even by her supporters. One even referred to her alcoholism as evidence against deception: "I have seen Margaret Fox Kane herself, when lying on a bed of sickness and unable to rise, produce 'rappings' in various parts of the room in which she was, and upon the ceilings, doors and windows several feet away from her. I have seen her produce the same effects when too drunk to realize what she was doing."[25] Spiritualism's skeptics and enemies seized on the alcohol-related deterioration of Maggie and Kate Fox's adult lives. Their brother-in-law Daniel Underhill remarked woefully, "They might both do well if they would only keep sober."[26] The Fox sisters' alcoholism was openly discussed by Spiritualism's devotees as well as its critics. John Bundy, the conservative Spiritualist editor of the *Religio-Philosophical Journal,* reported that Kate had lost custody of her children "because her drunken habits unfitted her to perform a mother's duty." He identified this sad series of events as part of what was wrong with some Spiritualists' morals: "There is among spiritualists . . . a class of maudlin sentimentalists ever on the alert for something that will pander to their diseased emotions, and who are only really in earnest when assisting weak and incorrigible criminals to escape the just consequences of their acts."[27] Spiritualists mortified by Maggie's 1888 repudiation of Spiritualism also pointed to her alcoholism and resulting pauperism as the motivator behind her disavowal. One Spiritualist conjectured: "I'll tell you what! I have heard that the Fox sisters are dreadfully addicted to drink. . . . Maybe she's out of money and thinks the spiritualists ought to do something for her. I shouldn't wonder."[28]

The Fox sisters' early deaths, likely stemming from alcohol-related health problems, along with their other struggles in the 1880s, were indirectly injurious to Spiritualism. While their decline may have marked the end of Spiritualism to its skeptics and enemies, the religion had already moved on from its beginnings in Hydesville. But the specter of alcoholism continued to haunt many of Spiritualism's star mediums in the United States and abroad. British mediums were equally vulnerable to alcoholism and other intoxicants, and reports of their scandals were splashed across the pages of American publications. Florence Cook was a materialization medium who became internationally known for her full-body materialization of a ghost named Katie King. Cook admitted that in the early years of her career, it was quite common for sitters to offer her stimulants and other intoxicants before a sitting in hopes that the substances would lubricate her mediumship. But she eventually understood them to be an impediment to true mediumship.[29]

Medium Mary Rosina Showers and her mother, Frederica Hurst Showers, also struggled very publicly with alcohol addiction.[30] Mary Rosina conducted private séances for pay as a teenager, and she was regarded as a gifted medium in the 1870s. Frederica was a devoted Spiritualist with an acid wit. She sparred tirelessly with other Spiritualists, and her spicy missives were often published in Britain's Spiritualist press. But by the mid-1890s, their reputations had been destroyed by their addictions. Mary Rosina was arrested for "being drunk and using bad language" in January 1895. Frederica appeared before the magistrate to testify on her daughter's behalf, asking that her behavior be excused because she "suffers from aberration," a euphemism for mental illness. Mary Rosina denied that she was mad and claimed to have been cleared by a physician. When asked to produce certificates attesting to her mental health, Mary Rosina said she was unable to do so because her physician was now dead. (You'd think this wouldn't have been an obstacle, given her line of work.) Frederica pressed the issue, arguing that Mary Rosina had suffered from hysteria since she was a teenager to the point where she had once temporarily lost the use of her legs. The authorities, however, noted that this was

Rosina's fourth arrest for public drunkenness in three months' time. Since she had been fined for her prior offenses, to no effect, the judge ordered that she be imprisoned for twenty-one days.[31]

Frederica died, as a result of her alcohol abuse, a pauper in January 1895, mere weeks after defending her daughter in court. A coroner's inquest further suggests that her mediumship, her authority within the Spiritualist movement, and her general celebrity had declined some time before her death, also because of her alcohol abuse. The *Coventry Evening Telegraph* reported the results of the inquest:

> Frederica Showers, who died somewhat suddenly[,] . . . was 69 years of age, lived alone, and was very eccentric in manners. She told a charwoman who waited upon her that she was a spiritualist. . . . It was shown in evidence that she drank large quantities of spirits, and the doctor stated that the disease and chronic inflammation which were the cause of death were the results of excessive drinking.[32]

Mary Rosina had already gone downhill before her mother's death, but she deteriorated further after Frederica's passing. In June 1895 she was found lying in the road, drunk. She resisted arrest and behaved abusively toward the constables, earning her twenty-one days' hard labor and a fine. She claimed to suffer from cataleptic fits and expressed suicidal thoughts.[33] There was no mention of her former life as a celebrated medium. For a brief time in 1898 and 1899, Mary Rosina attempted to resurrect her career, placing advertisements for her services in *Light*.[34] This abortive attempt ended with her very public exposure as a "fraudulent medium" in the same journal the following year by anonymous sitters who wrote letters to the editor denouncing her "rope trick." She tried to save her reputation by writing to the paper herself, but her effort was apparently unsuccessful. In October 1900 she wrote a letter, published in *Light*, asking for help: "For many years I and my dear mother devoted our lives to the cause of Spiritualism . . . but now, alas! matters are very different—I am almost destitute!"[35] The next month, a reader with the initials G. M. wrote that he and a friend were attempting to provide assistance, but he wanted it known that Mary Rosina was "largely to blame for the condition in which she now is."[36] Mary Rosina Showers disappears from the public record after 1900, so it is unclear how she fared. Her date of death is unknown.

British mediums and business partners Catherine Elizabeth Wood and Annie Fairlamb Mellon also struggled with alcohol abuse. In 1875 Wood and Mellon were purportedly "exposed" as frauds by Trinity College academics who later went on to found the Society for Psychical Research. Wood's and Mellon's purported fraudulence was tied to alcohol from the start. In 1877 Mellon resigned from her position as the official medium for the Newcastle Spiritual Evidence Society. Her critics cited her alcoholism as the primary reason for their parting ways.[37] One apologist argued instead that the medium was more a victim than a villain: "The fact is, Miss Fairlamb, after a great deal of insult and annoyance during the winter months of 1876–1877 from the alcoholic element introduced into the promiscuous séances of the society, over which she at the time had no control, tendered her resignation in March, 1877."[38] In 1895 Mellon was still practicing materialization mediumship, but now in Sydney, Australia, and it's unclear what her relationship to alcohol was at that point. Nonetheless, her career was ended by a particularly egregious exposure during a materialization séance in her Sydney home. Mellon was reportedly caught in the act of impersonating an infant materialization she called Cissie (sometimes Cissy) using a mask and muslin drapery.[39]

Some scholars argue that Spiritualist mediums were vulnerable to alcoholism because drinking helped them cope with the anxiety of knowingly perpetrating fraud. But this assumes that all Spiritualists were frauds, with no real belief in Spiritualist tenets.[40] But as the historian Marlene Tromp argues, we can take Spiritualists' faith seriously and also acknowledge the Victorian context in which women mediums worked. Spirit mediums, especially women, experienced liberty, authority, and celebrity in the séance room that allowed them to transcend the patriarchal bonds of the society in which they lived. Tromp is not the only historian to make this argument, but she takes this approach a step further and interprets the female mediums' struggles with alcoholism as a way to cope with the rude awakening they experienced when they left the séance room and entered a constraining world. She writes of one of the Fox sisters: "Kate's drinking was an attempt to sustain an environment outside the séance that she had otherwise only been able to create there. . . . Perhaps the act of drinking offered some mediums the opportunity to access an alternative reality, to realize an as-yet-unrealizable and othered space outside of the séance."[41]

Women mediums were indeed becoming more vulnerable outside the séance room after 1870. Psychiatry, rapidly on the rise in both the public consciousness and the medical establishment, sought to explain mediums' tendency toward substance abuse through diagnosis. Psychiatrists linked sexuality, alcoholism, and mediumship to madness, especially in women. Spiritualism's detractors were heavy-handed in using psychiatric diagnoses to criticize high-profile Spiritualists. For example, John Bundy took to the pages of the *Religio-Philosophical Journal* to attack Maggie Fox's alcohol use and question her sanity, alleging that "the ravings of these poor besotted [Fox] women have been eagerly published far and wide, as affording choice bits of sensationalism for a depraved press to feed the vitiated taste of an ill-informed public." Bundy excoriated both Fox sisters, who, like many of the young girl mediums, developed into adult women who could not be neatly slotted into Victorian ideals of femininity. He went on to dismiss the very notion of reproducing "the mutterings of the wreck which represents all that remains of the once innocent and modest little girl . . . [now] half demented, and only fit for an insane asylum."[42] More importantly, medical professionals were increasingly concerned about what they called an "epidemic of delusions."[43] The British psychiatrist Henry Maudsley, for example, wrote in 1886, "The unwholesome practice of inducing mesmeric, hypnotic, and so-called spiritualistic states undermines the moral energy and will of those who addict themselves to it, and leads surely towards badness or madness."[44]

L. Forbes Winslow, also a British psychiatrist, identified Spiritualism as the primary mechanism behind what he saw as America's struggle with madness, arguing that Spiritualism-induced mental illness was "very prevalent in America, and the asylums contain many of its victims." He clarified that the community of Spiritualists "contain[ed] a large proportion of weak-minded hysterical women, in whom the seeds of mental disorders, though for a time latent, [were] only waiting for a new excitement to ripen into maturity."[45] Winslow was a man on a mission, but most evidence suggests that his data were inaccurate. In the 1880s, California's Stockton State Asylum for the Insane published its patient census by "Cause of Insanity, as Stated in Commitment." Out of several thousand patients, only ten were admitted for "alcoholism"—eight men and two women. Four patients were admitted for "Spiritualism"—one man and three women. Another man was admitted for "Spiritualism and alcohol."

Alcohol features in other diagnoses as well: "masturbation and alcohol" or "cigarettes and alcohol," for example, were sometimes given as diagnoses.[46] While these instances suggest that alcoholism, Spiritualism, and madness were certainly linked, they do not suggest that Spiritualists were institutionalized in large numbers.

Nevertheless, institutionalization was always a looming danger to women mediums, and one that Spiritualists took seriously during the 1870s. British Spiritualist and automatic writer Louisa Lowe was incarcerated in an asylum, purportedly for her Spiritualist practices. When she was released in 1871, she wrote about her experience in the newspaper *Spiritualist:* "I was myself incarcerated and otherwise restrained as a lunatic for eighteen months, on the sole ground of claiming to be a passive or automatic writer. Mrs. — at Plymouth, and others, too numerous to name, have been and are constantly incarcerated for speaking of spiritual visions. In short, numbers are being daily severed from all usefulness and enjoyment in this life, because they claim communion with a higher."[47] Hers was a warning to other women in the transnational Spiritualist community that they were all vulnerable to accusations of madness.

In addition to wrongful incarceration, practicing Spiritualists recognized that substance abuse was another occupational hazard, especially for women mediums who could channel dangerous aspects of the minds of the dead. Medium Henry James Tresidder wrote in 1861: "The mental faculties and the moral perceptions lie down together in the same passive sleep. The subject is, therefore, equally liable to receive impressions from the minds of others, and from their passions and lusts."[48] The danger seemed especially worrying for the female sex. English medium William Chapman and American medium Alfred H. Firman described a sitting with a sixteen-year-old medium, Miss Abby Fetters, a "pale, delicate creature."[49] During the séance, the naïve Miss Fetters channeled a violent male alcoholic spirit named Joe Manton. During the session, Manton, via Miss Fetters, demanded alcohol, holding another spirit, that of the sixteenth-century Dutch theologian Erasmus, hostage as he waited in the wings to come forward via Miss Fetters, threatening: "I won't stand such meanness. I ha'n't come all the way here for nothin'. I'll knock Erasmus all to thunder if you go for to turn me out dry, and let him come in." Miss Fetters/Joe was handed a brandy, which she gulped down while in trance. With Manton's spirit satiated, Miss Fetters was able to channel Erasmus, who was much more of a gentleman.[50]

Mediums were also vulnerable to the physical and moral failings of their sitters. English materialization medium Elizabeth d'Espérance claimed to have suffered nicotine poisoning and hangovers whenever she performed séances for the spirits of smokers or drinkers.[51] D'Espérance was an innovative medium in many ways, but what is most notable to us here is her relationship to alcohol. D'Espérance operated as a materialization medium long after this practice had fallen out of favor within the larger Spiritualist community. Several high-profile debunkings made such physical mediumship a risky endeavor.[52] One of the things d'Espérance did to mitigate this risk was to avoid all intoxicants. She even went so far as to require that all sitters avoid alcohol and tobacco for six months prior to the sitting.[53] D'Espérance wanted to ensure that she had eliminated any possibility of passive mediumship or unintentional fraud. She needed a clear head and for her sitters to have clear heads. Substance use clouded the mind and damaged the effectiveness of the circle.

Criticizing female mediums' sanity and alcohol use amplified their already transgressive behaviors that were challenging the patriarchy: interacting with mixed audiences, materializing scantily clad female ghosts, experimenting with free love, financial independence, suffrage activism, and more. Their purported madness or alcoholism discredited not only them as mediums, and Spiritualism as a religion, but also women's rights more broadly. This explains why temperance women and even suffragists cultivated a conservative image: if they were beyond reproach according to Victorian norms, their enemies had very little ammunition to use against them. This was a hard lesson for some Spiritualists to learn.

The early years of the temperance movement were male dominated, centered on written tracts, and steeped in Christian morality. But during the 1860s, temperance was transformed from a fringe evangelical reformist movement into a mass movement. It gained momentum at precisely the moment when the Cassadaga Lake Free Association was incorporated in 1879. This same year, Frances Willard took over leadership of the WCTU. Under Willard's presidency, the WCTU became the largest and most powerful women's rights group in America, peaking at approximately 350,000 members. While to a contemporary reader, a freewheeling Spiritualist community and an austere temperance woman like Frances

Willard don't seem like natural allies, in 1879 in Cassadaga, New York, at that particular moment in history, their worlds were inextricably linked.

Temperance is easily misunderstood by the general public as conservative and sterile. Because of the abject failure of the Eighteenth Amendment to the US Constitution, which prohibited the production, importation, transportation, and sale of alcohol, temperance activists have been portrayed as straitlaced, conservative men and women railing against the evils of imbibing. Once Prohibition was achieved at the federal level in 1919, it became clear that the American public was unwilling to tolerate sobriety indefinitely. Alcohol smuggling operations and illegal speakeasies abounded, the illegality adding titillation to the drinking experience. The Prohibition amendment was repealed in 1933, and those who'd backed the amendment—the temperance activists—were cast as prudish anti-vice crusaders who rejected pornography, birth control, prostitution, masturbation, and essentially all things that were fun.

The relevance of temperance to women's rights might seem tenuous to us now, but to women at the time, the two were intertwined. Victorian women had few legal rights but could exercise some power as moral police. Women had little legal recourse if they suffered domestic violence. They had little control over their husbands' wages—and men often drank away their wages in the local tavern. Some men were violent drunks or indebted to creditors. Women's rights reformers reasoned that if someone in the family was going to be the moral enforcer, it needed to be a woman. Moreover, early feminists believed that the lives of women who suffered under abusive, bankrupt, alcoholic husbands would be improved by the criminalization of alcohol. In these endeavors they were partly successful. American reformers eventually achieved (short-lived) federal prohibition, enacted many local and state alcohol sales laws, and reduced alcohol use in both the United States and Britain.[54]

Starting in the 1870s, temperance activism came under the jurisdiction of the women's rights movement. During the movement's heyday between 1870 and 1900, temperance women deftly navigated a politically polarized public. Activists knew their rank and file were diverse, including everyone from religious radicals, political progressives, physicians, and health reformers to moderate Victorian housewives. They cleverly couched their progressive, perhaps even radical ideas in conservative language in order to amass the broadest possible coalition. Temperance challenged the patriarchal structure of Christianity because it proposed to endow wives with authority over their husbands. But although temperance activists' appeals to Christian morality allowed them to demand more rights for women in a way that was less of a threat to Victorian society, temperance was anything but conservative. After 1879, it acted as a gateway to increasingly radical positions. Temperance work forced moderates to consider issues like woman suffrage and gender equality. It also prepared women reformers for public life. Temperance was also more successful than many believe. The movement spearheaded the successful campaign to raise the legal age of consent for girls and, perhaps most important, brought the masses into the fold of woman suffrage. Finally, temperance gave Spiritualists a respectable, conservative-seeming venue for their freethinking activism.[55]

Therefore, Spiritualists' alliances with temperance women make sense. It is precisely *because* earlier Spiritualists struggled with reputations for libertinism, and *in response* to the damage that fraud investigations had done to Spiritualism's integrity, that Spiritualists spent the later 1870s rehabilitating their reputations. Lily Dale was established at this precise moment. By 1880, the year of Lily Dale's first full camp season, Spiritualists had wholeheartedly embraced the upstanding, morally superior, yet still progressive temperance movement and, in many cases, vice versa. This alliance meant that sexual radicals and throngs of moderates operated alongside conservative, traditional, and sometimes even reactionary forces. Their agendas were held together by the glue of pragmatism.

The temperance influence at Lily Dale became particularly evident in the 1890s. Isabella Beecher Hooker, suffragist and daughter of temperance bigwig Lyman Beecher, was a devoted Spiritualist.[56] While Isabella was pro-temperance, she spent most of her energies on women's suffrage and her Spiritualism. She allowed the WCTU, however, to use her as a symbol of the Beecher temperance legacy; she typically sat on the platform at national WCTU conventions.[57] Suffragist and Spiritualist Adeline Morrison Swain was also a member of the WCTU. She was born in Bath, New York, and lived for a long time in Buffalo but had left the area before the establishment of the CLFA. Still, she was pro-temperance and would have moved in the same circles as CLFA's original stockholders. Elizabeth J. French was a celebrated Spiritualist and faith healer. She was a member of the WCTU and an occasional temperance worker based in Philadelphia.

Temperance and Spiritualism may even share a common birthplace. There is a long-standing argument over where the WCTU was founded. The dominant narrative places its origins in Ohio, but a significant minority of scholars, and the WCTU itself, assert that Fredonia, New York, was where the organization was born. There is a lot of evidence that the Fredonia camp is correct. The temperance movement was sparked by an anti-alcohol address delivered in Fredonia by Boston physician Dio Lewis on December 13, 1873. The women in attendance were so inspired by his speech that they organized a meeting days later where they named themselves the Women's Christian Temperance Union of Fredonia.[58] Fredonia sits seven miles south of Lily Dale and twenty-two miles north of the Chautauqua Institution, so the Fredonia origin story fits conveniently with the premise that Spiritualism and First Wave feminism were inextricably intertwined, at least at Lily Dale.

The next year, in Cleveland, temperance crusaders established another organization called the WCTU; this one was declared a national organization from the start. The explicit national intentions of the Cleveland WCTU appear to be the only factor in favor of the Ohio origin story. Irrespective of where one falls on the WCTU origin debate, we can all agree that the worlds of the Fredonia WCTU, the Chautauqua lecture circuit, and Lily Dale Spiritualists were interwoven. Admittedly, there is little evidence that the CLFA prioritized temperance activism in any official or organized way during its earliest years, but those CLFA seasons were marketed particularly to Spiritualists in western New York, northern Pennsylvania, and eastern Ohio, three temperance hotbeds.

The 1885 season was the first time a self-proclaimed temperance activist, Elizabeth Lowe Watson, appeared on the program.[59] The CLFA embraced temperance-related programming in earnest starting in 1888. Temperance activist Anna Orvis was one of the season's speakers.[60] Orvis, a dedicated Spiritualist and founding member of Chicago's First Society of Spiritualists, was elected president of her local chapter of the WCTU in 1889.[61] Orvis later went on to help form the Women's Organization for National Prohibition Reform in Chicago in 1929. This organization was pro-temperance but opposed to the Republicans' handling of the Prohibition amendment.

Building on the natural partnership between temperance, women's rights, and Spiritualism, Marion Skidmore established the Cassadaga Lake branch of the Universal Cooperative Temperance Union in September 1888 at Lily Dale. It had twenty-five members. In the pattern of Women's Day, the CLFA launched its first dedicated Temperance Day on August 15, 1890.[62] This remained a beloved tradition until 1919, coincidentally (or not) the same year Congress ratified the Eighteenth Amendment, which prohibited alcohol nationwide.[63] The temperance cause continued to influence Lily Dale programming through the 1890s. As Elizabeth notes in chapter 4, Anna Howard Shaw, supporter of temperance as well as women's rights, spoke at the CLFA nearly every year from 1890 to 1910. By 1888, however, Shaw had been persuaded to dedicate all of her efforts to suffrage. Susan B. Anthony, temperance activist as well as suffragist, spoke at the CLFA in 1891 and 1892. The text of their speeches does not survive, but we can be fairly certain that they revolved around women's rights issues, temperance included but not the focus.[64] The 1890s seasons included several other temperance lecturers whose speeches have been lost to history, including appearances by Spiritualist temperance women Isabella Beecher Hooker in 1892 and Mary Seymour Howell in 1893.

Temperance continued to feature heavily in speeches during Lily Dale's first decade. On August 15, 1894, Helen Gouger delivered a talk titled "Why the Saloon?" Anna Howard Shaw and Henry Blackwell, the widower of the late bloomer-wearing Lucy Stone, were also on the docket. In 1895 Carrie Chapman Catt, head of the suffrage committee in the Iowa WCTU, spoke at the CLFA. That year Temperance Day was presided over by criminal lawyer, temperance activist, and Lily Dale booster Dr. Almond Benson Richmond.[65] It's no coincidence that one of Lily Dale's greatest defenders was a dedicated temperance man; temperance was a critical piece of Spiritualists' defense against accusations of fraud.

Feminists and temperance activists Mary Ellen Lease and May Wright Sewall spoke in 1897. Sewall was especially focused on temperance as one of the founders of the Indiana chapter of the WCTU, serving as its first president.[66] Initially fairly conservative, the Indiana WCTU (like the national WCTU) radicalized over time. Sewall and her colleagues presented a temperance petition to the Indiana legislature in 1875, only to be rudely chided and dismissed by the all-male body. This was when it became clear to the Indiana WCTU that they would need to add suffrage to their agenda if they were ever to have any hope of achieving their reformist goals.[67]

A similar scenario played out in other states and at the national level, tying suffrage to temperance throughout the 1880s and 1890s. For example, the national WCTU formally endorsed suffrage in 1881 at the national convention. By that time, President Frances Willard had been convinced that woman suffrage was crucial to achieving the goal of temperance.[68] It's tempting to remember women like Shaw, Anthony, and Willard as suffragists first and temperance women second, in the wake of suffrage's success and temperance's failure. But for most of them, the exact opposite was the case: temperance activism came first, and it was their dedication to temperance that made suffrage an overarching necessity. The marriage of suffrage and temperance played out at the Cassadaga Lake Free Association each camp season in the 1890s, as the regular temperance speakers were, overwhelmingly, suffragists as well.

The 1898 and 1899 season programs at Lily Dale were studded with suffragists: Carrie E. S. Twing, Elizabeth Lowe Watson, Anna Howard Shaw, Mary Ellen Lease, and Anna L. Robinson-Gillespie. During this time, Shaw was the chair of the Franchise Department at the WCTU. Lease was steeped in socialist and populist political movements, having moved on from her temperance work in the early 1890s.[69] Twing, Watson, and Robinson-Gillespie were just as much Spiritualists as they were women's rights activists. Twing proved crucial to the 1894 New York State suffrage campaign. In 1903, celebrated reformist Charlotte Perkins Gilman, granddaughter of Lyman Beecher and niece of Isabella Beecher, appeared among the CLFA speakers. At the time of her Lily Dale visit, Gilman would have been working on her book *The Home: Its Work and Influence*, wherein she argued that women should work outside the home.[70] This year may have been the apogee of progressive feminist activism at the camp. Abby Louise Pettengill was elected the CLFA's first female president that year, and WCTU member Laura Fixen was on the board of directors. Lily Dale was officially renamed the City of Light, a reference to the town's early adaptation of electric lighting but also to its commitment to modernity and progress.[71] What had started as a modest Spiritualist camp meeting had grown into a progressive feminist hub faithfully aligned with the Chautauqua Institution and the WCTU. Temperance was crucial to this positioning.

The City of Light continued in this vein, employing progressive rhetoric and espousing explicitly progressive principles for at least the next two decades. It is worth noting, however, that radical as Lily Dale may have been, the CLFA could have engaged more controversial, less refined temperance women like the combative bar-smasher Carrie Nation or militant British suffragette Emmeline Pankhurst, but never did. The Assembly instead reliably chose more respectable, reserved feminist figures, supporting the idea that they pursued temperance as part of an image rehabilitation rather than as a mark of radicalism.

Programming from 1903 to 1910 continued in this vein. The WCTU's Marie C. Brehm spoke at Women's Day in 1906, which that year was also Temperance Day and Peace Day, a testament to the interwovenness of these issues. The program's introduction for Brehm demonstrates the importance of appearance, respectability, and reputation to the City of Light Assembly's alignment with the temperance movement:

> Charming, dignified and graceful in appearance, with a well-modulated voice, a keen sense of humor, an eloquent and inspiring speaker and an energetic, courageous and tireless worker. She has the rare gift of getting everybody to work with her, and enthuses each of the thousands of white ribboners who compose her constituents. . . . Miss Brehm is a very spiritual woman, and it will be a treat to hear this level-headed, calmly superior leader, and to meet this most gracious womanly woman.[72]

Brehm was exactly the sort of activist that Lily Dale Spiritualists were courting in their bid for respectability. Temperance was given its own day again in 1907, this time presided over by speakers Laura Fixen and Mary Seymour Howell. But there's an indication that women and women's rights were slowly being marginalized at Lily Dale, perhaps because of the absence of Abby Louise Pettengill, who had moved to Pasadena in 1907. The next year, Lily Dale women founded the Ladies' Auxiliary. Auxiliaries are often touted as evidence of female authority in areas of reform, but they are also typically formed by women trying to carve out authority in gender-segregated, male-dominated organizations. The establishment of a Ladies' Auxiliary, along with the marginalization of women on the governing board which Averill discusses in chapter 2, suggests that women's primary avenues to power were narrowing.

At the same time that women were losing power in Lily Dale, there was a decline in temperance activism. There were still Women's Days with Anna Howard Shaw, Charlotte Perkins Gilman, and other speakers, but temperance activism was ceding ground to suffrage and socialism. But even as the political connections with temperance declined, Lily Dale clung to its prohibition of alcohol on Assembly grounds. By 1920, the ban served other purposes. The Assembly was concerned about, perhaps even preoccupied with, carefully managing its reputation. Most obviously this included abiding by federal laws, such as Prohibition from 1919 to 1933. But beyond following the law, prohibiting alcohol was the most effective way for the community to protect its true mediums from accusations of fraud. The Assembly needed to send the message that its mediums were not *those* kinds of occultists, like the Fox sisters, the Showers women, Cook, Mellon, and the Bangs sisters, whose drunken antics and exposure as frauds folks had read about in the papers. It was also in the Assembly's interest to maintain law and order in Lily Dale's public spaces; they did not want the kinds of audiences that the Fox sisters had experienced in Washington, DC. Banning alcohol from the premises checked all of these boxes at the same time.

Curbing the use of alcohol on the grounds was also a way of creating an orderly, family-friendly atmosphere. One correspondent during the tumultuous 1870s wrote that a visitor to Lily Dale would be impressed by the wholesome environment, as "he will observe the concourse of well-dressed, orderly, and intelligent people who throng its streets, lawns, and cottage porticoes; while music and song, and the mirthful voices of youth and childhood 'make the foliage of the ancient grove vibrate with the tones of joy and gladness.'" The writer seems impressed by the quality of people, adult and child, visitor and resident, who made up the village's sedate crowds, promising that if "visitors remain during the session, their favorable impressions will be increased with each passing day; they will see no policeman.... They will witness no unseemly sports or pastimes; only those innocent amusements approved by all, save those whose bigotry can hear sin in music, and see crime in youthful enjoyment."[73] Lily Dale was, in short, a paradise removed from the excesses of the world beyond.

The community's desire to keep order and preserve a good reputation are traceable in the language used to describe the prohibition of alcohol in the bylaws. In 1917, article 12 of the Lily Dale Assembly's bylaws banned all liquor from the grounds.[74] After the adoption of the Eighteenth

Amendment in 1919 outlawing the sale and purchase of intoxicating beverages, the language of article 12 remained absolute. This strong language was softened a little after the amendment was repealed in December 1933, presumably because the end of Prohibition limited the legal and criminal liability of the Assembly for alcohol use on the grounds. The Lily Dale Assembly joined the National Spiritualist Association of Churches on August 10 of that year.[75] While the NSAC doesn't strictly prohibit members from using intoxicants, one of its bylaws makes clear that the church does not condone drug and alcohol use.[76] By the 1990s, the Assembly's attitude toward alcohol appears to have softened even more, as evidenced by the 1995 recognition of private consumption, as well as wording limiting the prohibition of alcohol to public spaces only.[77] This suggests that by the close of the twentieth century, alcohol use by mediums, and its linkage to fraud and madness, was no longer a concern. Rather, it was the desire to maintain public law and order that kept article 12 on the books.

Five years after my first experience of Lily Dale, coincidentally on the anniversary of my father's death, I returned with a very different group of friends to the porch of the Maplewood Hotel. We didn't have to lament the lack of a hotel bar in town; we had a box of wine or two chilling in the mini fridge of our lodging house. The Maplewood felt like the center

Figure 17. The Leolyn Inn, date unknown. "Places and Spaces" folder, Lily Dale Museum.

of Lily Dale, its heart, which had welcomed thousands of Spiritualists, skeptics, and curious souls within its walls. But it wasn't the only hotel where our historical subjects had spent their time. The Leolyn Inn had also been part of the story.

During this trip, the Leolyn was closed because it was the off-season. But it was the Leolyn's hotel registers that contained the signatures of Anna Howard Shaw and Susan B. Anthony; we just *had* to see it.[78] With Averill serving as reluctant lookout, Elizabeth and I crept among the heavy foliage surrounding the Leolyn, peering into windows, surveying the interiors that had once surrounded our feminist icons. After being shooed away by Lily Dale security (thanks for nothing, Ave!), we hopped in the car and zipped down the road to the site of the Iroquois Hotel, now a gravel-blanketed boat launch. This hotel borrowed its name from the Haudenosaunee Confederacy, which had once inhabited the area. In our next chapter Sarah will discuss Spiritualism's affinity for Indigenous culture, a conspicuous theme in Lily Dale's past and present. But these connections weren't on my mind that day. As I stood looking at the gravel lot, I made a mental note to raise a glass of wine to Lily Dale's "wild bunch." My dad would have been a fan. And a glass of water to the straitlaced temperance women who paved the way. I'm indebted to you all. Cheers!

6

The Indian Village

Sarah

One fall, I made a solo return trip to Lily Dale to grab a few extra scans from the museum. The camp season was over, and the town was quiet and the weather crisp. I chatted with Ron Nagy and scanned the files, then wandered out of the museum for a walk before the drive back to Buffalo. I wanted to go past one particular house—the last house on East Street, not far from the entrance to the Leolyn Woods and just a short stroll south from the museum. There's nothing particularly noteworthy about the house now, but for a while in the mid-twentieth century, somewhere near this house was an area once called the "WigWam Indian Village." I'm not sure what the village looked like, or even quite what it offered visitors beyond an opportunity to purchase "authentic" Native American trinkets. During the 1940s and 1950s, when "cowboys and Indians" television shows and Western adventure novels proliferated, visitors to Lily Dale could stop here to have their own Indian encounter.

There's no Indian Village in Lily Dale anymore, but Native American imagery and spirituality are *everywhere*. There are paintings of Native "spirit guides" in the history museum and dream catchers in the gift shops. In the program for any given year, you'll find workshops led by folks claiming the authority to teach Native American spirituality. Most years I've visited, for example, the program has included events led by John Two-Hawks, a musician and speaker who claims—not without controversy—Lakota and Anishinaabe heritage.[1] Others, like the medium and energy worker Grandmother Spider, are white but use Native American–inspired names given to them in spirit quests. And others still, like longtime resident Neal Rzepkowski, do not claim to be Native Americans themselves but lead ceremonies based on Native American culture such as the sweat lodge.[2]

Something else stood out during our research trips to Lily Dale: bits of Native American spirituality and culture were everywhere, but there didn't seem to be any Indians.[3] This might also not be all that unusual except for the fact that the Cattaraugus Reservation, the largest in New York State and home to the Seneca Nation, is just a few miles away. The Seneca Nation is a powerful band of the Haudenosaunee (Iroquois), who operate three lucrative casinos in western New York and have a population of thousands throughout the region. Yet there aren't any real ties between the western New York Spiritualist community and the Seneca Nation. The souvenir shops are full of generic, not Haudenosaunee, Native American knickknacks. A survey of Lily Dale's camp season programs from the twentieth century shows an on-again, off-again relationship with the Seneca Nation specifically and Native Americans in general. As with Women's Day and Temperance Day, the village held themed Indian Day celebrations occasionally for decades, and in 1931 and 1970, for instance, it hosted lectures by local Seneca speakers (Wilbur Shongo and William Bluesky, respectively).[4] But far more often, they hosted vaguely Native American ceremonies and talks led either by white folks, by individuals who claimed to be Native American but whose legitimacy has been contested, or by Native Americans whom other Indians have labeled "plastic shamans" for bastardizing and selling their culture.[5]

And yet, for many years, there *was* an Indian in Lily Dale: Oskenonton (Mohawk), an internationally acclaimed opera singer, who lived in this modest house on East Street in the 1940s and early 1950s. Oskenonton traveled extensively, singing and lecturing, crossing the Atlantic some thirty-five times.[6] In the early 1940s, Oskenonton settled down to live in Lily Dale, purchasing the house near the entrance to the Leolyn Woods. The area near the house was fashioned as the "WigWam Indian Village," where Oskenonton sold souvenirs and crafts while serving as the "appointed Indian Healer" of the village. Oskenonton was a photogenic guy, so a significant amount of the Native American imagery in town actually consists of photographs of him at various stages of his life and career.

Native Americans, or perhaps more accurately the *idea* of Native Americans, are a huge part of Lily Dale's past as well as its present. As I tried to learn more about Oskenonton and understand how Native imagery became so integral to Lily Dale's culture, I was pulled into a complicated tangle of threads, leading back to the United States' project to eradicate Native Americans, the American Indian Movement of the 1970s, and the evolution of New Age religion. Those threads were woven together into complex debates over how to define Indian identity, the legitimacy of new religious movements, and accusations of spiritual exploitation. What might seem insignificant (like a dream catcher for sale in a tiny gift shop) or cringey (like a white New Age teacher using a Native American–sounding name) are actually manifestations of a much longer history of imperialism and exploitation.

In the Lily Dale Museum, amid spirit paintings of Indian princesses and carved wooden chiefs, there's a collection of photographs of Oskenonton. In some he's wearing leather breeches and a feathered headdress—not Haudenosaunee garments but Plains Indian clothing that was more recognizable for non-Indians. In others he's wearing a fashionable wool coat, scarf, and hat. One of his personal scrapbooks is kept under glass in a display case, and a short pamphlet relating his biography is available for visitors to take home. In the museum, Oskenonton is the one Native American who isn't the Spiritualist version of the infamous cigar store Indian.

Oskenonton was born near the banks of the St. Lawrence River in Quebec around 1886. His autobiography, which he titled "The Boy Stranger," recounts a blissful childhood: his parents taught him about herbal remedies, and he helped to care for the family's cows. As a boy, he was entranced when a visitor to the reservation brought an Edison phonograph. When he ran home to explain the wonders of the phonograph to his ailing father, the older man smiled and said to Oskenonton, "It is possible that one day you will sing into such an instrument."[7] His

The Indian Village 145

Figure 18. Oskenonton at Lily Dale, dressed in Plains Indian garb, likely in the 1940s. "Oskenonton," Lily Dale Museum.

spirituality also shines through his childhood memories. After his father's death, Oskenonton chose to live on his own, even as a child. His faith gave him strength: "The Great Spirit would be my guide. My father too, would be with me." He traveled with different groups of fur trappers for a while, but when he returned to his father's old cabin, he instantly felt his father's spirit. The cabin, though "desolate," was not empty after all. Oskenonton wrote: "I felt the spirit of my father present and a kind of spiritual elation surged through my being. . . . I felt that I was on holy ground."[8]

Figure 19. Oskenonton in a wool suit, undated. "Oskenonton," Lily Dale Museum.

His father's influence continued long after he died. "From what my father had told me," Oskenonton recalled, "I knew that I should roam the world and attain some measure of fame, whatever that might mean. . . . My father's point was that I should not allow others to do the manipulating or pulling the strings of my own fate." When struggling with a decision, he'd walk in the woods, among the spirits of the trees, and talk with his father. "In the silence of the forest," he wrote, "I listened for his assurance. I felt convinced it would come to me, in due course."[9] Eventually his journey took him to the Mount Elgin Residential School in Muncey, Ontario, which he believed would be a step toward the bright future his father had predicted for him, but when he graduated, he felt lost. Carpentry didn't work out, and neither did a career in the ministry. One day in 1912, while canoeing and contemplating his future, he sang out loud in gratitude to the Great Spirit. Two American women who happened to be camped along the river listened to him sing and called out to him. They spent the evening talking, and one of the women gave him a letter of introduction to a composer in New York City, encouraging him to consider singing as his trade.[10]

After years contemplating it, Oskenonton went to New York to seek out the composer, but he found the city overwhelming and his visit didn't come to much. Just a few months later, however, Oskenonton received a mysterious telegram from the composer: "Will you come to sing for me at the Christmas tree lighting in New York City? All expenses paid."[11] Oskenonton didn't have a clue what that meant—*what was a tree lighting?*—but took the chance. The next problem was that he didn't read music. He panicked: "I did not know if the manuscript was upside down or right side up." But the composer, a Mr. Farwell, "hammered" the music into him until he had it memorized, and in short order he was standing in front of a massive pine tree, wearing feathers, singing a solo in New York City. In an interview in 1925, Oskenonton reflected on his deep belief that this was the right move in his journey: "I felt, when I was a young boy, that the Great Spirit wanted me to sing. When I was singing, I had a terrible, happy feeling in my breast here that I was doing what I should be doing."[12] After that, he stayed in New York, training and working odd jobs to make ends meet. He was an usher at Carnegie Hall, a bellhop at the Astor Hotel, and a canoe instructor at a camp for girls. After years of scraping together a living, he finally found success—recitals and operas in New York, tours across Europe. He found a particular happiness in England, where he sang in over seven hundred engagements. Eventually he became internationally known for performing in the operatic adaptation of Longfellow's poem *Hiawatha*.

Unfortunately, this is where Oskenonton's unfinished autobiography ends and his story gets difficult to piece together. The records at Lily Dale consist largely of scattered newspaper clippings and photographs, and they mainly focus on his singing career, remaining silent on how and why he ended up connected to the world of Spiritualism, and Lily Dale in particular. What we do know is that in 1917, his journey brought him to Lily Dale to perform what became a somewhat standard offering in his career: a recital consisting of Native American songs, some of which he may have known from childhood and others that were probably modern creations. It's not clear how this concert came to be. There's no record of who was organizing bookings, or how the board might have heard of Oskenonton in the first place. But however it happened, it proved fateful, because

Oskenonton ended up in Lily Dale for a significant portion of his life. In the 1917 concert he was paired with a woman named Chinquilla, who claimed to be Cheyenne and Mohawk. The pair worked together often during this period, sometimes presenting themselves as brother and sister. (This is extremely unlikely to have been true, but we'll get to that later.) Sometimes the shows were big—like huge ensemble performances of *Hiawatha*, which Oskenonton continued to perform for several decades— and sometimes they were small, like the concerts for children the two performed at the behest of the National Kindergarten Association.[13] He continued to travel and perform into the 1930s, spending a great deal of time in the United Kingdom.

There's no record of when exactly Oskenonton became a resident of Lily Dale or when he began styling himself as a spiritual healer. In 1939 he wrote to a friend, Ted Blackmore, that he had performed and lectured at a Spiritualist church, and in 1941 he performed again in Lily Dale. His career stalled in 1939, when war made it impossible for him to return to the United Kingdom, where he had been so successful and happy. Years later he wrote to Ted Blackmore: "I have had a rough time since 1939. I can tell you that when I lived in England I lived like a Lord of Yorkshire. Over here—hand to mouth."[14] In 1944 he purchased a home in Lily Dale from Lula Freeborn, a resident medium, presumably the little cottage near the entrance to the Leolyn Woods. During the 1940s, he sold "genuine Indian Handicraft(s) & Souvenirs" in what the camp program called the "Wigwam Indian Village." Three afternoons a week, the "appointed Indian Healer" taught healing classes in the Assembly Hall.[15] Though we don't have a document explaining his decision to live in Lily Dale, hawking Indian souvenirs and teaching healing classes, we can reasonably assume he had few other choices for making a living as he aged and touring was hampered by war. His health suffered, making upstate New York winters difficult. In letters to his friends, he complained of problems with his lungs. He spent time in Florida, performing and speaking often at the Church of Spiritual Philosophy in St. Petersburg. The 1950s were hard: his career dwindled, and his health worsened despite the warm climate. He wrote to Ted Blackmore in April 1953: "Got a rejection from the conductor. Was in Saint Petersburg lung hospital during the winter—a difficult winter financially."[16] In 1955 he moved to Phoenix, where he hoped his health would improve—but in March he had a heart attack and died.

Oskenonton is a fascinating if not well-understood character in the story of Lily Dale. Taken at face value—a genuine Indian healer!—he serves as a kind of proof of authenticity for all the Native American history, culture, and spirituality that is pervasive in the town. But when read more critically, what we know—and don't know—about Oskenonton invites us to explore how Native Americans and their faith practices became so entwined with places like Lily Dale.

Native American faith traditions varied according to each group and subgroup's landscape and social structure. Across hundreds of unique Indigenous religions throughout North and Central America, there were sometimes similar mythologies. For instance, the Muskogee-Creek, Ashinaabeg, Ottawa, Cherokee, Delaware, Omaha, Seneca, Kansa, Shawnee, Hopi, Navajo, Acoma, and Onondaga, among others, share similar creation stories. Details differ, of course, but they all tell of an animal (sometimes a muskrat, sometimes a turtle or duck) that dove through a vast ocean, bringing up dirt to create the earth.[17] Many faiths emphasized respect and balance in all things. Native religions evolved over time, and when Europeans and Africans arrived in North America, traditions changed to make space for new people and objects. Glass beads, metal, and other imported goods were used in the creation of ceremonial items, for instance.

But newness also created tension. The voracious European appetite for beaver pelts and deer skins led to overhunting. European diseases decimated Indigenous populations, and European alcohol created social and health problems. Some Native Americans responded by converting to Christianity, from the early Massachusetts "praying towns" of converted Pequot to the Catholic saint Kateri Tekakwitha. Others responded by preaching a return to traditional ways of living. Among the Haudenosaunee, Handsome Lake (Tuscarora) promulgated a new law in the late eighteenth century, later formalized as the Code of Handsome Lake, which set moral codes for living but also commanded followers to learn the English language, indicating the need for peace and understanding with European Americans.[18] Other revivals were more concerned with reasserting Indian dominance over whites. The preaching of Neolin, a Delaware prophet, helped to bring about Pontiac's War against the English in 1763. Similarly, Tenskwatawa ("The Shawnee Prophet") urged followers to violently resist American imperialism, eventually ordering the Battle of Tippecanoe.[19]

Such violent clashes led whites to see Indigenous religion as a threat. This misunderstanding came to a head in the late nineteenth century. The reservation system, which had been the federal government's approach to Indian policy in the mid-nineteenth century, was failing, as frustrated Indians clashed with reservation authorities who limited their mobility and controlled them with food rations. During Ulysses Grant's administration, the United States government instead began to develop a policy of assimilation, heavily influenced by Christian reformers who believed that the salvation of "heathen Indians" was integral to American civilization. Grant created the Board of Indian Commissioners, made up exclusively of white Christian men, to help develop and implement Indian policy.[20] Their proposed solution was the destruction of tribal distinctions, the erasure of Native culture and language, and, of course, forced conversion to Christianity.

White Christian reformers, following the advice of leading anthropologists like John Wesley Powell and Alice Fletcher, saw this not just as the most humane solution to the "Indian problem" but as a natural process, one that all human groups underwent in the grand process of civilization.[21] Reformers across the United States—including Spiritualists, who sang the praises of assimilation efforts in the pages of *The Banner of Light*—likewise saw assimilation as a form of progress.[22] By helping tribes divide their land into individual allotments and removing their children to Indian schools where they could be reeducated and Christianized, white Americans could speed the process by which the "American Indian" would become the "Indian American," in the words of Alice Fletcher. Assimilationist efforts resulted in the 1887 General Allotment Act—or as it's more commonly known, the Dawes Act—which broke reservations up into individual plots, with all "extra" land sold off to white settlers.

Assimilation was cultural extermination, a concerted effort implemented by the United States government to erase Native Americans from the population. But there was literal extermination too, most of it also perpetrated by the federal government. Some of the deaths were a byproduct of forced removals. The Cherokee, Chickasaw, Seminole, Muscogee-Creek, and Choctaw lost thousands of lives on the Trail of Tears, forced to leave their ancestral homes by Andrew Jackson's administration in the 1830s. Encouraged by the federal government and aided by the army, hunters shot the buffalo into near extinction with the intention of hastening a solution to the "Indian problem."[23] But there were also outright campaigns of murder at the hands of white settlers and soldiers. Between the 1840s and 1870s, the California Gold Rush inspired a legally sanctioned genocide against Indigenous groups perpetrated by the state militia.[24] In Colorado in 1864, the army slaughtered about 150 men, women, and children camped on the banks of Sand Creek. The massacre wasn't an isolated incident; in the late nineteenth century, breathless reporting on "savage" brutality and calls to exterminate Plains tribes inspired violence from whites, and the army was dispatched to "control" the so-called problem.

In 1890 the parallel "solutions" of assimilation and extermination collided with Native American spirituality with horrific results at Wounded Knee Creek in South Dakota. Through the 1880s, the Plains Indian agencies (outposts that served as the point of contact between tribes and the federal government) had cracked down on religious expression. In 1883 the Office of Indian Affairs established the Code of Indian Offenses, later known as the Religious Crimes Code. The code banned cultural practices that whites believed kept Indians from assimilating, such as sacred dances and songs, plural marriage, shamanism, and medicine work. The Office of Indian Affairs saw the dances not merely as pagan acts that prevented Indians from assimilating but as exercises in savagery that riled them up to attack whites. The code had been in existence for only a couple of years when a Paiute man named Wovoka began to have visions of a future world with abundant game, where whites and Indians lived in peace.[25] These things, he learned, would come to pass only if Indians lived according to God's instruction that "they must be good and love one another, have no quarreling, and live in peace with the whites; that they must work, and not lie or steal; that they must put away all the old practices that savored war." God told the prophet to use a ceremonial dance to spread the message.[26] This became known as the Ghost Dance religion, a utopian revival that spread through western reservations. In 1889 Lakota leaders on the Rosebud Reservation in South Dakota sent a delegation to the Paiute—a journey of over a thousand miles—to listen to Wovoka preach. They returned with the message of peace for their people: "Work the ground so they do not get idle, help you agents, and get farms to live on . . . educate your children. Send them to schools." Further, Wovoka told the seekers to go to church, assuring them that the specific faith did not matter, for "all these churches are mine."[27]

The vision of an abundant future, with plenty of food and peace with whites, was understandably appealing to the Lakota. Things were particularly dire on the Pine Ridge and Rosebud Reservations in the late 1880s. The Dawes Act and its resulting land commissions had meant the loss of 9 million acres of Lakota land, and congressional belt-tightening had cut into the rations distributed by the agencies on the ground. When the Lakota started dancing—an act restricted under the Religious Crimes Code—agents began to get really anxious. Whites didn't understand the Ghost Dance religion, of course, and didn't care to learn. To them, all dancing was a prelude to war. Worried that trouble was brewing, the army dispatched soldiers to the Lakota reservations and required all residents to leave their homes in the bitter cold and set up temporary housing near their agencies, where they could be better supervised. Some of the most faithful dancers resisted, but as weeks went on, weather, sickness, and hunger forced most to report. One resistant band of Miniconjou Lakota agreed to move only if they could get a military escort to ensure their safe return to their agency. But when soldiers tried to disarm the band, a gun accidentally discharged. Even though no one was hurt and the discharge was clearly unintentional, the soldiers opened fire on the unarmed Lakota. After killing most of the men, the soldiers used their massive Hotchkiss gun to lob shells at women and children. When all those in camp were dead, soldiers went out to pick off any who had escaped. By the time they were done, around three hundred men, women, and children had been slaughtered by the US Army.[28]

While most histories leave the story of the Ghost Dance religion there, it didn't disappear after the killings at Wounded Knee Creek.[29] Many Plains tribes continued to dance into the 1920s. In Oklahoma, dances were held nearly every weekend through the early twentieth century, and even in the 1990s, Ghost Dance songs were performed at sacred occasions.[30] And while histories also sometimes treat Wounded Knee as the end of American Indian history, religious movements continued to appear and thrive well after 1890.

Peyotism, for instance, which centers on the vision-inducing effects of sacred peyote cacti, was pioneered by Quanah Parker (Comanche) and John Wilson (Delaware), who each developed their own ceremonies for using the drug at the end of the nineteenth century. The ceremonies combined Christianity with various Plains Indian traditions and ceremonies, creating an intertribal faith emphasizing peace and moral living.[31] Unlike the Ghost Dance, however, peyotism was formalized in 1918 as the Native American Church, which is now the most commonly practiced religion among Indians in the United States. But even formalized, the faith was subject to policing. Starting in 1896, the Bureau of Indian Affairs criminalized the use of peyote, and throughout the twentieth century, state governments followed suit, especially as recreational drug users popularized peyote. The American Indian Religious Freedom Act (AIRFA), passed in 1978, attempted to provide federal protection for Native American religious practice, especially when it came to prohibited substances. But it couldn't withstand the pressures of the war on drugs. In 1990 the Supreme Court upheld Oregon's ban on the religious use of peyote, with Justice Antonin Scalia arguing that religious belief could not excuse breaking "valid" laws. The decision enraged activists and inspired them to advocate for legislation that would protect Native Americans' religious freedom. In 1993 President Bill Clinton signed the Religious Freedom Restoration Act, intended to protect Indigenous religious practice, and the following year an amendment was added to AIRFA to specifically protect religious peyote use.[32]

Historically, then, spiritual beliefs and practices of Indians in America have been policed to the point of violent massacre. So how did sweat lodges and medicine wheels become key features of the Lily Dale camp season? Lily Dale is a Spiritualist community, but today the overall religious vibe of the town can also be described as New Age, an umbrella term for a loosely connected eclectic system of spiritual beliefs and practices—including the Spiritualist belief that the dead don't die. New Age religion isn't cohesive or organized, and often adherents don't even identify with the name "New Age." Instead they see themselves as spiritual seekers on highly individualized journeys of self-discovery, using spiritual tools and practices borrowed from or influenced by world religions. (This is why your medium might have a chakra chart hanging on the wall over a table that holds a Bible, some tarot cards, and a few turkey feathers.) By seeking personal spiritual enlightenment, some adherents—though not all—believe humans can help to usher in a "new age" or "age of Aquarius," which will offer expanded consciousness and other delights.[33] While we associate this kind of individualistic, eclectic religious seeking with the hippies of the 1960s and 1970s, the New Age has deep roots.

The ideas that eventually combined with the Fox sisters' discovery of spirit communication also helped to shape the New Age. Swedenborgianism, for instance, was based on the writings of Emanuel Swedenborg, eighteenth-century scientist turned Christian theologian, who taught that individuals carried the divine within themselves and that God could be found in nature.[34] Franz Anton Mesmer, who taught a form of energetic healing called mesmerism not unlike modern-day reiki, also began his work at the end of the eighteenth century. The early Spiritualist Andrew Jackson Davis began his career as a mesmerist. But while these were popular European movements at the time, Swedenborg's and Mesmer's theories didn't gain widespread traction in the United States until the Second Great Awakening. The new religious movements born out of the Second Great Awakening, such as Mormonism, as well as the Protestant Christian movements we've discussed throughout this book, expressed the hope that renewed personal faith, along with religious, individual, and societal reform, would bring about the millennium. And the Transcendentalists, Spiritualists, and Theosophists all sought individualized spiritual enlightenment outside established religions. These new movements nearly all drew on Swedenborg and Mesmer, updating them for a new era.[35]

It was the Theosophical Society, founded in 1875 by Helena Petrovna Blavatsky and Henry Steel Olcott, that innovated mixing elements of world religions—in this case, Asian religions—into something new. Blavatsky taught about a divine society of Ascended Masters, most of whom had lived human lives, achieved great wisdom, and developed supernatural powers before transitioning to Spirit. Masters included figures from world religions such as Jesus, Moses, Siddhartha Gautama, and Lao Tzu, but also two previously unknown men from India, Koot Hoomi and Morya, whom Blavatsky claimed to have learned from during her time traveling through India. (The real identity of the pair was contested, as was whether they had any supernatural powers.)[36] Reflecting the shift toward individualism, Blavatsky's and Olcott's Theosophical writings emphasized self-development, largely through learning from the Masters, that leaned hard on appropriated beliefs and practices. The Theosophists drew heavily on Southeast Asian culture and language, and they helped to spread interest in concepts like karma and reincarnation.[37]

Though Theosophy continued to gain new followers through the turn of the twentieth century, most of the other new religious movements of the nineteenth century dwindled until the 1920s and 1930s, when alternative religion was reinvigorated.[38] Edgar Cayce, a Christian trance medium from Kentucky whose writing continues to be one of the pillars of the New Age movement, was influenced by Theosophy to expand his extremely popular spiritual teaching to include elements of Asian religions, and Guy Ballard leaned on it in his popular "I AM" movement. But despite their popularity, religious experimentation was uncommon in the conformity-minded culture of the postwar years. Most Americans embraced Christianity as "America's civil religion" during the Cold War era and avoided experimentation under the pressure to focus on the family and state.[39] A counterculture existed: the Beats smoked pot and criticized mainstream culture, and UFO religions like the Aetherius Society and Scientology were founded, but to most Americans these groups were weird and marginal.[40]

Rejection of conformity and materialism spurred the counterculture of the 1960s, led by the children of the postwar baby boom. Disaffected boomers, eager for self-improvement and meaning, blended bits of teaching from folks like Blavatsky and Cayce and used pot and psychedelics to expand their minds. But while drugs opened a door to spiritual seeking, many desired even greater gravity and truth. For that they looked to world religions, blending aspects of different traditions that might expand the consciousness, including everything from yoga and astrology to crystals and aromatherapy. Many found that depth in Asian traditions, as had the Theosophists. Transcendental meditation, for instance, became enormously popular when the Beatles and the Beach Boys took the Maharishi Mahesh Yogi as their guru. Others, inspired by a burgeoning environmental movement, sought a connection to the earth and the ritual afforded by neopagan religions such as Wicca.[41]

The desire for deep spiritual connection and environmental consciousness also brought spiritual seekers back to the teachings of Indigenous Americans. In the 1970s, a series of books, all at least ostensibly based on anthropological research, introduced seekers to Indigenous religion. The two with the greatest impact were *Black Elk Speaks*, first published in 1931 but republished in 1972, and *The Teachings of Don Juan*, published in 1968. Both books featured an Indigenous elder sharing the wisdom of his people with a non-Indian, explaining their ancient beliefs and forgotten knowledge of the natural world. For non-Indians of the mid-twentieth century, raised in a culture where images of Indians were either the dangerous warriors of John Wayne movies or noble savages, these texts offered something deeper and more in tune with nature.

Black Elk Speaks was initially a relatively obscure anthropology text, republished thirty years after its original release. The text was based on extensive oral history interviews between the poet John G. Neihardt and Nicholas Black Elk, a member of the Oglala band of the Lakota who had converted to Catholicism in 1904. Before his conversion, Black Elk had been a leader of the Ghost Dance religion and had lived through both the Battle of Little Big Horn and the massacre at Wounded Knee. In the book, Black Elk tells his life story, but also clearly and beautifully describes Lakota spirituality, making Lakota religion legible to non-Indians by presenting it in Christian terms. For example, he compares Jesus to White Buffalo Cow Woman, whom Lakota credit with bringing the tribe the sacred ceremonies, including the sweat lodge and vision quest, from Wakantanka (the Great Spirit). The book had a quiet reception when it was first published in 1932, but its reissue was perfectly timed to meet an audience searching for ancient truth.

The second anthropology book that sparked interest in Indigenous spirituality was Carlos Castañeda's hugely popular *Teachings of Don Juan*. In 1968 the anthropology student Carlos Castañeda published his master's thesis (followed by several sequels), which purported to be the result of interviews he conducted with Don Juan Matus, a Yaqui shaman from Mexico. Castañeda recounts how Don Juan put him through shamanic training, leading him through ceremonies using peyote and other psychedelics. The book was a massively popular glimpse into Indigenous life, but it was Castañeda's drug-fueled spiritual adventures, guided by Don Juan, that really appealed to seekers. Castañeda's works found an eager audience with the counterculture: Jim Morrison was a fan, John Lennon referred to Yoko Ono as his personal "Don Juan," the writer William Burroughs referenced Don Juan numerous times in his writing, and George Lucas reportedly based Obi Wan Kenobi on the shaman.[42] Instead of staying in academia, Castañeda embraced shamanism. According to Castañeda, Don Juan named him the "last nagual" of the Yaqui, making the anthropology student heir to a centuries-old tradition of spiritual leadership. While *The Teachings of Don Juan* and its sequels were wildly popular, most scholars agree that they were more fiction than anthropological study.[43]

Both books were hugely successful because they tapped into two things happening in the 1970s: the boom in New Age interest in Indigenous faiths, yes, but also a growing Indian rights movement seeking to reclaim Native identity, including the revival of suppressed religious traditions. During the 1960s and 1970s, Indians across the United States began to push back against broken treaties and disrespect through direct action against governments.[44] When *Black Elk Speaks* and its companion book *The Sacred Pipe* were republished, they were hugely appealing to young Indians seeking to reconnect with ancestral traditions. Vine Deloria Jr., the Standing Rock Sioux writer and scholar, noted the importance of *Black Elk Speaks* on a generation of young Indians in his introduction to the 1979 edition: "The most important aspect of the book, however, is not its effect on the non-Indian populace . . . but upon the contemporary generation of young Indians who have been aggressively searching for roots of their own in the structure of universal reality. To them, the book has become a North American bible of all tribes."[45] In 1972, when members of the activist group the American Indian Movement (AIM) gathered on the Pine Ridge Reservation to participate in a Lakota Crow Dog sun dance, the political goals of the Indian civil rights movement became entwined with the revival in spirituality. Primed by *Black Elk Speaks*, when AIM embraced the sun dance, the movement adopted specifically Lakota spiritual beliefs, helping to make them accessible to all Indians seeking connection with older traditions. Just a few months later, AIM occupied Wounded Knee to protest a breakdown in treaty negotiations (among other issues), and while the occupation was violent and complicated, it drew public interest and helped usher in a series of reforms—including AIRFA and its amendments—intended to protect Native American religious freedom.[46]

As powerful as *Black Elk Speaks* was for Indians, it and *The Teachings of Don Juan* also sparked white people's interest in Indigenous spirituality. The 1972 edition of *Black Elk Speaks* was marketed specifically to spiritual seekers, with the promise on the cover that Black Elk's teaching made "an LSD trip pale by comparison."[47] The Lakota religion the book describes has become the template for the generic pan-Indian culture and faith endemic in New Age religion—the sweat lodges, medicine wheel ceremonies, and vision quests that have appeared so often on the program at Lily Dale over the decades. And not only did *Don Juan* spark general interest in shamanism and Indigenous teachers, but also it inspired Carlos Castañeda himself to join the New Age world. Castañeda transformed his (purportedly) anthropological research into a cultish religion, living on a compound with his female followers, alternately known as his "students" or his "witches."[48]

The interest sparked by *Black Elk Speaks* and *Don Juan* led some seekers to new religious movements. Both Indians and non-Indians capitalized on the interest in Native American spirituality, bringing it fully into the New Age world. Vincent LaDuke (Ojibwe), better known as Sun Bear, was born on the White Earth Reservation in northwest Minnesota. Sun Bear, an army deserter and actor, founded the Bear Tribe Medicine Society after he experienced a vision that told him he needed to bring the medicine wheel—a Lakota symbol used to facilitate healing and balance—to all people. In the 1970s, Sun Bear and his followers, the Bear Tribe, started a nature commune in Washington State. But within a few years, they also owned an office building and were making thousands of dollars a year selling "Indian ceremonial objects" through a mail-order catalog.[49]

A few years later, the Bear Tribe started holding "medicine wheel" gatherings where attendees could pay to hear Sun Bear preach, take part in "medicine wheel" ceremonies, and of course buy "sacred" Native American merch. One former member recalled followers "tying colored yarn onto chicken feathers while talking about the fools who would pay $1 apiece for them once they were 'blessed' by Sun Bear."[50] Most of Sun Bear's students and followers were white people. Noting that Sun Bear was rarely at his "Vision Mountain" commune, *Spokane Chronicle* columnist Doug Clark also pointed out that his audience was largely white folks. "He . . . keeps the busy schedule of a globe-trotting guru to his predominantly white admirers," Clark wrote in 1991.[51] Sun Bear's influence on New Age religion continues today. His heirs to the Bear Tribe, Marlise Wabun Wind (formerly Marlise James) and Wind Daughter, are both white women. They continue to teach widely. The fee for membership in the "tribe" is $60, and events can cost between $200 and $300.[52]

Native Americans were hugely critical of Sun Bear's blatant commercialization of a jumbled-up Indigenous spirituality. After Joseph Bruchac (Abenaki) attended a medicine wheel gathering in 1983, he wondered in the Native newspaper *Akwesasne Notes* whether the "tribe" was at risk of becoming a cult, asking if Sun Bear was "becoming the Maharishi or a Sun Myung Moon in a war bonnet? Will commercialism turn Native American sacred objects into supermarket items?"[53] In response to a Bear Tribe gathering in Ocala, Florida, in 1989, Ann Helms (Delaware), head of the American Indian Association of Florida, said that a "true medicine man would not give away such knowledge." She also worried about his acolytes: "I think a lot of his followers are groupies . . . these are people who are searching for something to hang on to, like the 1960s hippies. It's almost like a cult. It's a shame to have a self-promoter like Sun Bear presenting a mix of sacred teachings to such vulnerable people."[54]

The criticism of Sun Bear from Indian Country was focused on his identity as an "authentic Indian" in order to make a profit off selling a fictionalized mishmash of Native American spiritual traditions to white people. (Not to mention the allegations made against him that he used his reputation as a spiritual leader to coerce women into sexual relationships.)[55] But Sun Bear also accelerated another trend in New Age spirituality: white people claiming to be medicine men, shamans, and teachers of Native American culture and spirituality. Sometimes called the "female Carlos Castañeda," Lynn Andrews, a former art dealer from Los Angeles, published a book in 1981 called *Medicine Woman*, in which she detailed her supernatural (and unbelievable) path to becoming a white "medicine woman," taught by Native teachers.[56] Since then, Andrews has written over a dozen books in which she creates what Native American scholar Philip Deloria (Standing Rock Sioux) has called a "pastiche" of Indian cultures: "She finds, for example, a Choctaw woman living near a Canadian Cree community in a Pawnee earth lodge, described in such a way as to sound suspiciously like George Catlin's paintings of Mandan houses from 1832."[57] Andrews doesn't claim Native American identity—in other words, she never says that she is an enrolled member of a tribe or that she has Indian ancestry. Instead, she claims to have been taught by Native American women and initiated into a mysterious, vaguely Indigenous-sounding group. Like Castañeda, she claims she studied with Native elders, who blessed her and told her to spread the message. And like Sun Bear, Andrews has been repeatedly called out by Native American groups for being a spiritual huckster. Flora Zaharia (Kaiani), a member of one of the Canadian tribes Andrews supposedly studied with, told the *Boston Globe* in 1988 that Andrews was writing "falsehoods at the expense of native women." Attempts to shame Andrews into giving up her grift have been unsuccessful. More than thirty years after the *Boston Globe* piece, Andrews was still active. On her website, at the time of this writing, you could sign up for her Shaman Mystery School for a mere $2,495 tuition.

Spiritualism, specifically, has always included Indians—in spirit form, anyway. White mediums channeled Indians in séances, especially nationally famous ones like Black Hawk, the Sauk leader, who dictated a widely read memoir in 1833, or Red Jacket, the Seneca leader of the Revolutionary era.[58] Spirit chiefs spoke through white mediums to voice opposition to the white man's mistreatment of Native Americans. Maidens with names like White Fawn and Star Flower were another common feature, beautiful, tragically romantic, and sharing messages of universal love. Spirit Indians appeared most often during the Indian Wars, helping white Spiritualists spread the gospel of assimilation. This is reflected in Lily Dale's history museum, where spirit paintings and other imagery depict either powerful chiefs or beautiful young maidens, almost always wearing Plains Indian–style garb. And it's not an accident that Lily Dale's Florida sister camp, Cassadaga, was founded when medium George Colby was led to a patch of stolen Seminole land by an Indian spirit guide named Seneca.[59] While Natives had long appeared at Lily Dale, when Spiritualism collided with the New Age in the mid-twentieth century, it became more common for Lily Dale to offer programming on this new kind of Native American spirituality, usually presented by someone claiming Indigenous identity or claiming to have been taught or even adopted by an Indigenous person. The earlier séances presented messages that served white political ends and furthered Spiritualist goals. This newer shift, by contrast, came with mixed-up, made-up versions of stereotypical Native American culture presented by individuals with complex or contested identities.

I've never seen any evidence or suggestion that Oskenonton was anything other than who he said he was: a Mohawk born and raised on reservations in Canada. But Princess Chinquilla, Oskenonton's performing companion for several years, has been questioned and criticized for over a century. Not only is the controversy around Chinquilla interesting itself, but also her case is illustrative of just how complicated and, frankly, difficult it is to untangle the threads of Native American identity.

Princess Chinquilla appears many times in the playbills and newspaper clippings in the Lily Dale History Museum, and the most oft-repeated claim is the easiest to debunk: that Oskenonton and Chinquilla were brother and sister. Oskenonton was Mohawk (Haudenosaunee) and born in Quebec around 1886. But Chinquilla was born sometime around 1867 and identified throughout most of her life as Cheyenne, though after she connected with Oskenonton around 1917, she began to claim she was half-Mohawk.[60] Though it's not clear exactly how the sibling story was created, her claim to be partly Mohawk made it seem plausible to audiences. In Lily Dale and other Spiritualist circles, their relationship was taken at face value and was still repeated in Spiritualist media into the 1940s.[61]

Just as she altered her claims about her background to accommodate her partnership with Oskenonton, Chinquilla tailored herself to different audiences and changing times. Early in her career, she and her first husband had a slapstick vaudeville routine, which evolved into Chinquilla singing while dressed in traditionally masculine beaded breastplates and feathered headdresses, which audiences would recognize from stereotypical depictions of Indian men in Wild West shows.[62] When she performed in New York, she took to reciting Haudenosaunee work, such as the poetry of Tekahionwake (Mohawk) or a speech about Red Jacket.[63] Her life story changed too. In her earlier vaudeville career she spoke of having been orphaned and taken from the Cheyenne reservation in Oklahoma to perform in circuses before attending school in Kansas City. Later, while trying to get her son into Carlisle Indian School, she began to claim she had attended Carlisle, though the school denied it. In the late 1920s, she added even more detail to her story while traveling through Montana, apparently searching for family, saying she had been rescued from a burning Cheyenne village by white homesteaders and raised in Kansas.

Other Indians were suspicious of Chinquilla's ever-changing backstory. Indian political activists Gertrude Bonnin (also called Zitkala-Sa, Yankton Dakota) and her husband, Raymond Bonnin (Yankton Sioux), even suspected that her skin had been unnaturally tinted.[64] Gertrude Bonnin sent Charlotte Jones, a fellow member of the National Council of American Indians, to investigate Chinquilla, and the two exchanged a series of letters analyzing and criticizing her assertions. Jones questioned Chinquilla's claim of being both Cheyenne and Mohawk: "In looking over the material I am sending, I find that [Chinquilla] is called Cheyenne, Mohawk and Iroquois. How peculiar!"[65] But while there are lots of things about

Chinquilla's story that don't add up, context is also key. If she was Cheyenne, as she claimed, she was likely a very small child at a time when the Southern Cheyenne were under attack by the US Army. She could easily have been taken in, out of the carnage and flames, to be raised by whites, only to disappear later into the world of vaudeville—calling herself a princess and donning stereotypical clothing to appeal to white audiences, eking out a living, with only vague memories of who she was or where she was from.

It's almost impossible to pull apart the strands of Chinquilla's story to determine once and for all whether she was who she claimed to be. There's plenty of evidence that she was a fabulist, but within the context of the realities of life for a young Native American woman at the turn of the century, her ever-changing story looks more like that of a survivor skilled in crafting narratives to keep herself afloat in a hostile society. Identity is deeply fraught in the world of New Age Native Americans. Researching this chapter, I continually found myself being pulled down exhausting rabbit holes of identity, trying to learn whether the teachers of Native American spirituality who worked in Lily Dale were really Native. But as with Chinquilla, it's never that simple a question. As demonstrated by Sun Bear, even for undisputed Indians, identity can be problematic. "Plastic shamans," as Indian activists have called other Indians who pander to New Agers, are identified largely through Native whisper networks and message boards. When Vine Deloria Jr. was asked in 2003 about how he responded when he knew someone was fraudulently selling Native American spirituality, he replied, "Rather than make an issue with them, I just pass the word to other Indians that the person is a fraud."[66]

Take, for instance, a workshop led by a man named Howard Isaac at Lily Dale in 1985. In the workshop, Isaac performed the "Lily Dale Medicine Wheel of Stumps," in which he shared, according to the camp program, the "knowledge and wisdom of the Seneca Nation."[67] Isaac, who identified as a member of the Seneca Wolf Clan, appears to have done some amount of traveling during the 1980s and early 1990s talking about "Living the Wheel of Life" and Iroquois relationships to the natural world. While Howard Isaac doesn't seem to have been a very well-known writer or speaker, a quick search shows that he was a student of another Seneca spiritual teacher, Twylah Hurd Nitsch.[68] Nitsch was Seneca, grew up in Buffalo, and moved to the Cattaraugus Reservation as an adult.[69]

From the 1970s to the 1990s, Nitsch—often referred to as Grandmother Twylah—wrote or co-wrote pamphlets and books on Indian traditions and religions. Most were published by the Seneca Indian Historical Society, an imprint that certainly conveys a sense of authenticity. But while the Seneca Indian Historical Society was located on the Seneca Nation reservation, it was founded and run by Nitsch and her mother, Maude Shongo Hurd, and was located at the family home.[70] There's no evidence the society was endorsed by Seneca leadership, was affiliated with the nation, or existed outside of Nitsch and her followers. Nitsch and Jamie Sams, a Texas woman who claimed to be her granddaughter, co-wrote a book on Seneca creation mythology that received mixed reviews in major journals. Scholar Roger Weaver, for instance, remarked in his review for *Studies in American Indian Literatures* that the book made a "New Age incursion" on Seneca oral tradition.[71]

Twylah Nitsch's writing and public profile took on an increasingly New Age flavor, and she founded a spiritual school called the Wolf Clan Teaching Lodge, with the mission of "preserving and disseminating the teaching of the Seneca Indian Historical Society."[72] Nitsch seems to have declared a large number of non-Indians "adopted," who then went on to claim membership in the Seneca Wolf Clan—though they were referring to Grandmother Twylah's Wolf Clan Teaching Lodge, not the very real Seneca Wolf Clan. Those students often also connected with other New Age Indian teachers, typically Sun Bear.[73] Nitsch herself was a speaker at Sun Bear's medicine wheel gatherings, and it seems clear that she at some point started teaching Sun Bear's particular version of the medicine wheel, a Lakota—not Haudenosaunee—ceremony.[74] The medicine wheel, Sun Bear's New Age ceremony, is what Howard Isaac taught at his 1985 workshop at Lily Dale.

Twylah Nitsch and others accused of being "plastic shamans" taught at Lily Dale. Nitsch spoke on "sacred harmony" on Indian Day in 1984. She was back the next year, speaking on the "Wisdom of the Senecas," after which she led a medicine wheel ceremony.[75] Ed McGaa (Lakota), who had a bad reputation in Indian Country for packaging Native religion in New Age texts sold to outsiders, spoke at Lily Dale in 1997.[76] More recently a woman named Waynonaha Two Worlds lived in Lily Dale, leading women-only sweat lodges and retreats. Two Worlds claimed to be Lakota and Cheyenne but also stated that she was born into the "Bear Clan," and has claimed membership in the "Sisterhood of the Sacred Corn," which doesn't seem to exist outside her own author bios.[77]

For many Native New Agers, the question of identity is complex. Especially before DNA testing was ubiquitous, it was common for white people to claim Native American ancestry. Famously, something like a hundred thousand people have claimed Pocahontas as their ancestor—including Nancy Reagan.[78] In Lily Dale's history, the clearest example was Chief Ho-To-Pi, a contemporary of Oskenonton, who spent time at Lily Dale and was revealed in death to have been a Greek man named George Cutrulis.[79] To try to avoid folks claiming to be Native on the basis of a dodgy family story, most tribes require some proof, such as a genealogical study or a blood quantum. In addition to proving that relationship, most tribes require that a person be enrolled in the tribe in order to claim membership. Even with those protections, non-Natives continue to claim Indianness, such as prominent Native American studies scholar Andrea Smith, who was outed numerous times for fabricating Cherokee heritage.[80] But one can have the required genealogical lineage and still not be an enrolled member, or may be a member of a tribe that doesn't have federal recognition. Identity isn't simple.

Indian spiritual gurus who claim Native American spirituality are criticized in their own right, but they also create another problem when they symbolically "adopt" white adherents, endowing them with membership in newly invented "tribes" and "clans," which they then use to add authenticity to their own teaching. And Lily Dale regularly plays host to them. Grandmother Spider, who offered workshops often in recent years, is a medicine wheel teacher associated with Twylah Nitsch's Seneca Wolf Clan Teaching Lodge. Wind Daughter, the leader of Sun Bear's Bear Tribe Medicine Society, has visited Lily Dale several times. Not only is she Sun Bear's heir, but also she was "adopted" by another teacher, Bear Heart (Muskogee-Creek), and thus claims to be Muskogee-Creek. In 1995, Wind Daughter was the guest of honor during Native American Traditions Week at Lily Dale, though she is not Native American. Neal Rzepkowski, a white man, facilitated sweat lodges in Lily Dale throughout the 1990s and 2000s. Rzepkowski has made it clear that he is *not* Indian, but he uses a Native-sounding name (TiOmime) and conducts Lakota ceremonies on his property just a few miles from Lily Dale.[81] In 1989, while visiting sacred Lakota and Cheyenne territory, Rzepkowski was invited

Figure 20. Man, possibly Ho-To-Pi, dressed in Plains Indian attire, undated. "Places and Spaces" folder, Lily Dale Museum.

to attend a sweat lodge, then received messages from Spirit telling him to lead sweat lodges himself. When he asked Spirit why it didn't choose an Indian, it responded, "Well, you're here and there is not enough time."[82] Today he—like so many others—is affiliated with Sun Bear and Wind Daughter's Bear Tribe. It's not an accident that so many of these figures are interconnected through teachers and spiritual tribes. As the scholar Dagmar Wernitznig points out, the "secluded circle of New Agers" means that authors create a loop of justification and attribution: they get their expertise on Indian history, culture, and spirituality from one another in an endlessly interconnected web of pseudo-Indigenous spirituality.[83]

The most problematic aspect of Lily Dale's relationship with such figures is that Indian activists and spiritual elders have spoken out strongly against this kind of cultural theft for decades. In 1980, elders from several tribes signed the "Resolution of the 5th Annual Meeting of the Traditional Elders Circle," calling out individuals "purporting to be spiritual leaders" for sharing sacred objects and teaching non-Indians under false pretenses. They didn't object to sharing the faith; rather, they were concerned "with those people who use spiritual ceremonies with non-Indian people for profit" and argued that since sharing the faith was sacred, it needed to be offered with "great care by the Elders and the medicine people who carry the Sacred Trusts."[84]

The activist group AIM, at the urging of the Circle of Elders, passed its own resolution just four years later condemning exploitative spiritual leaders. That resolution condemned the sale of sacred ceremonies and items such as pipes and feathers. The 1984 resolution mentioned Sun Bear by name. Because he was Indian, Sun Bear touched a particular nerve with AIM for exploiting and bastardizing Native American spirituality. Richard Williams, president of the American Indian College Fund for over a decade, wrote that "Sun Bear isn't recognized as any sort of leader, spiritual or otherwise, among his own people. He's not qualified. It takes a lifetime of apprenticeship to become the sort of spiritual leader Sun Bear claims to be, and he never went through any of that." Matthew King, a Lakota spiritual elder, wrote that mixing together the beliefs of different tribes was "forbidden" because it destroyed balance. He explained that "the forbidden things are acts of disrespect, things that unbalance power. These things must be learned, and the learning is very difficult. This is why there are very few real 'medicine men' among us; only a few are chosen."[85] In other words, you can't just declare yourself a medicine person.

Protest went beyond resolutions and open letters to include direct actions and declarations of war. Not long after the 1984 resolution, the Colorado chapter of AIM protested a Sun Bear medicine wheel gathering, which participants had paid $500 each to attend. In 1993 the activist group SPIRIT (Support and Protection of Indian Religions and Indigenous Traditions) confronted Lynn Andrews at the Whole Life Expo in Los Angeles, asking her to "admit that what she was writing about was fantasy, not Indian spirituality."[86] That same year, members of SPIRIT drew up another document, endorsed by representatives of forty tribes of the Lakota, Dakota, and Nakota Nations of the United States and Canada. This resolution had a stronger name: "A Declaration of War against Exploiters of Lakota Spirituality." Like previous documents, this one described the abuses of the exploiters of Indian spirituality but was more pointed in calling out the New Age movement and the buying and selling of Indian culture. The resolution's authors decried seeing sacred pipes "at flea markets," "'sundances' for non-Indians . . . conducted by charlatans and cult leaders," and "wannabes . . . selling books that promote the systematic colonization of our Lakota spirituality." The declaration went on to "declare war" on "wannabes," charlatans, and "plastic medicine men," assuming a "posture of zero-tolerance for any white man's shaman who arises from within our own communities," stating that all such "plastic medicine men' are enemies of the Lakota, Dakota, and Nakota people" and calling upon Indians to "actively and vocally oppose this alarming takeover."[87] This criticism is widespread in the academic study of Native American religion and spirituality and is powerfully articulated by the Indian scholars Vine Deloria Jr. in *God Is Red* and Philip Deloria in *Playing Indian*.

American Indian writers, activists, and scholars have been vocal for decades about the problems with New Age versions of Indigenous spiritual practices. If folks in New Age circles were really as curious as their beliefs might suggest, there's plenty of information available to read and learn. Maybe someday one of the bookshops at Lily Dale will have *God Is Red* on the shelf instead of something by Sun Bear. Or host more events like one held in 2020, where artist Diane Shenandoah (Oneida) visited the village to give a talk about the history and cultural importance of the Haudenosaunee Thanksgiving address.[88]

Ron tells a story about how occasionally during his time in Lily Dale, Oskenonton would take a tent out and camp in the woods behind the Forest Temple to be alone. As with so much about Oskenonton's life, no archival source exists to tell me whether that's true, but something about that story strikes me as both lovely and sad. Even after decades of success, singing for crowds in the United States, Canada, and the United Kingdom, Oskenonton still thought of himself as a "Boy Stranger." In his autobiography, he is always wandering, and in his final letters to friends, he is a man with no home. And sometimes he slept out, alone, in the woods, to be away from camp season visitors. Yet when he needed it, Lily Dale offered him a home and a community, and though he wandered from Quebec to New York City and from London to Florida in his lifetime, it's here that Oskenonton is most celebrated and lovingly remembered. The threads of Native American history, spirituality, and New Age religion may be tangled, and sometimes in profoundly problematic ways, but when I look at the little house near the entrance to the Leolyn Woods, I hope that Oskenonton felt, at least temporarily, at home in Lily Dale.

Epilogue

The Lily Dale Museum

Averill

At this point, most of our time in Lily Dale, collectively and individually, has been spent in the Lily Dale Museum. The little yellow schoolhouse at the corner of Library and East Streets, which Pomfret children attended from 1889 until 1938, is two stories tall, narrow and long, with high ceilings and more bits of history packed along its walls than anywhere else in the town. It was a community center for the residents of Lily Dale for several decades, until 1995, when it was given over to the purpose of displaying the town's history in artifacts. Whether we were spending the night or just popping down for the day, we always ended up at the museum. Its caretaker and Lily Dale's historian, Ron Nagy, is the keeper of the town's history and secrets. He manages the file cabinets and plastic bins of records, hotel registers, photographs, newspaper clippings, and endless ephemera from 150 years of Spiritualist and western New York history. But he's also spent decades collecting the stories of Lily Dale from his friends and neighbors. In the off-season he writes books that record the happenings in the town from its inception to the present.[1]

Ours is a book about place, about the history of religion, activism, feminism, and emotion that's been churned up and paved over in the streets, bricked up and burned down in the buildings, and etched into every stone and plank of wood that makes up Lily Dale. Yet a place is more than the sum of its buildings and roads: a place is its people. It's the women and men who gathered at Alden's Grove in 1873 to picnic and commune with the dead. It's the mediums who've given demonstrations at Inspiration Stump for 130 years, and who've bought or rented cottages during camp season to accommodate their materializations or provide private readings to visitors. It's the radical suffragists who spoke in the auditorium to enthralled audiences and the temperance activists who made a dry town. It's the Lily Dale Assembly members and their elected board members who waged wars, big and small, over what Spiritualism meant here, what kinds of mediumship would be allowed, how big the butterfly garden would be, and who could buy houses on the property. Today, Lily Dale is its aging population, but also the thousands who visit each summer to participate in the workshops, religious services, ghost walks, messages at the Stump, private readings, and celebrations that still fill the robust annual camp program. Lily Dale is people like Ron, who experienced something that made them believe then moved to this town to be part of something meaningful. He's told us a couple of times that he wasn't converted, he was convinced. And Lily Dale is the spirits of all the dead who've lived, worked, and experienced Spiritualism in this town.

It took Ron a while to warm up to us. When we started archival research for this project in the summer of 2021, Lily Dale was still under COVID-19 restrictions. I had emailed Ron a few times in April and May, hoping that he'd be willing to let us into the archive before the height of camp season, when he and the museum would perhaps be too busy for us. But he said he wasn't allowed to let anyone into the museum before camp opened, so we had to wait till summer. By the time we could all carve out time for a group research trip, it was already August. We arranged to meet Ron at the museum as soon as he opened the doors in the morning. When Marissa and I walked in, in our T-shirts and shorts, armed with giant water bottles and iPhones, Ron laughed.

"I thought you were some 'Men in Black' coming to make my life difficult!" he said, waving a printout of my email at us. We introduced ourselves and made it clear that though "Averill" is a man's name (it means "wild boar hunter"), the person who had written the emails was me, the woman standing there in a "Liberal Feminist Witchcraft" T-shirt, not some intimidating suit coming to harass Ron Nagy. I like to think that he was more amused than annoyed by our arrival, but it's hard to say.

We were careful to let Ron lead the way over that first visit. He asked what we were looking for, and then brought us things he thought we'd be interested in. He pointed to the boxes we were allowed to retrieve from the back room, and watched carefully as we carried them back and forth. Lily Dale residents have been wary of outsiders writing books ever since journalist Christine Wicker published her unflattering history of Lily Dale in 2003. We'd all read it; we knew why folks would be a little closed off to outsiders. Profiles like Wicker's often present Spiritualists as fools out of step with reality or as frauds trying to scam a few bucks out of tourists. So we were cautious. We took what Ron was willing to show us, scanning everything so we could assemble a shared digital archive to read more closely in the snatches of time between teaching, service, and producing our podcast.

Slowly, though, Ron started to trust us. At one point he mentioned that he hoped to create a digital copy of all the archive's materials as well, so that he could read things from home on his computer in the winter while doing his own book writing. That fall, I organized all of our files into folders, put everything we'd digitized onto a thumb drive, and sent it to Ron with a Christmas card. When we finally got back to Lily Dale in May 2022, this tiny thank-you gift had helped us worm our way into his heart. He gave us access to materials I suspect he'd never shown outsiders before. He let us into the back room unsupervised. Sometimes he even left us in the museum alone while he ran copies of his book up to the gift shop or front office. It made us feel just a little more connected to Lily Dale, which was in the process of shifting in our hearts from research subject to old friend.

For months, we'd hoped to see the board meeting minutes. I imagined that they were detailed and packed with the ridiculous minutiae that went into planning camp every year, like picking colors for the signage, deciding what flowers to plant, and debating who to invite to speak. I wanted budgets and exact attendance numbers and controversies—not necessarily because we were going to include any of that in the book, but because I'm a nerd who loves archives.[2] There were a couple of presidents' reports in the materials Ron cared for at the museum, but as far as we could tell from our careful perusal of those filing cabinets, no meeting minutes. But we were also a little afraid to ask to see them. We were convinced that the board, understandably distrustful of outsiders and researchers, would be uncomfortable letting four strangers paw through the records of something as private as board meetings.

Finally, during one of our last trips, we worked up the courage to ask Ron if we might be able to see the minutes. He told us (at long last) that those were held in the Lily Dale front office, not in the archive. He offered to introduce us to the board president, Joanne Mansfield, and sure enough, when we made an appointment, he joined us there to smooth the way. According to Joanne, Ron had been showing people the Christmas card we'd sent him that previous winter, telling them what good gals we were and how thankful he was for all those digitized files. Our reputation preceded us! The staff showed us the bound books of board meeting minutes, kept on shelves in the basement. The oldest books were crumbling, and the collection wasn't organized. We took photos of what we could and, feeling dismayed at the history eroding in that building's basement, offered to come back and help do some light archival preservation of the books. We made recommendations about archive boxes, and indeed, Marissa and Elizabeth returned the following week to organize and better preserve those records for future generations of researchers. Ron hung out with us while we went through those books, his earlier grumbles of distrust replaced with friendly teasing and delightful stories.

From the very beginning, we had long conversations about how we would approach the writing of this book. Though our ruminations in each chapter of this book start in the present and connect to our own lives, we knew we wanted to write a *history* of Lily Dale, not an ethnography of contemporary Lily Dale. With very few exceptions, we have purposely not commented on the current lives or beliefs of Lily Dale's residents. Our biggest hurdle, though, has been figuring out how to discuss the more controversial elements of Spiritualism's history. We have friends and family members who are Spiritualists—Ron among them—and we are not interested in disparaging their religion. At its founding, Spiritualism was a faith of both rationalism and emotionalism. In the nineteenth century, as today, it purports to provide scientific evidence of life after death. At the same time, it tapped into the very human experiences of grief, isolation, and curiosity. Being both rational and emotional is a lot of work.

So too is grappling with the messy histories that come from the dual streams of rationalism and emotion. To do our jobs well as historians, we have had to acknowledge and confront the controversial elements of Spiritualism's history. We have applied the historical methodologies that we were trained in to subjects that challenge the bounds of historicity. Using the sources of both skeptic and Spiritualist, we have tried to reconstruct and make sense of inherently mysterious things. This is challenging work. But we never approached these issues lightly.

We discussed how to address these fraught histories when we were putting together the proposal for this book, every time we drove down to Lily Dale for group trips, and each night as we debriefed after a day in the archive. Even as I write this epilogue, we're having a group chat over text about how to navigate "truths" when the history of a place is so tied up in its mythology. Why, for example, is there a memorial to the ashes of the Fox Cottage but no markers celebrating the space where Maggie Fox actually performed séances when she visited for the camp season in 1882? Or, similarly, when *The Banner of Light* reported on Maggie's various visits to Spiritualist camps in the summers during the 1880s, for example, why did the newspaper acknowledge her fame but not offer anything substantive about her presence?[3] In the same newspaper that only briefly mentioned the ripple of pleasure Maggie brought to Lily Dale in 1882, there was at least one article about the Fox family and their initial experiences of Spiritualism in nearby Hydesville in 1848. Often in Spiritualist histories, the girl versions of the Fox sisters are distinct from the adult versions. After many conversations, we concluded that it was because the adult Fox sisters struggled with alcohol abuse, were constantly embroiled in charges of fraud, and even confessed that their famed spirit rappings were all a hoax. The innocent little girls who had lived in the Hydesville cottage were heralded as the founders of Spiritualism by its earliest chroniclers, and so the tale was preserved as an essential part of Lily Dale's curated history. The adult sisters, by contrast, were a threat to the very heart of the faith.

We're historians, not journalists. This book isn't an exposé. Acknowledging the flawed, painful, and upsetting parts of our history is how we better understand the present. History is complicated, and histories of religion all the more so. There are histories of fraud, alcoholism, and spiritual hucksters in Lily Dale. Despite these painful passages—or perhaps because of them—Lily Dale continues to be the largest Spiritualist camp in the world. It is, of course, not the same as it was in 1882, when Maggie Fox was in residence. Visitors today are more likely to be interested in a contemplative cup of coffee on the balcony of a guesthouse than a dance on a floating platform on the lake. In mediums' homes, instead of blacked-out windows and spirit cabinets, you'll find a well-lit, comfortable office with a couple of armchairs and some burning incense. In 1979 an advertisement for the camp season promised "dancing, concerts, and entertainment," but in 2000 Joyce LaJudice, Ron's predecessor, cautioned that "[Lily Dale] is not a psychic fair. . . . [R]esidents are serious about privately practicing the religion of Spiritualism . . . not here for entertainment."[4] Change is inevitable, whether an adaptation to external circumstances or a self-reflexive transformation driven by an evolving collective philosophy. The histories we've written in this book will help readers make sense of the past that helped create Lily Dale as it stands today.

Many Spiritualists acknowledge the messiness of their history, just as many of their nineteenth-century forebears faced fraud accusations head-on and welcomed parapsychology investigators into the séance room. On the ghost tour we took in Lily Dale, for instance, the guide forthrightly discussed Maggie Fox's "confession" of fraud. But undoubtedly there will be believers who feel we've been unfair or unduly critical because we've included controversial elements in this book. It would have been hard to leave those stories out. When we got to our chapter on the Fox Cottage, we realized it was impossible *not* to talk about the role of professional skeptics, allegations of fraud, and scientific investigations in the history of Spiritualism and Lily Dale. But what's more important than the veracity of fraud allegations is the historical moment in which those conversations were taking place across the United States and Europe. Lily Dale's first decades occurred at the moment when branches of science were invested in proving that there was life after death, when women claimed public space to speak and be heard in a patriarchal world, and when the women's suffrage and temperance movements were helped to grow through the radical feminist networks of Spiritualists. We wanted to tell those histories, the tangled, complex histories that have grown out of this little intentional community of Spiritualists, to the best of our ability. The results of our effort are before you.

Hours spent collecting and digitizing archival material at the museum meant spending quality time with the museum's irreverent caretaker. Ron keeps the best stories about Lily Dale in his brain, probably stored next to his "proprietary filing system" of the archive. His best stories likely started as gossip and rumor, and might be verifiable, but with the records long lost, they're unfit to publish.[5] He spends his days during the camp season answering people's random questions about family members who once visited there ("How the heck should I know?" Ron might say, as he pulls out a hotel registry with that person's signature) and keeping an eye on the carefully curated and ever-changing collection of artifacts that chronicle the history of Lily Dale. The walls are hung floor to ceiling with spirit paintings, business signs from mediums gone but not forgotten, sepia photographs of the founders of Lily Dale. Glass-fronted apothecary cabinets house curiosities, everything from the charred remnants of the Fox Cottage to bits and bobs of suffrage paraphernalia.

The history of Lily Dale has been lovingly cared for by residents, the hamlet, and students of the movement, though perhaps not centrally preserved. Josh Ramsdell and Carrie Twing were among the first to try to write the story of Lily Dale at the close of the nineteenth century.[6] Some histories of the town are housed in the Skidmore Library, a legacy left by the founding grande dame, Marion Skidmore. The official meeting records are still in the basement of the Assembly offices, though now slightly more organized thanks to Elizabeth and Marissa. Most of Lily Dale's recorded history is kept in cold green file drawers, folders stuffed with yellowing loose-leaf paper, newspaper clippings, and black-and-white photographs. The archives in the museum were originally curated by the former town historian, Joyce LaJudice, who passed in 2005. Neither she nor Ron was formally trained in library science, though they've done their best as self-taught archivists. There isn't a catalog or formal database of the records held in the museum or the front office, as is often the case in these very small archives, run entirely by volunteers who make do with shoestring budgets and more donated artifacts than they know what to do with. But even without indexes and finding aids, the museum is painstakingly maintained, preserving Lily Dale's history for future generations of seekers.

Lily Dale is special to so many people. It's a kind of capital for Spiritualists and a beacon for non-Spiritualists seeking to connect with their dead. Folks in western New York and northeastern Pennsylvania are particularly connected to this little town. Sarah's family, from the Syracuse area, made their way to Lily Dale and Spiritualism. When I told friends from the area that we were writing this book, they were familiar with Lily Dale already, and one even had an aunt who used to be a medium who lived in Lily Dale. On one of our early visits to the museum, I located her aunt's sign on the wall and sent her a photo. This is a town that is a family history touchstone for many, and Ron regularly gets donations from people of their deceased relatives' possessions, and even more frequently he gets requests for information about long-dead relatives who spent time in Lily Dale over the decades. And of course, it's so much more than just a regional archive and resort town. During one of our visits, we happened to attend a message service where a group of student mediums were practicing delivering readings. They had come, brimming with excitement, from all over the country to Lily Dale to learn the trade, following in the footsteps of generations of mediums. At its founding, Lily Dale was the nexus of nineteenth-century radical social activism, religious revival, and utopian ideals. It was, and in many ways remains, a beacon of light.

The last time I was in Lily Dale was a little chaotic. After a few hours at the museum, Elizabeth, Marissa, and I met Ron at the front office so we could get started photographing Assembly minutes. We moved quickly, capturing as much as we could before they closed up for the night. It didn't dawn on me until much later that it could be my last visit to Lily Dale ever, or at least for a very long time. Now that Marissa and I have taken jobs about as far from western New York as you can get, we can't all just pop down to Lily Dale for the day. Even when we were all based in western New York, the logistics of planning so much as a day trip were onerous. I regret not taking one last moment to appreciate being in that place with my dearest friends.

Loss is part of life. We do what we can to mitigate it. We put the crumbling records of a Free Association into archival boxes to slow their decay. We share the silly stories and frustrations of our daily lives in a group chat to stay connected when it feels like our jobs and families have sent us to the farthest corners of the earth. We sit with mediums, hoping—even through skepticism—to make contact with a parent who died too soon. Some of these measures bring us a little peace, maybe even joy. The loss is still there, though, an emptiness that can't be filled, a tangible thing that is reduced to its echoes in photographs and digital copies. Lily Dale exists, at its core, to help us cope with losing loved ones. At any given reading or message service, visitors can be seen weeping, hugging, sharing memories. Those who have lost a beloved pet are also invited to contemplate as they walk through the small pet cemetery. If nothing else, Lily Dale forces its visitors—even the most hardened doubters—to consider their own losses.

As historians, we are also trying to mitigate loss. We intervene where we can in order to prevent the loss of physical historic artifacts in archives and museums. But when we do this work, when we go into those archives and pull together the threads of historical memory and documentation, we are combatting the loss of something even greater. When we forget or deny or ignore the foundations on which our world was built, we lose ourselves. Historians do the work to remind us where we came from, how we got here, and why we must continue to grapple with those truths.

In 2022 more of the town was reopened, and there were significantly more visitors than we'd seen in 2021. Loss and disaster were very much on our minds as we spent time in Lily Dale on the heels of the worst pandemic in a century. Will Spiritualism—and Lily Dale—experience a resurgence in the wake of COVID-19? It's possible. Just as this town and this religious movement provided solace across the United States after the Civil War and across the Atlantic after World War I, the COVID-19 pandemic might swell Lily Dale's summer visitor numbers once again. Or maybe not. We've shown you a movement and a town that have changed dramatically from its founding. Lily Dale holds on to its Victorian charm and offers a range of services and workshops every summer that might seem radical to some, but perhaps not in the way that Spiritualism was radical in 1880 or even 1919. It both is and isn't the same place, just as Spiritualism is and isn't the same religious movement built on the talents of the Fox sisters.

The last time we were all at the museum together was a stark contrast to our first research trip to Lily Dale. We'd earned Ron's trust, and instead of watching us warily, he made jokes and teased us like old friends. We knew those creaky green filing cabinets almost as well as Ron did. Elizabeth persuaded Ron to open a glass-front cabinet where the Women's Day and suffrage materials were on display—off limits to regular visitors. He even took us up into the schoolhouse attic, where yet more artifacts are stored. We took more breaks than we did at the beginning of the project, a little less desperate to collect as much as we could for winter examination.

Instead, we spent more time just walking around the museum, appreciating the accumulated ephemera that Ron has displayed for visitors seeking a little history with their spiritual experience.

We had a blast writing this book. Don't get me wrong—there were a lot of panicked moments. As with the "copy week" that we often chat about at the end of a podcast episode, there was a lot of furious writing, revising, and rewriting in the week before the manuscript was due at our publisher's. But we got to spend time together in a beautiful town in western New York, taking evening strolls by the lake, eating delicious meals at the Lily, and shoring up our friendship and partnership. We got to think about the very real and surprising ways that we connected to this history, demonstrating again and again why this was such a perfect project for the four of us to take on. And we got to *do* history—sometimes challenging, cringey, and uncomfortable history, but history nonetheless—for the joy of it. For me and Marissa, at least, this book is so far afield from our formal areas of scholarship that it was like starting a new career trajectory. It's been as enjoyable a writing project as anything else I've done to date, and I know my friends agree. We hope that you've enjoyed the journey with us. We want to thank you for being curious, for taking the time to learn something new, and for joining us on this trip to Lily Dale. And since this is the stand-in for our traditional podcast sign-off, as always, you can find us on social media @dig_history and you can join the official Dig Pod Squad group on Facebook. You can support the podcast (and our future book projects?) by becoming a patron. Look for us at patreon.com/digpodcast to learn more.

Thank you.

Notes

Introduction

1. Don't get us wrong: We all love a horror story that might produce a haunting or, in Marissa's case, an unsolved murder that she can spend hours investigating on the Internet. But we're historians, so of course we also love history tours.

2. The Lyceum was a school dedicated to the instruction of children. It seems that this served as a sort of day care center and spiritual school for families that visited Lily Dale during the summer.

3. Physical mediumship refers to those mediums who purported to be able to demonstrate proof of the afterlife through various physical manifestations.

4. "Camp meetings" are a particular feature of the American Second Great Awakening, which Sarah talks about extensively in chapter 1.

5. The official Lily Dale history timeline, held in the Lily Dale Museum (hereafter LDM), states that the first Spiritualist picnic on Alden's property was in 1873. A note on the museum archive: there is no uniform filing system nor finding aid. We have listed a folder name if one exists; otherwise anything cited LDM without a folder name is housed somewhere in the museum.

6. Jan Prymus, "Lily Dale Then and Now," *The Summit of Spiritual Understanding* 55, no. 590 (November 1973): 6.

7. For examples of Victorian entertainment culture, and particularly the growth of the "seaside resort" and other country-based getaways, see Andrea Inglis, *Beside the Seaside:*

Victorian Resorts in the Nineteenth Century (Carlton South, Victoria: Miegunyah Press of Melbourne University Press, 1999); Lee Jackson, *Palaces of Pleasure: From Music Halls to the Seaside to Football: How the Victorians Invented Mass Entertainment* (New Haven: Yale University Press, 2019); and John K. Walton, ed., *Histories of Tourism: Representation, Identity and Conflict* (Bristol, UK: Channel View Publications, 2005). Sarah also discusses the long history of religious camp meetings in chapter 1.

8. Sarah discusses the Burned Over District extensively in chapter 1.

9. But I am the opposite of a religious radical.

10. Gretchen Clark, "Inspiration Stump," *Light Bridges Magazine*, 2007. This is a clipping held in the LDM.

11. From a random piece of paper in the "Places and Spaces" folder, LDM.

12. Official program, 1931, Camp Program Collection, LDM.

13. Quoted in Lisa Morton, *Calling the Spirits: A History of Séances* (London: Reaktion Books, 2021), 225.

14. Marissa discusses the Iroquois Hotel's liquor license (which was unusual, as Lily Dale was a dry town by its own Assembly's bylaws) in chapter 5.

15. Is it a coincidence that, as we were writing this book, Marissa moved to the state where Lily Dale's sister community, Cassadaga, is, and my new home in the Twin Cities of Minneapolis–Saint Paul is a stone's throw from both a Buffalo *and* a Lily Dale? Well, you're either open to hearing the universe tell you everything is going to work out, or you're not . . .

1. Welcome to Lily Dale

1. National Spiritualist Association of Churches, "Declaration of Principles," https://nsac.org/what-we-believe/principles/.

2. For examples, see Ella Morton, "Lily Dale: The Gated Community for People Who Talk to the Dead," *Slate*, June 11, 2014; Penelope Green, "Meet the Mediums of Lily Dale," *New York Times*, August 4, 2018; Frank Bruni, "A Booming Little Ghost Town," *New York Times*, August 25, 1997. The best-known book on Lily Dale is Christine Wicker, *Lily Dale: The Town That Talks to the Dead* (New York: HarperSanFrancisco, 2004). Lily Dale has also been the subject of MA and PhD theses, such as one by Mary Catherine Gaydos Gabriel, "Ordinary Spirits in an Extraordinary Town: Finding Identity in Personal Images and Resurrected Memorial in Lily Dale, New York" (MA thesis, Utah State University, 2010).

3. Josh D. Ramsdell, *A Souvenir of Cassadaga Lake* (Erie, PA: Herald Printing and Publishing Co., 1889), 3, LDM.

4. Ron Nagy, "History of Lily Dale," http://ronnagy.net/ronsblog/2010/02/history-of-lily-dale-1st-handout/.

5. William Denevan, "The Pristine Myth: The Landscape of the Americas in 1492," *Annals of the Association of American Geographers* 82 (September 1992): 369–85. On the Erie and how they were conquered by the Haudenosaunee, see Harry Leopold, *The Forgotten People: The Woodland Erie* (New York: Exposition Press, 1975); Alan Axelrod, *A Savage Empire: Trappers, Traders, Tribes, and the Wars That Made America* (New York: Thomas Dunne, 2011).

6. Laurel Thatcher Ulrich, *The Age of Homespun: Objects and Stories in the Creation of an American Myth* (New York: Doubleday, 2001), 16.

7. For spirit communication in America before the founding of Spiritualism, see Erik Seeman, *Speaking with the Dead in Early America* (Philadelphia: University of Pennsylvania Press, 2019).

8. Daniel K. Richter, *The Ordeal of the Longhouse: The Peoples of the Iroquois League in the Era of European Colonization* (Chapel Hill: University of North Carolina Press, 1992).

9. See Alan Taylor, *The Divided Ground: Indians, Settlers, and the Northern Borderland of the American Revolution* (New York: Knopf, 2006), 98–100; Mark M. Mintz, *Seeds of Empire: The American Revolutionary Conquest of the Iroquois* (New York: New York University Press, 1999); Glenn Williams, *The Year of the Hangman: George Washington's Campaign against the Iroquois* (Yardley, PA: Westholme, 2005).

10. Whitney Cross, *The Burned-over District: The Social and Intellectual History of Enthusiastic Religion in Western New York, 1800–1850* (Ithaca: Cornell University Press, 1950), 5.

11. Paul E. Johnson, *A Shopkeeper's Millennium: Society and Revivals in Rochester, New York, 1812–1837* (New York: Hill and Wang, 1978), 17.

12. Joanne Reitano, *New York State: Peoples, Places, and Priorities* (New York: Routledge, 2016), 73.

13. Reitano, *New York State*, 73.

14. Peter L. Bernstein, *The Wedding of the Waters: The Erie Canal and the Making of a Great Nation* (New York: W. W. Norton, 2005), 31.

15. Daniel Walker Howe, *What Hath God Wrought: The Transformation of America, 1815–1848* (New York: Oxford University Press, 2007), 118.

16. Bernstein, *The Wedding of the Waters*, 325.

17. Bernstein, *The Wedding of the Waters*, 348.

18. Johnson, *A Shopkeeper's Millennium*, 17–18.

19. See Jon Butler, *Awash in a Sea of Faith: Christianizing the American People* (Cambridge: Harvard University Press, 1992); Nathan O. Hatch, *The Democratization of American Christianity* (New Haven: Yale University Press, 1989); John Howard Smith, *The First Great Awakening: Redefining Religion in British America, 1725–1775* (Lanham, MD: Fairleigh Dickinson Press, 2014).

20. Cross, *The Burned-over District*, 8. See also Shelby Balik, *Rally the Scattered Believers: Northern New England's Religious Geography* (Bloomington: University of Indiana Press, 2014), 76–80.

21. Cross, *The Burned-over District*, 31; Lester Langley, *The Shaker Experience in America* (New Haven: Yale University Press, 2009), 10–14.

22. Cross, *The Burned-over District*, 31; Langley, *The Shaker Experience in America*, 66–76.

23. Séan Alonzo Harris, "The Last Shakers," *Deseret News*, March 25, 2022; Katherine Lucky, "The Last Shakers: Keeping the Faith in a Community Facing Extinction," *Commonweal Magazine*, November 28, 2019.

24. Though the Friend did not seem to have a preference regarding pronouns, and different followers used different pronouns—some male, some female—I have chosen to use gender-neutral pronouns to describe the Friend.

25. Paul B. Moyer, *The Public Universal Friend: Jemima Wilkinson and Religious Enthusiasm in Revolutionary America* (Ithaca: Cornell University Press, 2015), 11–20.

26. Moyer, *The Public Universal Friend*, 142–48.

27. Moyer, *The Public Universal Friend*, 166–88.

28. Cross, *The Burned-over District*, 45–50.

29. Charles Grandison Finney, *An Autobiography* (Bloomington, MN: Bethany House Publishing, 1977), 16.

30. Marianne Perciaccante, for instance, notes that there was a culture of revivalism in Jefferson County before the onset of the "Second Great Awakening" in 1830, and Cross emphasizes that much of the population of New York was already active in Christian worship, if not a member of a church. For a nice overview of the historiography on the Great Awakenings in New York, see Rachel Cope, "From Smoldering Fires to Revitalizing Showers: Historiographical Overview of Revivalism in Nineteenth-Century New York," *Wesley and Methodist*

Studies 4 (2012): 25–49; and Nathan O. Hatch, "Redefining the Second Great Awakening: A Note on the Study of Christianity in the Early Republic," in *The Democratization of American Christianity* (New Haven: Yale University Press, 1989), 220–26.

31. Paul E. Johnson, *Sam Patch, the Famous Jumper* (New York: Hill & Wang, 2003), 128.

32. Johnson, *Sam Patch*, 133.

33. Cross, *The Burned-over District*, 155.

34. See, for example, Christine Leigh Heyrman, *Southern Cross: The Beginnings of the Bible Belt* (Chapel Hill: University of North Carolina Press, 1998); Hatch, *Democratization of American Christianity*; Matthew Dennis, *Seneca Possessed: Indians, Witchcraft, and Power in the Early American Republic* (Philadelphia: University of Pennsylvania Press, 2010); Jon Butler, *Awash in a Sea of Faith: Christianizing the American People* (Cambridge: Harvard University Press, 1990); Albert J. Raboteau, *Slave Religion: The Invisible Institution* (Oxford: Oxford University Press, 1978).

35. The region was not really discussed in those terms before Whitney Cross's foundational book *The Burned-over District*, published in 1950. When the name was used during the era, it was not meant as a compliment. Fiery imagery regarding the region came from Henry Ward Beecher, who suggested that the intensity of revivalism left behind moral ruin, much as a raging fire might. Charles Grandison Finney also talked about the "fires of revival" in negative terms, suggesting that past revivals had burned hot but left behind hardened, unreceptive citizens. Cross argued that "the history of the twenty-five years following Finney's early campaigns suggests that the burning-over process fertilized luxuriant new growths rather than merely destroying old ones." Cross passed away just five years after the book was published, but his influence on American religious history was profound. See Cope, "From Smoldering Fires to Revitalizing Showers," 30–35. For more on Cross and his work on the Burned Over District, see Judith Wellman, "Crossing over Cross: Whitney Cross's Burned Over District Social History," *Reviews in American History* 17 (1989): 159–74.

36. Cross, *The Burned-over District*, 307.

37. David L. Rowe, *God's Strange Work: William Miller and the End of the World* (Grand Rapids: Eerdmans Publishing, 2008), 193.

38. Richard Bushman, *Joseph Smith: Rough Stone Rolling* (New York: Vintage Books, 2005), 39.

39. On treasure digging, see Max Perry Mueller, *Race and the Making of the Mormon People* (Chapel Hill: University of North Carolina Press, 2017), 1; Bushman, *Joseph Smith*, 50–54, 30–57; Ronald V. Huggins, "From Captain Kidd's Ghost to the Angel Moroni: Changing *Dramatis Personae* in Early Mormonism," *Dialogue: A Journal of Mormon Thought* 36 (2003): 17–42; Noel A. Carmack, "Joseph Smith, Captain Kidd Lore, and Treasure Seeking in New York and New England during the Early Republic," *Dialogue: A Journal of Mormon Thought* 46 (2013): 78–153.

40. Several of Smith's biographers have suggested that Smith fabricated the plates himself, or that he passed off bags filled with sand as the "plates," but Richard Bushman, a faithful Mormon who is considered his leading biographer, urges historians to take Smith at his word. See Bushman, *Joseph Smith*, 59. For an accessible introduction to the criticisms of Bushman's interpretation, see "Examining Mormon Truth Claims," https://www.mormonstories.org/truth-claims/.

41. Bushman, *Joseph Smith*, 109, 113–14.

42. Bushman, *Joseph Smith*, 122.

43. Bushman, *Joseph Smith*, 126.

44. Cross, *The Burned-over District*, 132.

45. Spencer Klaw, *Without Sin: The Life and Death of the Oneida Community* (New York: Penguin, 1993); Louis J. Kern, *An Ordered Love: Sex Roles and Sexuality in Victorian Utopias; The Shakers, the Mormons, and the Oneida Community* (Chapel Hill: University of North Carolina Press, 1981); Lawrence Foster, *Women, Family, and Utopia: Communal Experiments of the Shakers, the Oneida Community, and the Mormons* (Syracuse: Syracuse University Press, 1991).

46. Robert Cox, *Body and Soul: A Sympathetic History of American Spiritualism* (Charlottesville: University of Virginia Press, 2003), 16–17.

47. Cox, *Body and Soul*, 6.

48. Cox, *Body and Soul*, 7.

49. Ann Braude, *Radical Spirits: Spiritualism and Women's Rights in Nineteenth-Century America* (Bloomington: Indiana University Press, 1989), 64–67.

50. Braude, *Radical Spirits:* 65.

51. Braude, *Radical Spirits,* 64–67.

52. Barbara Weisberg, *Talking to the Dead: Kate and Maggie Fox and the Rise of Spiritualism* (New York: HarperCollins, 2005), 41.

53. Cox, *Body and Soul,* 10.

54. Emma Hardinge Britten, *Modern American Spiritualism: A Twenty Years' Record of the Communion Between Earth and the World of Spirits* (New York, self-published, 1872), 61.

55. Britten, *Modern American Spiritualism*, 547.

56. Britten, *Modern American Spiritualism*, 19.

57. Bradley J. Longfield, *Presbyterians and American Culture: A History* (Louisville: Westminster John Knox Press, 2013), 55.

58. Samuel Avery-Quinn, *Cities of Zion: The Holiness Movement and Methodist Camp Meeting Towns in America* (Lanham, MD: Lexington Books, 2019), xiv.

59. *Buffalo Daily Republic,* July 29, 1858, 2.

60. Emma Hardinge Britten, *Nineteenth Century Miracles; or Spirits and Their Work in Every Country of the Earth. A Complete Historical Compendium of the Great Movement Known as Modern Spiritualism* (New York: William Britten, 1884), 542.

61. Newspaper reports suggest there was a camp meeting held in July 1858 in Illinois, but nearly every secondary source consulted still considered Pierpont Grove the first Spiritualist camp meeting. It's also clear that many American Spiritualists at the time considered it the first camp meeting—including attendees.

62. "The First Great Spiritualist Camp Meeting at Pierpont Grove," *Banner of Light*, September 15, 1866, 4.

63. *Banner of Light*, September 22, 1866, 3–4.

64. *Vermont Record and Farmer*, July 3, 1874, 8.

65. "New Spiritualist Camp-Ground," *Fall River Daily Evening News*, January 8, 1877, 2; William D. Moore, "To Hold Communion with Nature and the Spirit-World: New England's Spiritualist Camp Meetings, 1865–1910," *Vernacular Architecture Forum* 7 (1997): 235–36; *Baltimore Sun*, July 17, 1877, 4.

66. Moore, "To Hold Communion with Nature and the Spirit-World," 232.

67. "Onset Bay," *Boston Globe*, July 26, 1880, 1.

68. Britten, *Nineteenth Century Miracles*, 543.

69. Moore, "To Hold Communion with Nature and the Spirit-World," 238.

70. Britten, *Nineteenth Century Miracles,* 544.

71. "The First Great Spiritualist Camp Meeting," *Banner of Light,* September 15, 1866, 4.

72. See W. Douglas McCombs, "Therapeutic Rusticity: Antimodernism, Health, and the Wilderness Vacation, 1870–1915," *New York History* 76 (1995): 409–28.

Notes to Pages 35–45

73. Nettie Pease Fox, "Camp Meetings," *Spiritual Offering*, April 1879, 375–76.
74. Flora B. Cabell, letter to the editor, *Banner of Light*, August 8, 1885, 8.
75. Moore, "To Hold Communion with Nature and the Spirit-World," 239.
76. Ron Nagy and Joyce LaJudice, *Chronicles of Lily Dale: Free Thinkers and Spiritualism—Courage and Determinism—The Early Years* (self-published using CreateSpace Independent Publishing Platform, 2017), 4–5.
77. Nagy and LaJudice, *Chronicles of Lily Dale*, 18.
78. Ramsdell, *A Souvenir of Cassadaga Lake*, 3.
79. Jan Prymus, "Lily Dale Then and Now," *The Summit of Spiritual Understanding* 55 (November 1973): 6; Nagy and LaJudice, *Chronicles of Lily Dale*, 20; official program, 1939, Camp Program Collection, LDM; Ron Nagy with Joyce LaJudice, *The Spirits of Lily Dale* (Lakeville, MN: Galde Press, 2010), 14
80. Nagy and LaJudice, *Chronicles of Lily Dale*, 48.
81. Nagy and LaJudice, *The Spirits of Lily Dale*, 14.
82. A. G. Smith, "Lily Dale Twenty-Four Years Ago," *The Sunflower* (Lily Dale, NY), August 22, 1903.

2. Little Victorian Cottages

1. Once, to save money, Marissa and I slept on a very firm air mattress on the floor of our friends' very tiny DC studio apartment, literally an arm's length from their bed. Marissa, in classic repose, reached out to our friend to re-create Michelangelo's *Creation of Adam*. There was a lot of silly whispering in the dark and giggling that night. Sleepovers with your friends are the best, even when you're much too old for them.
2. "Places and Spaces" folder, LDM.
3. Maxwell Stevenson Nobisch, "'To Free Thought, Free Speech, and Free Investigation': The Cultural Landscape of Lily Dale, New York" (PhD diss., University of Georgia, 2020), 115–16.
4. Ann Braude, *Radical Spirits: Spiritualism and Women's Rights in Nineteenth-Century America* (Bloomington: Indiana University Press, 1989).
5. Every year since at least 1885, the Lily Dale Assembly has published a program of summer events. The earliest of these just identified the top-billed speakers who came to town. By the 1920s they included all sorts of officially sanctioned events, including workshops and a range of guest speakers. Camp Program Collection, LDM.
6. Hereward Carrington, "Report of a Two-Weeks' Investigation into Alleged Spiritualistic Phenomena, Witnessed at Lily Dale, New York," *Proceedings of the American Society for Psychical Research* 2, pt. 1 (1908): 97. Of course Carrington, on his two-week investigation of Lily Dale mediums in 1908, was interested in scientific testing of the various physical phenomena produced by Lily Dale's summer mediums, and presented a report that can only be described as an exposé of rampant fraud (95–117).
7. The idea of the "domain of women" in American society was observed and reported on by Alexis de Tocqueville in *Democracy in America* (1840). Though of course women's experiences were largely shaped by individual circumstances, as well as class, race, region, religion, and so on, the idea that women belonged in the home and out of public (democratic) participation was used to limit access for the majority of women to citizenship and participation in public life.
8. Simone Natale, *Supernatural Entertainments: Victorian Spiritualism and the Rise of Modern Media Culture* (State College: Pennsylvania State University Press, 2017), 13.
9. See Judith Flanders, *Inside the Victorian Home: A Portrait of Domestic Life in Victorian England* (New York: W. W. Norton, 2005); and John Tosh, *A Man's Place: Masculinity and the Middle-Class Home in Victorian England* (New Haven: Yale University Press, 2007).

10. See, for example, Florence Hartley, *The Ladies' Book of Etiquette and Manual of Politeness* (Boston: G. W. Cottrell, 1860), accessed January 27, 2023, https://www.gutenberg.org/files/35123/35123-h/35123-h.htm; George Washington Burnap, *The Sphere and Duties of Woman*, 3rd ed. (Baltimore: J. Murphy, 1848); and Professor De la Banta, *De la Banta's Advice to Ladies Concerning Beauty* (Chicago: S. Junkin, 1878).

11. Natale, *Supernatural Entertainments*, 6.

12. Braude, *Radical Spirits*, 25.

13. Elana Gomel, "'Spirits in the Material World': Spiritualism and Identity in the *Fin de Siècle*," *Victorian Literature and Culture* 35, no. 1 (2007): 192.

14. Lisa Morton, *Calling the Spirits: A History of Séances* (Chicago: University of Chicago Press, 2021), 151; see also John Warne Monroe, *Laboratories of Faith: Mesmerism, Spiritism, and Occultism in Modern France* (Ithaca: Cornell University Press, 2007), 85.

15. Barbara Weisberg, *Talking to the Dead: Kate and Maggie Fox and the Rise of Spiritualism* (New York: HarperOne, 2005).

16. Arthur Conan Doyle, *The History of Spiritualism*, vols. 1 and 2 (London: Cassell & Company, 1926), 1:73.

17. Simone Natale points to Corinthian Hall as the "beginning" of Spiritualism in *Supernatural Entertainments*. Eliab Capron, Robert Davis Owen, Uriah Smith, and Arthur Conan Doyle all point back to the Hydesville house.

18. Uriah Smith, *Modern Spiritualism* (Battle Creek, MI: Review and Herald Publishing, 1896), 19.

19. Official program, 1933, Camp Program Collection, LDM.

20. In 1920 it was the first attraction listed but in 1921 was buried in the middle of the program again. Official programs, 1916–1920 and 1922–1925, Camp Program Collection, LDM.

21. Official program, 1927, Camp Program Collection, LDM. In 1934 and 1935 the Fox Cottage wasn't included in the program,.

22. Official programs, 1936 and 1939, Camp Program Collection, LDM.

23. Robert S. Cox, *Body and Soul: A Sympathetic History of American Spiritualism* (Charlottesville: University of Virginia Press, 2003).

24. Braude, *Radical Spirits*, 23.

25. Harrison D. Barrett, *The Life Work of Mrs. Cora L. V. Richmond* (Chicago: Hack & Anderson Printers, 1895), 9–10.

26. Barrett, *The Life Work of Mrs. Cora L. V. Richmond*, 11–12.

27. Braude, *Radical Spirits*, 67 and 196.

28. Diane Skolfield, "Harrison D. Barrett," Camp Etna, accessed January 4, 2023, https://www.campetna.com/harrison-d.-barrett.html.

29. I haven't been able to figure out if Barrett brought her to the Cassadaga Lake Free Association to perform or if they met there. She is listed in the 1887 CLFA program and every program thereafter until the 1910 Lily Dale Assembly program. Camp Program Collection, LDM.

30. Barrett, *The Life Work of Mrs. Cora L. V. Richmond*, 2. It seems likely that Barrett wrote the biography with Scott, though she is not listed as a coauthor. Barrett did collect stories and impressions of Scott from dozens of notables in the Spiritualist community, as evidenced by those notes being addressed to him. But throughout Barrett uses "we" when pontificating on the philosophical elements of the biography, which might be the royal we, but perhaps—and this is giving him a lot of credit—he and Scott collaborated on those sections and he acknowledges her through this pronoun.

31. Barrett, *The Life Work of Mrs. Cora L. V. Richmond*, 3–4.

32. Arthur Conan Doyle, "Playing with Fire," https://www.arthur-conan-doyle.com/index.php/Playing_with_Fire.

33. Gomel, "Spirits in the Material World," 200.

34. Doyle, "Playing with Fire."

35. Nina Shandler, *The Strange Case of Hellish Nell* (Cambridge: Da Capo Press, 2006), 154.

36. Peter Lamont, "Spiritualism and a Mid-Victorian Crisis of Evidence," *Historical Journal* 47, no. 4 (December 2004): 897; Ira Davenport, *Davenport Brothers: World-Renowned Spiritual Mediums* (Boston: William White and Company, 1869); Braude, *Radical Spirits*.

37. Carrington, "Report of a Two-Weeks' Investigation," 8.

38. Carrington, "Report of a Two-Weeks' Investigation," 8.

39. Letter from Warne to Hyslop, September 23, 1907, reproduced in *Proceedings of the American Society for Psychical Research*, 75.

40. This isn't saying much, because today the area around Lily Dale could only with the most generous possible definition be called "built up."

41. Carrington, "Report of a Two-Weeks' Investigation," 9.

42. Carrington, "Report of a Two-Weeks' Investigation," 9.

43. Carrington, "Report of a Two-Weeks' Investigation," 14.

44. Carrington, "Report of a Two-Weeks' Investigation," 26–28.

45. Carrington, "Report of a Two-Weeks' Investigation," 10.

46. Carrington, "Report of a Two-Weeks' Investigation," 20–24.

47. "About Us," Lily Dale Assembly, accessed August 3, 2022, https://www.lilydaleassembly.org/about-us.

48. Braude, *Radical Spirits*, 25. This number is also repeated in Bridget Bennett's *Transatlantic Spiritualism and Nineteenth-Century American Literature* (New York: Palgrave Macmillan, 2007), 7.

49. Braude, *Radical Spirits*, 28.

50. See Emily Suzanne Clark, *A Luminous Brotherhood: Afro-Creole Spiritualism in Nineteenth-Century New Orleans* (Chapel Hill: University of North Carolina Press, 2016); Mary Ann Clark, "Spirit Is Universal: Development of Black Spiritualist Churches," in *Esotericism in African American Religious Experience*, ed. Stephen Finley, Margarita Guillory, and Hugh Page Jr. (Boston: Brill, 2014), 86–101; and Braude, *Radical Spirits*, 25–39.

51. It is likely that there were some Native American–identifying individuals who were members of the church as well, though it's not clear if, as Sarah points out later in this book, the most famous Native Americans associated with Spiritualism, like Oskenonton, were actually Spiritualists themselves.

52. Clark, *A Luminous Brotherhood*. I haven't found any records of the members of the French-speaking Cercle visiting Lily Dale, and as the Cercle practiced only from 1858 to 1877, it seems unlikely that they did.

53. "2835 National Colored Spiritualist Association of Churches," in *Melton's Encyclopedia of American Religions*, ed. J. Gordon Melton, 9th ed., vol. 2 (Farmington Hills, MI: Gale, 2017), 1452.

54. Significantly, most of the NCSAC-affiliated members and churches referred to the Black-led movement as "spiritual" to explicitly differentiate themselves from the predominantly white "spiritualist" movement. See Clark, "Spirit Is Universal," 86–101.

55. Rev. Marguerite Hanny to Carol Littlebrandt, New York State Division of Human Rights, November 30, 1982, Board of Directors folder, LDM.

56. Charter of the Lily Dale Assembly, August 14, 1928, LDM. A copy of this charter is included in a series of correspondence between Ed Bodin, the Lily Dale board of directors, and the New York State Office of the Attorney General, Board of Directors folder, LDM.

57. Charter of the Lily Dale Assembly, August 14, 1957, LDM, emphasis added.

58. Hanny to Littlebrandt, November 30, 1982. Lily Dale was originally established as a joint stock corporation in 1879 before changing to a membership corporation in 1925.

59. According to an official timeline housed in the Lily Dale Museum, Lily Dale became the headquarters of NSAC in 1933.

60. See correspondence between Ed Bodin, the Lily Dale board of directors, and the New York State Office of the Attorney General, Board of Directors folder, LDM.

61. *Cowen v. Lily Dale Assembly*, 44 A.D.2d 772 (N.Y. App. Div. 1974), Board of Directors folder, LDM.

62. "Can a Spiritualist Accept the Teaching of Jesus?" accessed December 7, 2022, https://nsac.org/ufaqs/can-a-spiritualist-accept-the-teaching-of-jesus/.

63. See correspondence of Rev. Marguerite Hanny to various persons, 1976–1982, Board of Directors folder, LDM.

64. "Eviction Dispute Splits Community of Mediums," *New York Times,* October 6, 1984. According to the Lily Dale annual programs for 1970–1982, Sabol's presidency began in late 1974. and lasted until 1981. Camp Program Collection, LDM.

65. "Eviction Dispute Splits Community of Mediums."

66. "Lily Dale Dispute Centers on By-Laws," *Jamestown (NY) Post-Journal,* May 2, 1977.

67. Agnes Palazzetti, "Lily Dale Family Wins Court Order Permitting Free Access to Grounds," *Evening Observer* (Dunkirk-Fredonia, NY), April 7, 1977.

68. Palazzetti, "Lily Dale Family Wins Court Order."

69. Stan Ludine, Member of Congress, to George Hanny, Marguerite's son and plaintiff in *Lily Dale Assembly v. Hanny*, Board of Directors folder, LDM.

70. "Eviction Dispute Splits Community of Mediums."

71. While there are certainly nonwhite Spiritualists who are members of the NSAC, few if any live in Lily Dale. The NSAC doesn't make its demographics public.

72. Mary Catherine Gaydos Gabriel, "Ordinary Spirits in an Extraordinary Town: Finding Identity in Personal Images and Resurrected Memories in Lily Dale, New York" (MA thesis, Utah State University, 2010).

73. "Correspondence," *Journal of the American Society for Psychical Research* 2 (1908): 410.

74. "Eviction Dispute Splits Community of Mediums."

75. President Report addition, 1903, Presidents' Reports, LDM.

76. Home and other male mediums were often mocked for their perceived femininity. See David Allen Harvey, "Elite Magic in the Nineteenth Century," in *The Cambridge History of Magic and Witchcraft in the West: From Antiquity to the Present*, ed. David Collins (Cambridge: Cambridge University Press, 2015), 572.

77. Braude, *Radical Spirits,* 168.

78. Official programs, 1906–1925, Camp Program Collection, LDM.

3. The Fox Cottage

1. "Fire Destroys Fox Cottage," *Rochester Democrat and Chronicle*, September 22, 1955.

2. "Cassadaga Lake Camp," *Banner of Light*, August 19, 1882, 12. Ron Nagy also briefly references Fox's visit to the camp in *The Spirits of Lily Dale* (Lakeville, MN: Galde Press, 2017), 12. The August 19 edition is the first of the "Camp Notes" to mention Maggie Fox. She isn't mentioned again in the August 26 edition. In the final summary article at the end of the season (September 9), she is mentioned once more, but only to say that she and the other mediums were particularly well patronized. The reports from Thomas Lees (September 9) gush more about speakers like Mrs. Field, Mrs. R. S. Lillie, Mrs. A. H. Colby, and other figures on the Spiritualist circuit.

3. Thomas Lees, "Lake Cassadaga Camp-Meeting," *Banner of Light,* September 9, 1882, 12.
4. "Fifth Annual Camp Meeting," *Mind and Matter* (Philadelphia), July 7, 1883, 6.
5. Quoted in David Walker, "The Humbug in American Religion: Ritual Theories of Nineteenth-Century Spiritualism," *Religion and American Culture: A Journal of Interpretation* 23, no. 1 (2013): 30.
6. Simone Natale, *Supernatural Entertainments: Victorian Spiritualism and the Rise of Modern Media Culture* (State College: Pennsylvania State University Press, 2017), 1.
7. "What We Believe," National Spiritual Association of Churches, www.nsac.org//what-we-believe/definining-spiritualism/.
8. Quoted in Lisa Morton, *Calling the Spirits: A History of Séances* (Chicago: University of Chicago Press, 2021), 90.
9. James Hyslop, introduction to "Report of a Two-Weeks' Investigation into Alleged Spiritualistic Phenomena, Witnessed at Lily Dale, New York," *Proceedings of the American Society for Psychical Research* 2 (1908): 1.
10. Arthur Conan Doyle, "The Psychic Quest," in *Memories and Adventures* (London: Hodder & Stoughton, 1924), 401.
11. Barbara Weisberg, *Talking to the Dead: Kate and Maggie Fox and the Rise of Spiritualism* (New York: HarperOne, 2005), 67.
12. As an aside, those names—Flint, Lee, and Coventry—are all familiar to anyone who has visited the University at Buffalo today.
13. For more on the process of professionalization of medicine in the United States, see Paul Starr, *The Social Transformation of American Medicine: The Rise of a Sovereign Profession and the Making of a Vast Industry* (New York: Basic Books, 1982).
14. Weisberg, *Talking to the Dead,* 123.
15. Austin Flint, Charles Lee, and C. B. Coventry, "Discovery of the Source of the Rochester Knockings," *Buffalo Medical Journal* 6 (March 1851): 628–42; see also Rev. H Mattison, *Spirit Rapping Unveiled!* (New York: Mason Brothers, 1853), 176; Emma Hardinge Britten, *Modern American Spiritualism* (New York: published by the author, 1870), 92–93.
16. Weisberg, *Talking to the Dead,* 191. While Maggie and Elisha never married, Maggie used the Kane name and lived as a widow for the remainder of her life. Their relationship is discussed in David Chapin, *Exploring Other Worlds: Margaret Fox, Elisha Kent Kane, and the Antebellum Culture of Curiosity* (Amherst: University of Massachusetts Press, 2004).
17. Emily Ogden, *Credulity: A Cultural History of Mesmerism* (Chicago: University of Chicago Press, 2018), 238.
18. "The Present Condition of Spiritualism," *The Liberator* 1, no. 2 (September 15, 1898): 1, accessed January 3, 2023, http://iapsop.com/archive/materials/liberator_sfo/liberator_v1_n2_sep_15_1898.pdf.
19. *Preliminary Report of the Commission Appointed by the University of Pennsylvania to Investigate Modern Spiritualism, In According with the Request of the Late Henry Seybert* (Philadelphia: J. B. Lippincott & Co., 1887), 5.
20. For more on the writing of the report, see Elizabeth Schleber Lowry, *The Seybert Report: Rhetoric, Rationale, and the Problem of Psi Research* (London: Palgrave Macmillan, 2017).
21. *Preliminary Report of the Commission,* 47.
22. *Preliminary Report of the Commission,* 48.
23. Lowry, *The Seybert Report,* 39.
24. Lowry, *The Seybert Report,* 36–37. See also the Biography/History note on the Seybert Commission for Investigating Modern Spiritualism Records finding aid, University of Pennsylvania Special Collections, Rare Books and Manuscripts, https://findingaids.library.upenn.edu/records/UPENN_RBML_PUSP.MS.COLL.412.

25. "T. R. Hazard's Spiritual Experiences," *The Medium and Daybreak: A Journal Devoted to the History, Phenomena, Philosophy and Teachings of Spiritualism*, September 1885, 613.

26. "The Seybert Commission and Mrs. Kane," *Light: A Journal of Psychical, Occult, and Mystical Research*, September 10, 1887, 426.

27. *The Banner of Light*, April 9, 1887, 5.

28. John Michael Andrick, "Modern Mecca of Psychic Forces: The Psychical Science Congress and the Culture of Progressive Occultism in Fin-de-Siècle Chicago, 1885–1900" (Ph.D. diss., University of Illinois at Urbana-Champaign, 2016), 60–64; "Lesson of the Suspended Slates," *Religio-Philosophical Journal*, May 3, 1890.

29. A. B. Richmond, *What I Saw at Cassadaga Lake: A Review of the Seybert Commissioners' Report*, 3rd ed. (Boston: Colby & Rich, 1890); A. B. Richmond, *What I Saw at Cassadaga Lake: Addendum to a Review in 1887 of the Seybert Commission's Report* (Boston: Colby & Rich Publishers, 1889).

30. Richmond, *What I Saw at Cassadaga Lake: Addendum*, 9–10, 14.

31. "An Evening with the Bangs Children," *Religio-Philosophical Journal*, August 3, 1872.

32. Richmond, *What I Saw at Cassadaga Lake: Addendum*, 20–24.

33. "Hon. A. B. Richmond at Cassadaga," *Religio-Philosophical Journal*, May 21, 1890, 8. For an interesting explanation of the perspective of the *Religio-Philosophical Journal* and its editors, see Andrick, "Modern Mecca of Psychic Forces," 60–64.

34. "*Quaestor Vitae* and the Bangs Sisters," *Light*, May 13, 1899, 223; "Statement of the Case," *The Progressive Thinker*, August 16, 1890, 3.

35. "Mediums Arrested," *Stark County Democrat* (Canton, OH), April 5, 1888.

36. "Mediums Arrested." This story was reproduced in newspapers across the country, a common practice in the nineteenth century; see, for example, "Bogus Mediums," *Atchison (Kansas) Daily Champion*, April 4, 1888; "Caught Spirits Napping," *Daily Inter Ocean* (Chicago), April 2, 1888.

37. As reproduced in "*Quaestor Vitae* and the Bangs Sisters," 223.

38. "*Quaestor Vitae* and the Bangs Sisters," 223.

39. "That Wonderful Picture," *The Light of Truth*, November 27, 1897, 6.

40. "May Bangs Denial of Mediumship," *Light*, October 9, 1909, 483.

41. Weisberg, *Talking to the Dead*, 235, 238.

42. "Spiritualism Exposed," *New York World*, October 21, 1888.

43. "The Foxes and Their Foxings," *Light*, December 15, 1888, 619. Many secondary sources report that Maggie received $1,500 from a journalist in exchange for her story, but we find no primary evidence to support this. The only mention of that sum comes from Kate, who states that it was the profit generated from Maggie's sold-out show. Later, Maggie does say her manager, Frank Stechen, paid her $550 at the beginning of their contract but doesn't specify whether this was for that event or for multiple events.

44. As quoted in Arthur Conan Doyle, "The Mystery of the Three Fox Sisters," *Quarterly Transactions of the British College of Psychic Science* 1 (October 1922): 229.

45. Love M. Willis, "Letter from Mrs. Willis," *Banner of Light*, March 18, 1893.

46. Isaac Funk, *The Widow's Mite and Other Psychic Phenomena* (New York: Funk & Wagnalls Co., 1904), 241.

47. Hereward Carrington, *Personal Experiences in Spiritualism: Including the Official Account and Record of the American Palladino Séances* (London: T. Werner Laurie, 1913), 24.

48. Carrington, "Report of a Two-Weeks' Investigation," 35.

49. Carrington, *Personal Experiences*, 25

50. Carrington, "Report of a Two-Weeks' Investigation," 14.
51. Carrington, *Personal Experiences*, 45.
52. Carrington, "Report of a Two-Weeks' Investigation," 66–67.
53. Carrington, "Report of a Two-Weeks' Investigation," 97.
54. Warne's letter to Hyslop is reproduced in *Proceedings of the American Society for Psychical Research* 2 (1908): 75.
55. Carrington, "Report of a Two-Weeks' Investigation," 98.
56. Abby Louise Pettengill, President's Report to the Board, 1903, Presidents' Reports, LDM.
57. Letter from Warne to Hyslop, 75.
58. Carrington, "Report of a Two-Weeks' Investigation," 98.
59. "Correspondence," *Journal of the American Society for Psychical Research* 2 (1908): 416–22.
60. "Correspondence," *Journal of the American Society for Psychical Research*, 416.
61. "Correspondence," *Journal of the American Society for Psychical Research*, 416.
62. "Correspondence," *Journal of the American Society for Psychical Research*, 417.
63. "Correspondence," *Journal of the American Society for Psychical Research*, 417.
64. Jan Prymus, "Lily Dale Then and Now," *The Summit of Spiritual Understanding* 55, no. 590 (November 1973): 7.
65. Official program, 1906, Camp Program Collection, LDM.
66. Official program, 1916, Camp Program Collection, LDM.
67. *Some Account of the Vampires of Onset, Past and Present* (Boston: Press of S. Woodberry, 1892).
68. President's Report to the Lily Dale Assembly Stockholders, August 15, 1910, Presidents' Reports, LDM.
69. Peter Lamont, "Spiritualism and a Mid-Victorian Crisis of Evidence," *Historical Journal* 47, no. 4 (2004): 898.
70. "Is there to be no end to the war on mediums, by the R-P Journal, but with its destruction?" *Mind and Matter* 2, no. 48, (October 23, 1880): 5; see also Arthur Conan Doyle, chap. 2 in *The History of Spiritualism*, vol. 2 (London: Cassell, 1926), 319.
71. *Light*, April 8, 1899, 167.
72. Elizabeth d'Espérance, *ShadowLand, or Light from the Other Side* (London: Geo. Bedway, 1897), 339.
73. Elizabeth d'Espérance, "What I Know of Materializations from Personal Experience," *Light*, November 14, 1903, 547. The text was transcribed from an address that d'Espérance delivered to the London Spiritualist Association.
74. D'Espérance, *ShadowLand*; Marlene Tromp, *Altered States: Sex, Nation, Drugs, and Self-Transformation in Victorian Spiritualism* (Albany: State University of New York Press, 2006), 179.
75. Tromp, *Altered States*, 191.
76. Estelle Wilson Stead, *My Father: Personal and Spiritual Reminiscences* (New York: George H. Doran Company, 1913), 302.
77. Stead, *My Father*, 303.
78. "Prove Your Paranormal Powers and Win $250,000 from the CFI Investigations Group," Center for Inquiry, June 26, 2020, https://centerforinquiry.org/press_releases/prove-your-paranormal-powers-and-win-250000-from-the-cfi-investigations-group/.
79. Burkhard Bilger, "Waiting for Ghosts," *The New Yorker*, December 23 and 30, 2002, 86–100.
80. May Wright Sewall, *Neither Dead nor Sleeping* (Indianapolis: Bobbs-Merrill, 1920), 11–15.

4. The Auditorium

1. Ann Braude, *Radical Spirits: Spiritualism and Women's Rights in Nineteenth-Century America* (Bloomington: Indiana University Press, 1989), 192.
2. "Twenty-Fourth Annual Season Opens July 8, Closes September 2, 1903," *The Sunflower,* June 6, 1903.
3. Official program, 1911, Camp Program Collection, LDM.
4. Susan B. Anthony et al., eds., *A History of Woman Suffrage,* 6 vols. (Rochester: Fowler and Wells, 1881–1922), 1:70–71. Hereafter cited as *History of Woman Suffrage.*
5. Braude, *Radical Spirits,* 60.
6. The historiography of the Seneca Falls convention and the suffrage movement which followed is vast. For recent interpretations, see Martha S. Jones, *Vanguard: How Black Women Broke Barriers, Won the Vote, and Insisted on Equality for All* (New York: Basic Books, 2020), 43–68; Lisa Tetrault, *The Myth of Seneca Falls: Memory and the Women's Suffrage Movement, 1848–1898* (Chapel Hill: University of North Carolina Press, 2014); Tricia Franzen, *Anna Howard Shaw: The Work of Woman Suffrage* (Chicago: University of Illinois Press, 2014).
7. See Spencer McBride and Jennifer Hull Dorsey, eds., *New York's Burned-over District: A Documentary History* (Ithaca: Cornell University Press, 2023), 253–54, for a discussion of women in the Shaker religion. For women in the early Church of Jesus Christ of Latter-day Saints, see Laurel Thatcher Ulrich, *A House Full of Females: Plural Marriage and Women's Rights in Early Mormonism, 1835–1870* (New York: Knopf, 2017).
8. Quoted in Braude, *Radical Spirits,* 119.
9. Nancy Hewitt, *Radical Friend: Amy Kirby Post and Her Activist Worlds* (Chapel Hill: University of North Carolina Press, 2018).
10. Ellen Carol Dubois, ed., *Elizabeth Cady Stanton, Susan B. Anthony: Correspondence, Writing, Speeches* (New York: Schocken Books, 1981), 76.
11. Julia Schlesinger, *Workers in the Vineyard: A Review of the Progress of Spiritualism, Biographical Sketches, Lectures, Essays, and Poems* (San Francisco, 1896), 121–24.
12. Schlesinger, *Workers in the Vineyard,* 121–24.
13. Schlesinger, *Workers in the Vineyard,* 121–24.
14. At this point her name was Cora Scott.
15. "Mrs. Cora L. V. Richmond Going to Washington," *Kansas City Journal,* September 6, 1897; Hewitt, *Radical Friend,* 203.
16. Obed Edson, *History of Chautauqua County, New York* (Boston: W. A. Fergusson, 1894), 901–2.
17. "Spirit Oil Gushers," *Pittsburg Dispatch,* May, 18, 1891; "A Pioneer Gone," *Titusville Herald,* June 18, 1894; Alicia Puglionesi, *In Whose Ruins: Power, Possession, and the Landscapes of American Empire* (New York: Scribner Press, 2022), 134.
18. Eugene Taylor Sawyer, *History of Santa Clara County, California: With Biographical Sketches of the Leading Men and Women of the County Who Have Been Identified with Its Growth and Development from the Early Days to the Present,* vol. 2 (Los Angeles: Historic Record Company, 1922), 928; E. L. Watson to Amy Kirby Post, March 9, 1868, Rare Books, Special Collections and Preservation, University of Rochester Exhibits, accessed January 30, 2023, https://rbscpexhibits.lib.rochester.edu/viewer/4054; "National Liberal League," *New York Times,* October 29, 1877.
19. Puglionesi, *In Whose Ruins,* 134; "A Pioneer Gone."
20. Sawyer, *History of Santa Clara County,* 928; Schlesinger, *Workers in the Vineyard,* 124.
21. Edson, *History of Chautauqua County,* 901–2; "Ideal Home," in *A Souvenir of Cassadaga Lake Free Association Camp Grounds,* illustrated by Josh D. Ramsdell (Erie, PA: Herald Printing and Publishing Co., 1889), 21.

22. Sawyer, *History of Santa Clara County*, 928.
23. Sawyer, *History of Santa Clara County*, 928; Schlesinger, *Workers in the Vineyard*, 124.
24. Edson, *History of Chautauqua County*, 901–2.
25. "Marion H. Skidmore," *Banner of Light*, February 16, 1895; Edson, *History of Chautauqua County*, 901–2.
26. Edson, *History of Chautauqua County*, 901–2; "Marion H. Skidmore"; "Children's Lyceum," loose-leaf paper, "Lily Dale Assembly History," Marion Skidmore Library, Lily Dale.
27. John Phillip Downs, *History of Chautauqua County, New York, and Its People* (New York: American Historical Society, 1921), 351.
28. Downs, *History of Chautauqua County*, 351, 353.
29. "Constitution of American Equal Rights Association," 1866, *Proceedings of the first anniversary of the American Equal Rights Association, held at the Church of the Puritans, New York, May 9 and 10* (New York: Robert J. Johnston, Printer, 1867), https://lccn.loc.gov/ca10003542.
30. Ida Husted Harper, *The Life and Work of Susan B. Anthony Including Public Addresses, Her Own Letters and Many from Her Contemporaries during Fifty Years*, 3 vols. (Indianapolis: Bowen-Merrill Company, 1898–1908), 1:302.
31. *History of Woman Suffrage*, 1:95, fn. 51.
32. Anna Howard Shaw, *The Story of a Pioneer* (New York: Kraus Reprint Co., 1970), 182; Franzen, *Anna Howard Shaw*, 61–64.
33. *The Selected Papers of Elizabeth Cady Stanton and Susan B. Anthony: An Awful Hush, 1895 to 1906*, vol. 6, ed. Ann D. Gordon (New Brunswick: Rutgers University Press, 2012), 287; "Notes from Cassadaga Camp," *Banner of Light*, August 13, 1892, 8.
34. Downs, *History of Chautauqua County*, 353.
35. "Notes from Cassadaga Camp," *Banner of Light*, August 13, 1892.
36. Harper, *Life and Work of Susan B. Anthony*, 2:710; "Cassadaga Lake, N.Y.," *Banner of Light*, July 18, 1891.
37. "Cassadaga Camp," *Banner of Light*, August 29, 1891; for Wyoming and women's suffrage, see Cathleen Cahill, *Recasting the Vote: How Women of Color Transformed the Suffrage Movement* (Chapel Hill: University of North Carolina Press, 2020), 11, 21, 24.
38. Harper, *Life and Work of Susan B. Anthony*, 2:711.
39. Harriet Bartnett, "Abby Louise Pettengill: A Tribute," pamphlet, n.d., ephemera, Marion Skidmore Library, Lily Dale.
40. Gertrude Van Rensselaer Wickham, *The Pioneer Families of Cleveland, 1796–1840*, vol. 2 (Cleveland: Evangelical Publishing House, 1914), 591.
41. Bartnett, "Abby Louise Pettengill."
42. "Affairs in Cleveland," *Cincinnati Enquirer*, March 14, 1879; "Mrs. Josephine Pettingill [sic] Everett," accessed December 4, 2022, http://robertstrongwoodward.com/Scrapbook/Everett.html.
43. "Widow of Rail Pioneer Dies," *Los Angeles Times*, July 5, 1937.
44. Untitled scrapbook clipping from *Jamestown Post Journal*, August 25, 1892, Women's Suffrage binder, Marion Skidmore Library, Lily Dale.
45. "Cassadaga Camp," *Banner of Light*, August 20, 1892; "Cause of Women," *Buffalo Express*, August 24, 1892.
46. Barbara A. White, *The Beecher Sisters* (New Haven: Yale University Press, 2003), 233.
47. *History of Woman Suffrage*, 4:194.
48. "Cause of Women," *Buffalo Express*, August 24, 1892.
49. The New Departure was a strategy used by the NWSA which interpreted the Fourteenth Amendment as granting all naturalized and native-born Americans citizenship,

inherently conferring suffrage rights. This interpretation was rejected in the 1875 Supreme Court decision *Minor v. Happersett*.

50. "Cause of Women," *Buffalo Express*, August 24, 1892.

51. *Proceedings of the Twenty-Fifth Annual Convention of the National American Woman Suffrage Association, held in Washington, D.C., January 16, 17, 18, 19, 1893*, (Washington, DC: Stormont & Jackson, Printers, 1893), 82.

52. "Cassadaga Camp," *Banner of Light*, August 26, 1893.

53. "Echoes from Cassadaga Camp," *Banner of Light*, July 22, 1893.

54. *History of Woman Suffrage*, 4:850.

55. *History of Woman Suffrage*, 4:849, 383; *The Complete House Builder with Hints on Building* (Chicago: Donohue, Henneberry & Co., 1890), 116.

56. *History of Woman Suffrage*, 4:850–52; New York State Woman Suffrage Association, Report of the Annual Convention, 1894, ephemera, LDM, 13.

57. *History of Woman Suffrage*, 4:772.

58. "Newsy Notes and Pithy Points," *Banner of Light*, February 3, 1894.

59. "Woman's Day," *Buffalo Express*, August 22, 1894.

60. "Woman's Day," *Buffalo Express*, August 22, 1894.

61. Susan B. Anthony Papers: Daybook and Diaries, to 1906 (1894), Manuscript/Mixed Material, accessed June 6, 2022, https://www.loc.gov/item/mss11049017/.

62. "Amusements," *The Sunflower*, June 6, 1903.

63. "Editor Observer," *Evening Observer* (Dunkirk, NY), October 8, 1894.

64. "Twenty-Fourth Annual Season Opens July 8, Closes September 2, 1903," *The Sunflower*, June 6, 1903.

65. Leolyn Louise Everett Spelman, Spelman Family Papers, Sheridan Library Special Collections, MS-0392, Johns Hopkins University, https://aspace.library.jhu.edu/repositories/3/resources/391.

66. "Cassadaga Camp," *Banner of Light*, July 16, 1892.

67. "Transition and Funeral of Mrs. Marion H. Skidmore," *Banner of Light*, February 16, 1895.

68. *The Cassadagan* 5, no. 6 (February 1895).

69. *The Cassadagan* 5, no. 6 (February 1895).

70. *History of Woman Suffrage*, 4:259.

71. "The Pioneer Meeting," *The Cassadagan* 6, no. 12 (August 1896).

72. Elizabeth Lowe Watson, "The Needs of the Hour," in *Song and Sermon* (San Francisco: Hicks-Judd Co., 1906), 155.

73. "The Pioneer Meeting," *The Cassadagan* 6, no. 12 (August 1896).

74. Shaw, *The Story of a Pioneer*, 273.

75. *History of Woman Suffrage*, 4:288.

76. Braude, *Radical Spirits*, 58.

77. "Spiritualist Semi-Centennial," *El Paso Daily Herald*, May 25, 1898.

78. "Spiritualism and Christianity," *Rochester Democrat and Chronicle*, May 30, 1898; *Selected Papers of Elizabeth Cady Stanton and Susan B. Anthony*, 237, fn. 5.

79. *Selected Papers of Elizabeth Cady Stanton and Susan B. Anthony*, 237.

80. Harper, *Life and Work of Susan B. Anthony*, 3:1259.

81. Official programs, 1901, 1903, 1904, 1907, Camp Program Collection, LDM.

82. Harper, *Life and Work of Susan B. Anthony*, 3:1373.

83. "Lily Dale News," *The Sunflower*, August 26, 1905.

84. Bartnett, "Abby Louise Pettengill."

85. "Suffragettes Choose Heads," *Los Angeles Herald*, October 3, 1909.

86. "Suffragists Are in Cheerful Mood," *Salt Lake Tribune*, October 21, 1911.

87. Anna Howard Shaw, "Stand on the Principle of Justice," speech delivered at Lily Dale, August 19, 1914, in "The Speeches of Anna Howard Shaw: Collected and Edited with Introduction and Notes," ed. Wilmer Albert Linkugel (PhD diss., University of Wisconsin, 1960), 203.
88. "Annual Convention of State W.C.T.U.," *Berkeley Daily Gazette*, October 22, 1919.
89. Bartnett, "Abby Louise Pettengill."
90. Women of color did vote and hold office after the passage of the Nineteenth Amendment, but their numbers were small. For women of color and the vote, see Jones, *Vanguard*; Cahill, *Recasting the Vote*.
91. Official programs, 1930, 1931, Camp Program Collection, LDM.
92. Tetrault, *The Myth of Seneca Falls*, 181–84.
93. *Selected Papers of Elizabeth Cady Stanton and Susan B. Anthony*, 38.
94. Bartnett, "Abby Louise Pettengill."
95. Susan B. Anthony to Rachel Foster Avery, January 22, 1900, in Susan B. Anthony Papers: Correspondence, 1846–1905, https://www.loc.gov/item/mss11049017/.
96. "Mrs. Josephine Pettingill [*sic*] Everett," accessed December 4, 2022, http://robertstrongwoodward.com/Scrapbook/Everett.html.

5. The Maplewood Hotel

1. "Straight edge" is a subculture that refrains from using alcohol, tobacco, and recreational drugs and is most often associated with hardcore punk.
2. William James, *Varieties of Religious Experience: A Study in Human Nature* (London: Longmans, Green & Co., 1902), 300.
3. Citizens for a Better Cassadaga, "Historic Walking Tour of Cassadaga," pamphlet, LDM.
4. Ebenezer Alden, *Memorial of the descendants of the Hon. John Alden* (1861), accessed January 29, 2023, https://quod.lib.umich.edu/m/moa/AGV3178.0001.001?rgn=main;view=fulltext.
5. Collector Elton Brumfield owns a copy of the 1879 bylaws—the only known copy—but the item is inaccessible in storage. The oldest original copy of the bylaws we could locate at Lily Dale was from 1917.
6. John J. Guthrie, "Seeking the Sweet Spirit of Harmony: Establishing a Spiritualist Community at Cassadaga, Florida, 1893–1933," *Florida Historical Quarterly* 77, no. 1 (Summer 1998): 1–38, esp. 12–13.
7. "Jacob Scheu—Lily Dale," Directory of Liquor Tax Certificate Holders (1898), accessed January 30, 2023, https://www.google.com/books/edition/Directory_of_Liquor_Tax_Certificate_Hold/LAxQAAAAYAAJ?hl=en&gbpv=1&dq=%22liquor+tax+certificate%22+%22lily+dale%22&pg=PA32&printsec=frontcover.
8. Directory of Liquor Tax Certificate Holders, 1908, accessed January 30, 2023, https://www.google.com/books/edition/_/b_xPAAAAYAAJ?gbpv=1&bsq=louisa%20scheu. For details about how the liquor tax certificate replaced licensing, see New York State Legislature Assembly, Documents of the Assembly of the State of New York, issues 23–30, 1898, accessed January 30, 2023, https://www.google.com/books/edition/Documents_of_the_Assembly_of_the_State_o/WHQyAitpDQgC?hl=en&gbpv=1&bsq=%22liquor%20tax%20certificate%22.
9. Iroquois Hotel ads appear in many issues, but you can find examples in these specific issues: "The Iroquois," *The Sunflower*, July 18, 1903; "Iroquois Hotel," *The Cassadagan*, March 1901.
10. Louisa Scheu lost a corner cottage on the grounds to fire. "Fire at Lily Dale," *The Sunflower*, January 1, 1901.

11. Lily Dale Assembly, "Rules and Regulations," 1995, LDM.

12. "The Art of Dreaming," *Light: A. Journal of Psychical, Occult, and Mystical Research* 20, no. 1001 (March 17, 1900): 132.

13. "Life After Death," *Portsmouth (UK) Evening News*, February 19, 1903, accessed January 18, 2023, link-gale-com.i.ezproxy.nypl.org/apps/doc/GR3218832724/BNCN?u=nypl&sid=bookmark-BNCN&xid=355100a1.

14. George Fox, *The Great Mistery of the Great Whore Unfolded: And Antichrist's Kingdom Revealed Unto Destruction . . .* (London: Theodore Simmons, 1659).

15. Barbara Weisberg, *Talking to the Dead: Kate and Maggie Fox and the Rise of Spiritualism* (New York: HarperOne, 2005), 152–53; Jacqueline Jones-Hunt, *Moses and Jesus: The Shamans* (Winchester, UK: Moon Books, 2011), 122; Marlene Tromp, "Spirited Sexuality: Sex, Marriage, and Victorian Spiritualism," *Victorian Literature and Culture* 31, no. 1 (2003): 67–81.

16. Mariam Buckner Pond, *The Unwilling Martyrs: The Story of the Fox Family* (London: Spiritualist Press, 1947), 183.

17. Marion Meade, *Free Woman: The Life and Times of Victoria Woodhull* (New York: Knopf, 1976). See also Molly McGarry, "Spectral Sexualities: Nineteenth-Century Spiritualism Moral Panics, and the Making of U.S. Obscenity Law," *Journal of Women's History* 12, no. 2 (2000): 8–29.

18. Cathy Gutierrez, "Sex in the City of God: Free Love and the American Millennium," *Religion and American Culture: A Journal of Interpretation* 15, no. 2 (2005): 187.

19. American Spiritualist Association, "Report of the Proceedings of the Annual Meeting," *Religio-Philosophical Journal*, September 27, 1874.

20. "Freeloveism—The Universal Association of Spiritualists Assembled at the Hub . . . ," *Religio-Philosophical Journal*, October 10, 1874, http://iapsop.com/spirithistory/1874_universal_association_of_spiritualists.html.

21. Thomas Low Nichols, *Free Love: A Doctrine of Spiritualism* (Cincinnati: F. Bly, 1856), 3.

22. Joel Tiffany, *Spiritualism Explained* (New York: Graham and Ellinwood Publishers, 1856), 190. We photographed this rare book in the Marion Skidmore Library, Lily Dale.

23. William Hepworth Dixon, *Spiritual Wives* (Philadelphia: J. B. Lippincott, 1868), 257.

24. Official programs, 1880–1899, Camp Program Collection, LDM.

25. Reuben Briggs Davenport, *The Death-Blow to Spiritualism: Being the True Story of the Fox Sisters* (New York: C. W. Dillingham, 1888), 48.

26. Davenport, *The Death-Blow to Spiritualism*, 42.

27. *Religio-Philosophical Journal*, October 20, 1888, extracted in *The Two Worlds*, November 16, 1888, 7.

28. Davenport, *The Death-Blow to Spiritualism*, 45–46.

29. "William Crookes and the Physical Phenomena of Mediumship," *Proceedings of the Society for Psychical Research* 54, pt. 195 (March 1964): 32.

30. Alex Owen, *The Darkened Room: Women, Power, and Spiritualism in Late Victorian England* (Chicago: University of Chicago Press, 2004), 65–66.

31. "Mrs. Paul Sent to Prison," *Worthing Gazette*, January 30, 1895, 5.

32. "Death of an Eccentric Lady," *Coventry Evening Telegraph*, March 23, 1895.

33. "Lady's Strange Conduct," *Lincolnshire Echo*, June 8, 1895.

34. "Mrs. Paul," *Light*, December 3, 1898.

35. "Help Wanted," *Light*, October 13, 1900.

36. "An Appeal for Help," *Light*, November 3, 1900.

37. William Armstrong, "Mrs. Mellon and the Newcastle Society," *The Medium and Daybreak*, October 25, 1878, 6.

38. *The Medium and Daybreak*, October 25, 1878, 678.

39. Thomas Shekleton Henry, *Spookland: A Record of Research and Experiment in a Much-talked-of Realm of Mystery, with a Review and Criticism of the So-called Spiritualistic Phenomena of Spirit Materialization, and Hints and Illustration as to the Possibility of Artificially Producing the Same* (Chicago: Clyde Publishing Company, 1902), 50–72.

40. This thesis was first expounded by Reuben Briggs Davenport in *Death-Blow to Spiritualism*, but debunkers, biographers, and scholars built on this theme. See, for example, Pond, *The Unwilling Martyrs*.

41. Marlene Tromp, *Altered States: Sex, Nation, Drugs, and Self-Transformation in Victorian Spiritualism* (Albany: State University of New York Press, 2006), 175.

42. "The Foxonian Cataclysm," *Religio-Philosophical Journal*, October 20, 1888, 4.

43. Quoted in Judith Walkowitz, *City of Dreadful Delight: Narratives of Sexual Danger in Late-Victorian Britain* (Chicago: University of Chicago Press, 2013), 172.

44. Henry Maudsley, *Natural Causes and Supernatural Seemings* (London: Kegan Paul & Co., 1886), 333.

45. Quoted in Alex Owen, *The Darkened Room*, 147.

46. Appendix to the *Journals of the Senate and Assembly of the Legislature of the State of California* vol. 2 (1891), 41.

47. "Lunacy Law Reform Association," *The Spiritualist*, May 15, 1874.

48. [William Chapman], *Confessions of a Medium* (New York: E. P. Dutton & Co., 1882), 18. This book was published anonymously, but the author has since been identified as English medium William Chapman and his American partner Alfred H. Firman.

49. [Chapman], *Confessions*, 9.

50. [Chapman], *Confessions*, 19.

51. Elizabeth d'Espérance, *ShadowLand, or Light from the Other Side* (London: Geo. Bedway, 1897), 307–8.

52. See chapter 3.

53. Tromp, *Altered States*, chap. 7.

54. Ruth Bordin, *Frances Willard: A Biography* (Chapel Hill: University of North Carolina Press, 1986), 7; Nancy Hardesty, *Women Called to Witness: Evangelical Feminism in the Nineteenth Century* (Nashville: Abingdon Press, 1984); Scott C. Martin, introduction to *Devil of the Domestic Sphere: Temperance, Gender, and Middle-Class Ideology, 1800–1860* (DeKalb: Northern Illinois University Press, 2008).

55. See Ellen Carol DuBois, *Suffrage Women's Long Battle for the Vote* (New York: Simon & Schuster, 2021); and Elaine Frantz Parsons, *Manhood Lost: Fallen Drunkards and Redeeming Women in the Nineteenth-Century United States* (Baltimore: Johns Hopkins University Press, 2010).

56. Susan Campbell, *Tempest-Tossed: The Spirit of Isabella Beecher Hooker* (Middletown, CT: Wesleyan University Press, 2014), 49–53.

57. Campbell, *Tempest-Tossed*, 155.

58. "History of the WCTU," https://www.wctu.org/history.

59. Official program, 1885, Camp Program Collection, LDM.

60. Official program, 1888, Camp Program Collection, LDM.

61. *Dunkirk (NY) Observer*, August 27, 1889; H. D. Barrett, *Life Work of Cora D. Richmond* (Chicago: Hack & Anderson Printers, 1895).

62. Advertisement for 1890 Lily Dale Camp Meeting, LDM.

63. Official program, 1916, Camp Program Collection, LDM.

64. Official programs, 1890s, Camp Program Collection, LDM; Trisha Franzen, *Anna Howard Shaw: The Work of Woman Suffrage* (Urbana: University of Illinois Press, 2014), 65.

65. This is the same A. B. Richmond who conducted an investigation at the CLFA in 1887 and wrote a rejoinder to the Seybert Commission report, which we discussed in chapter 3.

66. Ray Boomhower, *Fighting for Equality: The Life of May Wright Sewall* (Indianapolis: Indiana Historical Society Press, 2007).

67. Lindsey Beckley, "Zerelda G. Wallace and May Wright Sewall: A Study," paper presented at Hoosier Women at Work: Studies in Indiana Women's History, Indianapolis, April 2018, https://www.in.gov/history/files/Lindsey-Beckley.pdf.

68. Bordin, *Frances Willard*, 98–102; Janet Zollinger Giele, *Two Paths to Women's Equality: Temperance, Suffrage, and the Origins of Modern Feminism* (New York: Twayne, 1995).

69. Mary Elizabeth Lease, "Speech to the Women's Christian Temperance Union" (1890), accessed January 30, 2023, http://www.historyisaweapon.com/defcon1/marylease2.html.

70. Charlotte Perkins Gilman, *The Home: Its Work and Influence* (New York: Co-Operative Press, 1910), digitized by Project Gutenberg, https://www.gutenberg.org/files/44481/44481-h/44481-h.htm.

71. Ron Nagy and Joyce LaJudice identify 1903 as the year the Cassadaga Lake Free Association changed its name to the City of Light Assembly in the official Lily Dale timeline, LDM; this is confirmed by the official publications produced by the Assembly that year under the name City of Light Assembly, advertised in *The Sunflower* and *The Cassadagan*. The City of Light Assembly changed its name again in 1906 to Lily Dale Assembly. The town had colloquially been referred to as Lily Dale for years.

72. Official program, 1906, Camp Program Collection, LDM.

73. A. B. Richmond, *What I Saw at Cassadaga Lake: Addendum to a Review in 1887 of the Seybert Commission's Report* (Boston: Colby & Rich Publishers, 1889), 6.

74. Lily Dale bylaws, 1917, courtesy of Elton Brumfield, personal correspondence.

75. This is the date identified by Lily Dale historians Ron Nagy and Joyce LaJudice in the official Lily Dale timeline, LDM.

76. "Report of Committee on Revision of Constitution and By-Laws," *The Summit of Spiritualist Understanding* 55, no. 591 (December 1973): 6.

77. Lily Day Assembly bylaws, 1991, LDM.

78. Leolyn Inn registration book, LDM.

6. The Indian Village

1. John Two-Hawks, who also goes by John Allen Hill, has claimed Native American ancestry in his memoir and other outlets. At least two websites run by Native Americans, however, have questioned the legitimacy of Two-Hawks's ancestral claims. See, for example, http://ancestorstealing.blogspot.com/2016/10/john-allen-hill-aka-john-two-hawks.html.

2. You can learn more about Grandmother Spider on her website, http://spidersmedicine.com/. Neal Rzepkowski, a physician who lives in Lily Dale, was the subject of a biography published by fellow medium Ruth Shilling. See Ruth Shilling, *Through a Medium's Eyes. About Life, Love, Mediumship, and the Spirit World*, vol. 3, *Neal Rzepkowski, MD* (West Kingston, RI: All One World Publishing, 2018).

3. Many Native American people have reclaimed the name "Indian" and, particularly since the American Indian Movement of the mid-twentieth century, have used it to refer to themselves. I use the terms "Indian," "Native American," "Indigenous," and "Native" interchangeably throughout this chapter, following the precedent set by scholars like Vine Deloria Jr. and Philip Deloria. For a quick guide to usage, see the Smithsonian Museum of the American Indian's terminology guide, https://americanindian.si.edu/nk360/informational/impact-words-tips#:~:text=American%20Indian%20or%20Native%20American,would%20like%20to%20be%20addressed.

4. William Bluesky (Seneca) was one of the first American Indians to become a doctor of osteopathic medicine. Wilbur Shongo (Seneca) was a relative of Twylah Nitsch, discussed later in this chapter. Nathan Lefthand, "NCAIHP Honors First American Indian to Graduate from ATSU's KCOM," *ATSU News*, January 27, 2014, https://www.atsu.edu/news/ncaihp-honors-first-american-indian-to-graduate-from-atsus-kcom; "W. Clifford Shongo," *Buffalo Courier Express*, May 1, 1968.

5. Official programs, 1931 and 1970, Camp Program Collection, LDM.

6. "Chief Running Deer," *Darwen (UK) News*, February 26, 1937, Oskenonton Collection, LDM.

7. Oskenonton, "The Boy Stranger, Being the Autobiography of the Famous Mohawk Singer Chief Os-Ke-Non-Ton," unpublished ms., Oskenonton Collection, LDM.

8. Oskenonton, "The Boy Stranger."

9. Oskenonton, "The Boy Stranger."

10. Gregory Clark, "He Has Sung the Songs of Canada's Northland to the Princes and Nobles of Old England," *Daily Standard* (Kingston, Ontario), October 19, 1925; Oskenonton, "The Boy Stranger."

11. Oskenonton, "The Boy Stranger."

12. Clark, "He Has Sung the Songs of Canada's Northland."

13. "To Acquaint Children with Indian Customs," *Brooklyn Standard Union*, January 16, 1920.

14. Oskenonton to Edward "Ted" Blackmore, November 27, 1953, private collection of Elizabeth Graham. I am deeply indebted to Elizabeth Graham and Jennifer Mills for their willingness to share these letters with me.

15. "Visit Oskenonton Wigwam Indian Village," copy of pamphlet, undated, Oskenonton Collection, LDM.

16. Oskenonton to Edward "Ted" Blackmore, April 7, 1953, private collection of Elizabeth Graham.

17. Joel W. Martin, *The Land Looks After Us: A History of Native American Religion* (New York: Oxford University Press, 2001), 17–19.

18. Arthur C. Parker and Handsome Lake, *The Code of Handsome Lake, the Seneca Prophet* (Albany: University of the State of New York, 1913); Martin, *The Land Looks After Us*, 53.

19. Martin, *The Land Looks After Us*, 54–55.

20. Michael D. McNally, *Defend the Sacred: Native American Religious Freedom beyond the First Amendment* (Princeton: Princeton University Press, 2020), 36. See also Frederick E. Hoxie, *A Final Promise: The Campaign to Assimilate the Indians, 1880–1920* (1984; repr., Lincoln: University of Nebraska Press, 2001), 3.

21. Hoxie, *A Final Promise*, 17–25.

22. Kathryn Troy, *The Specter of the Indian: Race, Gender, and Ghosts in American Séances, 1848–1890* (Albany: State University of New York Press, 2017), 115–49.

23. See David D. Smiths, "The Frontier Army and the Destruction of the Buffalo, 1865–1883," *Western Historical Quarterly* 25, no. 3 (Autumn 1994): 312–38.

24. For some truly brutal firsthand accounts of the white slaughter of Californian Native Americans, see Clifford E. Trafzer and Joel R. Hyer, *Exterminate Them: Written Accounts of the Murder, Rape, and Enslavement of Native Americans during the California Gold Rush* (East Lansing: Michigan State University Press, 1999).

25. Scholars disagree over whether this happened in 1887 or 1889. Louis Warren, *God's Red Son: The Ghost Dance Religion and the Making of Modern America* (New York: Basic Books, 2017), 104.

26. James Mooney, *The Ghost-Dance Religion and the Sioux Outbreak of 1890* (Lincoln: University of Nebraska Press, 1991), 772, originally published as part 2 of the *Fourteenth Annual Report of the Bureau of Ethnology, 1892–93* (Washington, DC: Government Printing Office, 1896).

27. Quoted in Warren, *God's Red Son*, 186.

28. Warren, *God's Red Son*, 284–89.

29. For an analysis, see Vine Deloria Jr., *God Is Red: A Native View of Religion* (Wheat Ridge, CO: Fulcrum Publishing, 2003), 23–45.

30. Warren, *God's Red Son*, 370–72.

31. Carolyn Nestor Long, *Religious Freedom and Indian Rights: The Case of Oregon v. Smith* (Lawrence: University Press of Kansas, 2000), 11.

32. Over the course of the twentieth century, Native Americans have also been in ongoing conflict with the Department of the Interior over the use of feathers from protected bird species, including bald and golden eagles. See Adair Martin Smith, "Native American Use of Eagle Feathers under the Religious Freedom Restoration Act," *University of Cincinnati Law Review* 84 (2018): 575–94.

33. Hugh Urban notes that the phrase "New Age" was first used in this sense by Alice Bailey in her book *Discipleship in the New Age*, "where it refers to the transition from the astrological sign of Pisces to the sign of Aquarius." Hugh Urban, *New Age, Neopagan, and New Religious Movements: Alternative Spirituality in Contemporary America* (Berkeley: University of California Press, 2015), 223.

34. Urban, *New Age, Neopagan, and New Religious Movements*, 70. Swedenborg's writings remain one of the single greatest influences on spiritualism to this day.

35. Sarah M. Pike, *New Age and Neopagan Religions in America* (New York: Columbia University Press, 2004), 47, 49.

36. See K. Paul Johnson, *The Masters Revealed: Madame Blavatsky and the Myth of the Great White Lodge* (Albany: State University of New York Press, 1994), 2–3. Johnson's historical study of Blavatsky's life shows convincingly that she developed the mythology of the divine Masters to lend a mystical air to what was essentially a synthesis of her own lifelong spiritual quest, learning from teachers of various faiths around the world.

37. Pike, *New Age*, 57.

38. There's a difference between new religious movements and New Age spirituality, though they're often intertwined. New religious movements, says religious studies scholar Hugh Urban, are more organized and clearly defined, typically center on a particular thought leader, and have boundaries between members and non-members. New Age religion is diverse and nebulous and has no system of membership. See Urban, *New Age, Neopagan, and New Religious Movements*.

39. Pike, *New Age*, 68–69.

40. Pike, *New Age*, 70.

41. Ethan Doyle White, *Wicca: History, Belief and Community in Modern Pagan Witchcraft* (Liverpool: Liverpool University Press, 2022).

42. Hadley Meares, "The Witches of Westwood and Carlos Castañeda's Sinister Legacy," *LAist*, September 2, 2021; Robert Marshall, "The Dark Legacy of Carlos Castañeda," *Salon*, April 12, 2007; *Trickster: The Many Lives of Carlos Castañeda*, https://tricksterpodcast.com/.

43. Philip J. Deloria, *Playing Indian* (New Haven: Yale University Press, 1998), 169; Deloria, *God Is Red*, 35–36.

44. Vine Deloria Jr. gives a clear and concise explanation of the background of the Indian movement in *God Is Red*, 1–22.

45. Vine Deloria Jr., foreword to John G. Neihardt, *Black Elk Speaks: The Complete Edition* (Lincoln: University of Nebraska Press, 2014), xiii.

46. Lee Irwin, "Freedom, Law, and Prophecy: A Brief History of Native American Religious Resistance," *American Indian Quarterly* 21 (Winter 1997): 43–45.

47. As quoted in Deloria, *Playing Indian*, 168.

48. See Meares, "The Witches of Westwood"; Marshall, "The Dark Legacy of Carlos Castañeda"; *Trickster*.

49. Judy Mills, "Life with the Tribe," *Spokane Spokesman-Review*, February 19, 1984.

50. Mills, "Life with the Tribe."

51. Doug Clark, "For Sun Bear, 'Green Energy' Fuels Forecasts," *Spokane Chronicle*, January 17, 1991.

52. Fees for events are typically styled as "love offerings"; www.winddaughter.com.

53. Joseph Bruchac, "Spinning the Medicine Wheel: The Bear Tribe in the Catskills," *Akwesasne Notes* 15, no. 5 (1983), quoted in Mills, "Life with the Tribe."

54. Michelle Bearden, "The Mystique of the Medicine Man," *Tampa Bay Times*, September 16, 1989.

55. Mills, "Life with the Tribe."

56. On the Andrews oeuvre, see Lynn Andrews, *Medicine Woman* (New York: HarperCollins, 1981); Beth Ann Krier, "The Medicine Woman of Beverly Hills," *Los Angeles Times*, November 23, 1987; Maralyn Lois Polak, "In Quest of Ancient Powers," *Philadelphia Inquirer*, November 23, 1986; Mark Munro, "Lynn Andrews: Sharing Spiritual Adventures," *Boston Globe*, November 23, 1991. Someone more New Agey than me would note the "synchronicity" of the fact that each of those articles was published on November 23. As far as I can tell, there's no evidence that either of the women Andrews claimed as teachers actually existed, and members of the tribes the women supposedly belonged to have denied ever meeting or working with Andrews.

57. Deloria, *Playing Indian*, 174. Andrews has since expanded her repertoire to include Anglo-Saxon pagan "magic" cultures. For a great analysis of the Andrews theological universe, see Nano Riley, "Incredible Journey," *Tampa Bay Times*, October 21, 1990.

58. Troy, *Specter of the Indian*, 31. See also Molly McGarry, *Ghosts of Futures Past: Spiritualism and Cultural Politics in Nineteenth-Century America* (Berkeley: University of California Press, 2008), 66–93.

59. "Cassadaga: Who We Are," https://www.cassadaga.org/who-we-are.html. See also Jamie Loftus's podcast *Ghost Church*.

60. "Indian Life Study," *Buffalo Enquirer*, September 11, 1917.

61. "Indian Recognizes Sister's Psychic Portrait," undated and unattributed newspaper clipping, Oskenonton Collection, LDM; D. Hird Minty, "They Say," *New York Spiritualist Leader,* January 11, 1942. These articles both also suggest that Oskenonton maintained the story that Chinquilla was his sister.

62. Christine Bold, *Vaudeville Indians on Global Circuits, 1880s–1930s* (New Haven: Yale University Press, 2022), 193–216.

63. "Oskenonton and Princess Chinquilla in a Genuine Indian Program," program printed by the Lily Dale Press, 1917, Oskenonton Collection, LDM; Bold, *Vaudeville Indians*, 207.

64. Bold, *Vaudeville Indians*, 208; Cari M. Carpenter, "Detecting Indianness: Gertrude Bonnin's Investigation of Native American Identity," *Wicazo Sa Review* 20 (Spring 2005): 139–59.

65. Carpenter, "Detecting Indianness," 148.

66. Ray A. Hemachandra, "Selling the Sacred? American Indians and the New Age," *New Age Retailer*, November–December 2003, 3.

67. Lily Dale "Calendar of Events, Lectures, Workshop, and Films," 1985, LDM.

68. Howard Isaac appears in a photograph taken at Nitsch's Cattaraugus home; https://www.geomancy.org/index.php/sacred-space/new-sacred-spaces. Isaac's "Medicine Wheel of Stumps" might refer to a medicine wheel made out of tree stumps on Nitsch's property.

69. *Fourteenth Census of the United States, 1920*, Bureau of the Census, Record Group 29, National Archives, Washington, DC; *Fifteenth Census of the United States, 1930*, Bureau of the Census, Record Group 29, National Archives, Washington, DC; *Sixteenth Census of the United States, 1940*, Bureau of the Census, Record Group 29, National Archives, Washington, DC; 1913 US Indian Census Rolls, 1885–1940, Records of the Bureau of Indian Affairs, Record Group 75, National Archives, Washington, DC.

70. "Mrs. Hurd Dies, Red Jacket Descendant," *Evans Journal* (Angola, NY), May 20, 1971.

71. Roger Weaver, "Review of *Other Council Fires Were Here Before Ours*," *Studies in American Indian Literatures* 5 (Spring 1993): 115–16. It's hard to say definitively whether Sams was really Nitsch's granddaughter, not only because she was born in Texas when Nitsch was thirty-eight and living in Buffalo with small children, but also because Nitsch "adopted" many people and asked people to call her "Gram."

72. Today, both the teaching lodge and the Seneca Indian Historical Society are incorporated in Florida. Most of the listed board members and staff are members of the Nitsch family. The website seems no longer to exist but can be accessed through the Wayback Machine; see https://web.archive.org/web/20110209073230/http://wolfclanteachinglodge.org/.

73. Many Native American tribes, including the Haudenosaunee, have cultures of adoption. Robert Wagner, "2 Seek Balance between Man, Nature's Way," *Buffalo News*, September 10, 1980; Brad Steiger, *Medicine Talk: A Guide to Walking in Balance and Surviving on the Earth Mother* (New York: Doubleday, 1974).

74. "California Medicine Wheel Gathering," *LA Weekly*, October 15, 1987. The medicine wheel was popularized by Sun Bear, but how it became a pan-Indian ceremony is a little more complex, dating back to the popularity of Black Elk's memoir. For more on the appropriation of the medicine wheel, see Suzanne Owen, *The Appropriation of Native American Spirituality* (London: Continuum Books, 2008).

75. Official program, 1985, Camp Program Collection, LDM.

76. Deloria, *Playing Indian*, 171.

77. Official program, 2005, Camp Program Collection, LDM. The "Bear Clan" may be a reference to Sun Bear's Bear Tribe. She also advertised her teaching connections to Twylah Nitsch's Wolf Clan. A discussion of Two Worlds can be found at http://www.newagefraud.org/smf/index.php?topic=696.0.

78. "Laying Claim to Pocahontas," *Washington Post*, July 9, 1995; Virginia Rollings, "Pocahontas Is a Popular Grandmother to Claim," *Newport News Daily Press*, April 1, 2006.

79. "'Indian' Chief Ho-To-Pi Dies," *Miami Herald*, February 22, 1973; "George Cutrulis, 78, Was Chief Ho-To-Pi," *Miami Herald*, February 23, 1973; Eliot Kleinberg, "Greek-Turned-'Indian' Wowed Kids," *Palm Beach Post*, June 17, 2010; Eliot Kleinberg, "Wild West Roots Were Just a Show," *Palm Beach Post*, June 21, 2010.

80. Sarah Viren, "The Native Scholar Who Wasn't," *New York Times*, May 25, 2021.

81. "Neal TiOmime Rzepkowski," www.winddaughter.com/neal-rzepkowski.

82. Shilling, *Through a Medium's Eyes*.

83. Dagmar Wernitznig, *Going Native or Going Naive? White Shamanism and the Neo-Noble Savage* (Lanham, MD: University Press of America, 2003), 64–65.

84. Irwin, "Freedom, Law, and Prophecy," 15–16.

85. Ward Churchill, "Spiritual Hucksterism: The Rise of Plastic Medicine Men," *Cultural Survival Quarterly Magazine*, June 2003, https://www.culturalsurvival.org/publications/

cultural-survival-quarterly/spiritual-hucksterismthe-rise-plastic-medicine-men, originally published in *Z Magazine*, December 1990.

86. Owen, *The Appropriation of Native American Spirituality*, 64.

87. Wilmer Stampede Mesteth (Oglala Lakota), Darrell Standing Elk (Sicangu Lakota), Phyllis Swift Hawk (Kul Wicasa Lakota), and Tiospaye Wounspe Waokiye, "A Declaration of War against Exploiters of Lakota Spirituality." The full text can be found at https://www.digitalhistory.uh.edu/disp_textbook.cfm?smtid=3&psid=730.

88. "Seneca Spirituality," https://www.lilydaleassembly.org/event-details/seneca-spirituality-the-importance-of-the-thanksgiving-address-with-diane-shenandoah.

Epilogue

1. Ron Nagy and Joyce LaJudice, *The Chronicles of Lily Dale* (self-published using CreateSpace Independent Publishing Platform, 2017); Ron Nagy and Joyce LaJudice, *Spirits of Lily Dale* (Hendersonville, NC: Galde Press, 2017); Ron Nagy, *Precipitated Spirit Paintings* (Hendersonville, NC: Galde Press, 2006); Ron Nagy, *Slate Writing: Invisible Intelligence* (Hendersonville, NC: Galde Press, 2012).

2. Sadly, the minutes contained almost none of these juicy boring details.

3. "Cassadaga Lake Camp," *Banner of Light*, August 19, 1882. Nagy also briefly references Fox's visit to the camp in *The Spirits of Lily Dale*, 12.

4. *National Spiritualist Summit* 61, no. 656 (June 1979): 16; "The Draw of Healing Tranquility: Tens of Thousands Visit Spiritualist Community in N.Y.," *Deseret News*, September 9, 2000, accessed January 26, 2023, https://www.deseret.com/2000/9/9/19527766/the-draw-of-healing-tranquility.

5. For example, when Marissa asked why the owners of the Iroquois Hotel got a liquor license when the town was dry, he wrote back in an email that they "ran with a wild bunch." Now, isn't that exactly the sort of story you'd want to read about? Alas, Marissa has found nothing to verify this particular gem.

6. Carrie Twing, *A History of Cassadaga Camp* (Lily Dale: The Sunflower Print, July 1899).

Bibliography

Primary Sources

Archives and Unpublished Sources

Ancestry.com
Elizabeth Graham's private Oskenonton collection
iapsop.com (International Association for the Preservation of Spiritualist and Occult Periodicals)
Lily Dale Museum, Lily Dale, NY (LDM)
National Spiritualist Association of Churches Headquarters, Lily Dale, NY
New York Directory of Liquor Tax Certificate Holders, google.com
New York State Court of Appeals, casetext.com
Newspapers.com
OldFultonPostcards.com
Sheridan Library Special Collections, Johns Hopkins University

Bibliography

Susan B. Anthony Papers: Daybook and Diaries, to 1906. Manuscripts/Mixed Material, Library of Congress
US Census Records

Periodicals

Baltimore Sun
Banner of Light
Berkeley Daily Gazette
Boston Globe
Brooklyn Standard Union
Buffalo Daily Republic
Buffalo Express
The Cassadagan
Cincinnati Enquirer
Courier Express (Buffalo)
Coventry Evening Telegraph
Daily Inter Ocean (Chicago)
Daily Standard (Kingston, Ont.)
Darwen (UK) News
Dunkirk (NY) Observer
El Paso Daily Herald
Evans Journal (Angola, NY)
Evening Observer (Dunkirk, NY)
Fall River Daily Evening News
Jamestown (NY) Post-Journal
Journal of the American Society for Psychical Research
Kansas City Journal
The Liberator
Light: A Journal of Psychical, Occult, and Mystical Research
Light
Light Bridges Magazine
The Light of Truth
Lincolnshire Echo
Los Angeles Times
Mind and Matter

New York Spiritualist Leader
New York Times
New York World
The New Yorker
Philadelphia Inquirer
Pittsburg Dispatch
Proceedings of the American Society for Psychical Research
The Progressive Thinker
Religio-Philosophical Journal
Rochester Democrat and Chronicle
Salt Lake Tribune
Spiritual Offering
Spokane Chronicle
Stark County Democrat
The Summit of Spiritual Understanding
The Sunflower
Tampa Bay Times
Titusville Herald
Vermont Record and Farmer
Washington Post
Worthing (UK) Gazette

Books and Essays

Alden, Ebenezer. *Memorial of the descendants of the Hon. John Alden*. 1861. Accessed January 29, 2023. https://quod.lib.umich.edu/m/moa/AGV3178.0001.001?rgn=main;view=fulltext.

Barrett, Harrison D. *Life Work of Mrs. Cora L. V. Richmond*. Chicago: Hack & Anderson Printers, 1895.

Bartnett, Harriet. "Abby Louise Pettengill: A Tribute." Skidmore Library, Lily Dale, NY.

Britten, Emma Hardinge. *Modern American Spiritualism: A Twenty Years' Record of the Communion Between Earth and the World of Spirits*. New York: published by the author, 1870.

———. *Nineteenth Century Miracles; or Spirits and Their Work in Every Country of the Earth, a Complete Historical Compendium of the Great Movement Known as Modern Spiritualism*. New York: William Britten, 1884.

Carrington, Hereward. *Personal Experiences in Spiritualism: Including the Official Account and Record of the American Palladino Séances*. London: T. Werner Laurie, 1913.

———. "Report of a Two-Weeks' Investigation into Alleged Spiritualistic Phenomena, Witnessed at Lily Dale, New York." *Proceedings of the American Society for Psychical Research* 2, pt. 1 (1908): 7–116.

Castañeda, Carlos. *The Teachings of Don Juan: A Yaqui Way of Knowledge*. 30th Anniversary Edition. Berkeley: University of California Press, 2016.

[Chapman, William.] *Confessions of a Medium*. New York: E. P. Dutton & Co., 1882.

The Complete House Builder with Hints on Building. Chicago: Donohue, Henneberry & Co., 1890.

Davenport, Ira. *Davenport Brothers: World-Renowned Spiritual Mediums*. Boston: William White and Company, 1869.

Davenport, Reuben Briggs. *The Death-Blow to Spiritualism: Being the True Story of the Fox Sisters*. New York: C. W. Dillingham, 1888.

De la Banta, Professor. *De la Banta's Advice to Ladies Concerning Beauty*. Chicago: S. Junkin, 1878.

d'Espérance, Elizabeth. *ShadowLand, or Light from the Other Side*. London: Geo. Bedway, 1897.

Dixon, William Hepworth. *Spiritual Wives*. Philadelphia: J. B. Lippincott, 1868.

Downs, John Phillip. *History of Chautauqua County, New York, and Its People*. New York: American Historical Society, 1921.

Doyle, Arthur Conan. *The History of Spiritualism*. Vols. 1 and 2. London: Cassell, 1926.

———. *Memories and Adventures*. London: Hodder & Stoughton, 1924.

Dubois, Ellen Carol, ed. *Elizabeth Cady Stanton, Susan B. Anthony: Correspondence, Writing, Speeches*. New York: Schocken Books, 1981.

Edson, Obed. *History of Chautauqua County, New York*. Boston: W. A. Fergusson, 1894.

Finney, Charles Grandison. *An Autobiography*. Bloomington, MN: Bethany House Publishing, 1977.

Flint, Austin, Charles Lee, and C. B. Coventry. "Discovery of the Source of the Rochester Knockings." *Buffalo Medical Journal* 6 (March 1851): 628–42.

Funk, Isaac. *The Widow's Mite and Other Psychic Phenomena*. New York: Funk & Wagnalls Co., 1904.

Hardice, Emma. *Modern American Spiritualism*. New York: Published by the Author, 1870.

Harper, Ida Husted. *The Life and Work of Susan B. Anthony Including Public Addresses, Her Own Letters and Many from Her Contemporaries during Fifty Years*. 3 vols. Indianapolis: Bowen-Merrill Company, 1898–1908.

Hartley, Florence. *The Ladies' Book of Etiquette and Manual of Politeness*. Boston: G. W. Cottrell, 1860.

James, William. *Varieties of Religious Experience: A Study in Human Nature*. London: Longmans, Green & Co., 1902.

Maudsley, Henry. *Natural Causes and Supernatural Seemings*. London: Kegan Paul & Co., 1886.

Nichols, Thomas Low. *Free Love: A Doctrine of Spiritualism*. Cincinnati: F. Bly, 1856.

Oskenonton. "The Boy Stranger, Being the Autobiography of the Famous Mohawk Singer Chief Os-Ke-Non-Ton." Oskenonton Collection, Lily Dale History Museum.

Parker, Arthur C., and Handsome Lake. *The Code of Handsome Lake, the Seneca Prophet*. Albany: University of the State of New York, 1913.

Preliminary Report of the Commission Appointed by the University of Pennsylvania to Investigate Modern Spiritualism, In According with the Request of the Late Henry Seybert. Philadelphia: J. B. Lippincott & Co., 1887.

Proceedings of the Twenty-Fifth Annual Convention of the National American Woman Suffrage Association, held in Washington, D C., January 16, 17, 18, 19, 1893. Washington, DC: Stormont & Jackson, Printers, 1893.

Ramsdell, Josh D. *A Souvenir of Cassadaga Lake*. Erie, PA: Herald Printing and Publishing Co., 1889.

Richmond, A. B. *What I Saw at Cassadaga Lake: Addendum to a Review in 1887 of the Seybert Commission's Report*. Boston: Colby & Rich Publishers, 1889.

——. *What I Saw at Cassadaga Lake: A Review of the Seybert Commissioners' Report*. 3rd ed. Boston: Colby & Rich, 1890.

Schlesinger, Julia. *Workers in the Vineyard: A Review of the Progress of Spiritualism, Biographical Sketches, Lectures, Essays and Poems*. San Francisco: self-published, 1896.

Sewall, May Wright. *Neither Dead nor Sleeping*. Indianapolis: Bobbs-Merrill Publishing Company, 1920.

Shaw, Anna Howard. *The Story of a Pioneer*. New York: Kraus Reprint Co., 1970.

——. "Stand on the Principle of Justice." Speech delivered in Lily Dale, NY. August 19, 1914. In Wilmer Albert Linkugel, ed., "The Speeches of Anna Howard Shaw: Collected and Edited with Introduction and Notes." PhD diss., University of Wisconsin, 1960.

Smith, Uriah. *Modern Spiritualism*. Battle Creek, MI: Review and Herald Publishing, 1896.

Some Account of the Vampires of Onset, Past and Present. Boston, Press of S. Woodberry, 1892.

Stanton, Elizabeth Cady, Susan B. Anthony, Matilda Joslyn Gage, and Ida Husted Harper, eds. *A History of Woman Suffrage*. 6 vols. Rochester: Fowler and Wells, 1881–1922.

Stead, Estelle Wilson. *My Father: Personal and Spiritual Reminiscences*. London: George H. Doran Company, 1913.

Tiffany, Joel. *Spiritualism Explained*. New York: Graham and Ellinwood Publishers, 1856.

Watson, Elizabeth Lowe. *Song and Sermon*. San Francisco: The Hicks-Judd Co., 1906.

Wickham, Gertrude Van Rensselaer. *The Pioneer Families of Cleveland, 1796–1840*. Vols. 1 and 2. Cleveland: Evangelical Publishing House, 1914.

Secondary Sources

Andrick, John Michael. "Modern Mecca of Psychic Forces: The Psychical Science Congress and the Culture of Progressive Occultism in Fin-de-Siècle Chicago, 1885–1900." PhD diss., University of Illinois at Urbana-Champaign, 2016.

Avery-Quinn, Samuel. *Cities of Zion: The Holiness Movement and Methodist Camp Meeting Towns in America*. Lanham, MD: Lexington Books, 2019.
Axelrod, Alan. *A Savage Empire: Trappers, Traders, Tribes, and the Wars That Made America*. New York: Thomas Dunne, 2011.
Bennett, Bridget. *Transatlantic Spiritualism and Nineteenth-Century American Literature*. New York: Palgrave Macmillan, 2007.
Bernstein, Peter L. *The Wedding of the Waters: The Erie Canal and the Making of a Great Nation*. New York: W. W. Norton, 2005.
Bold, Christine. *Vaudeville Indians on Global Circuits, 1880s–1930s*. New Haven: Yale University Press, 2022.
Bordin, Ruth. *Frances Willard: A Biography*. Chapel Hill: University of North Carolina Press, 1986.
Boomhower, Ray. *Fighting for Equality: The Life of May Wright Sewall*. Indianapolis: Indiana Historical Society Press, 2007.
Braude, Ann. *Radical Spirits: Spiritualism and Women's Rights in Nineteenth-Century America*. Bloomington: Indiana University Press, 1989.
Bushman, Richard. *Joseph Smith: Rough Stone Rolling*. New York: Vintage Books, 2005.
Butler, Jon. *Awash in a Sea of Faith: Christianizing the American People*. Cambridge: Harvard University Press, 1992.
Cahill, Cathleen. *Recasting the Vote: How Women of Color Transformed the Suffrage Movement*. Chapel Hill: University of North Carolina Press, 2020.
Campbell, Susan. *Tempest-Tossed: The Spirit of Isabella Beecher Hooker*. Middletown, CT: Wesleyan University Press, 2014.
Carmack, Noel A. "Joseph Smith, Captain Kidd Lore, and Treasure Seeking in New York and New England during the Early Republic." *Dialogue: A Journal of Mormon Thought* 46 (2013): 78–153.
Carpenter, Cari M. "Detecting Indianness: Gertrude Bonnin's Investigation of Native American Identity." *Wicazo Sa Review* 20 (Spring 2005): 139–59.
Chapin, David. *Exploring Other Worlds: Margaret Fox, Elisha Kent Kane, and the Antebellum Culture of Curiosity*. Amherst: University of Massachusetts Press, 2004.
Clark, Emily Suzanne. *A Luminous Brotherhood: Afro-Creole Spiritualism in Nineteenth-Century New Orleans*. Chapel Hill: University of North Carolina Press, 2016.
Clark, Mary Ann. "Spirit Is Universal: Development of Black Spiritualist Churches." In *Esotericism in African American Religious Experience*, edited by Stephen Finley, Margarita Guillory, and Hugh Page Jr., 86–101. Boston: Brill, 2014.
Collins, David, ed. *The Cambridge History of Magic and Witchcraft in the West: From Antiquity to the Present*. Cambridge: Cambridge University Press, 2015.
Cope, Rachel. "From Smoldering Fires to Revitalizing Showers: Historiographical Overview of Revivalism in Nineteenth-Century New York." *Wesley and Methodist Studies* 4 (2012): 25–49.
Cox, Robert. *Body and Soul: A Sympathetic History of American Spiritualism*. Charlottesville: University of Virginia Press, 2003.
Cross, Whitney R. *The Burned-over District: The Social and Intellectual History of Enthusiastic Religion in Western New York, 1800–1850*. Ithaca: Cornell University Press, 1950.

Deloria, Philip J. *Playing Indian*. New Haven: Yale University Press, 1998.
Deloria, Vine, Jr. *God Is Red: A Native View of Religion*. Wheat Ridge, CO: Fulcrum Publishing, 2003.
Denevan, William. "The Pristine Myth: The Landscape of the Americas in 1492." *Annals of the Association of American Geographers* 82 (September 1992): 369–85.
Dennis, Matthew. *Seneca Possessed: Indians, Witchcraft, and Power in the Early American Republic*. Philadelphia: University of Pennsylvania Press, 2010.
DuBois, Ellen Carol. *Suffrage Women's Long Battle for the Vote*. New York: Simon & Schuster, 2021.
Flanders, Judith. *Inside the Victorian Home: A Portrait of Domestic Life in Victorian England*. New York: W. W. Norton, 2005.
Foster, Lawrence. *Women, Family, and Utopia: Communal Experiments of the Shakers, the Oneida Community, and the Mormons*. Syracuse: Syracuse University Press, 1991.
Franzen, Trisha. *Anna Howard Shaw: The Work of Woman Suffrage*. Urbana: University of Illinois Press, 2014.
Gabriel, Mary Catherine Gaydos. "Ordinary Spirits in an Extraordinary Town: Finding Identity in Personal Images and Resurrected Memorial in Lily Dale, New York." MA thesis, Utah State University, 2010.
Gomel, Elana. "'Spirits in the Material World': Spiritualism and Identity in the *Fin-de-Siècle*." *Victorian Literature and Culture* 35, no. 1 (2007): 189–213.
Guthrie, John J. "Seeking the Sweet Spirit of Harmony: Establishing a Spiritualist Community at Cassadaga, Florida, 1893–1933." *Florida Historical Quarterly* 77, no. 1 (Summer 1998): 1–38.
Gutierrez, Cathy. "Sex in the City of God: Free Love and the American Millennium." *Religion and American Culture: A Journal of Interpretation* 15, no. 2 (2005): 187–208.
Hardesty, Nancy. *Women Called to Witness: Evangelical Feminism in the Nineteenth Century*. Nashville: Abingdon Press, 1984.
Hatch, Nathan O. *The Democratization of American Christianity*. New Haven: Yale University Press, 1989.
Hewitt, Nancy. *Radical Friend: Amy Kirby Post and Her Activist Worlds*. Chapel Hill: University of North Carolina Press, 2018.
Heyrman, Christine Leigh. *Southern Cross: The Beginnings of the Bible Belt*. Chapel Hill: University of North Carolina Press, 1998.
Howe, Daniel Walker. *What Hath God Wrought: The Transformation of America, 1815–1848*. New York: Oxford University Press, 2007.
Hoxie, Frederick E. *A Final Promise: The Campaign to Assimilate the Indians, 1880–1920*. 1984. Repr., Lincoln: University of Nebraska Press, 2001.
Huggins, Ronald V. "From Captain Kidd's Ghost to the Angel Moroni: Changing *Dramatis Personae* in Early Mormonism." *Dialogue: A Journal of Mormon Thought* 36 (2003): 17–42.
Inglis, Andrea. *Beside the Seaside: Victorian Resorts in the Nineteenth Century*. Carlton South, Australia: Miegunyah Press of Melbourne University Press, 1999.
Jackson, Lee. *Palaces of Pleasure: From Music Halls to the Seaside to Football: How the Victorians Invented Mass Entertainment*. New Haven: Yale University Press, 2019.
Johnson, K. Paul. *The Masters Revealed: Madame Blavatsky and the Myth of the Great White Lodge*. Albany: State University of New York Press, 1994.

Johnson, Paul E. *A Shopkeeper's Millennium: Society and Revivals in Rochester, New York, 1812–1837.* New York: Hill and Wang, 1978.

———. *Sam Patch, the Famous Jumper.* New York: Hill and Wang, 2003.

Jones, Martha S. *Vanguard: How Black Women Broke Barriers, Won the Vote, and Insisted on Equality for All.* New York: Basic Books, 2020.

Jones-Hunt, Jacqueline. *Moses and Jesus: The Shamans.* Winchester, UK: John Hunt Publishing, 2011.

Kern, Louis J. *An Ordered Love: Sex Roles and Sexuality in Victorian Utopias; The Shakers, the Mormons, and the Oneida Community.* Chapel Hill: University of North Carolina Press, 1981.

Klaw, Spencer. *Without Sin: The Life and Death of the Oneida Community.* New York: Penguin, 1993.

LaJudice, Joyce, and Paula M. Vogt. *Lily Dale: Proud Beginnings.* Lily Dale, NY: self-published, 1984.

Lamont, Peter. "Spiritualism and a Mid-Victorian Crisis of Evidence." *Historical Journal* 47, no. 4 (December 2004): 897–920.

Langley, Lester. *The Shaker Experience in America.* New Haven: Yale University Press, 2009.

Leopold, Harry. *The Forgotten People: The Woodland Erie.* New York: Exposition Press, 1975.

Long, Carolyn Nestor. *Religious Freedom and Indian Rights: The Case of Oregon v. Smith.* Lawrence: University Press of Kansas, 2000.

Longfield, Bradley J. *Presbyterians and American Culture: A History.* Louisville: Westminster John Knox Press, 2013.

Lowry, Elizabeth Schleber. *The Seybert Report: Rhetoric, Rationale, and the Problem of Psi Research.* London: Palgrave Macmillan, 2017.

Lucky, Katherine. "The Last Shakers: Keeping the Faith in a Community Facing Extinction." *Commonweal Magazine*, November 28, 2019.

Martin, Joel W. *The Land Looks After Us: A History of Native American Religion.* New York: Oxford University Press, 2001.

Martin, Scott C. *Devil of the Domestic Sphere: Temperance, Gender, and Middle-Class Ideology, 1800–1860.* DeKalb: Northern Illinois University Press, 2008.

McBride, Spencer W., and Jennifer Hull Dorsey, eds. *New York's Burned-Over District: A Documentary History.* Ithaca: Cornell University Press, 2023.

McCombs, W. Douglas. "Therapeutic Rusticity: Antimodernism, Health, and the Wilderness Vacation, 1870–1915." *New York History* 76 (1995): 409–28.

McDowell, Bill. *Banner of Light: The Lily Dale Photographs.* Syracuse: Light Work, 1998.

McGarry, Molly. *Ghosts of Futures Past: Spiritualism and the Cultural Politics of Nineteenth-Century America.* Berkeley: University of California Press, 2008.

———. "Spectral Sexualities: Nineteenth-Century Spiritualism, Moral Panics, and the Making of U.S. Obscenity Law." *Journal of Women's History* 12, no. 2 (2000): 8–29.

Meade, Marion. *Free Woman: The Life and Times of Victoria Woodhull.* New York: Knopf, 1976.

Mintz, Mark M. *Seeds of Empire: The American Revolutionary Conquest of the Iroquois.* New York: New York University Press, 1999.

Monroe, John Warne. *Laboratories of Faith: Mesmerism, Spiritism, and Occultism in Modern France*. Ithaca: Cornell University Press, 2007.

Mooney, James. *The Ghost-Dance Religion and the Sioux Outbreak of 1890*. Lincoln: University of Nebraska Press, 1991.

Morton, Lisa. *Calling the Spirits: A History of Séances*. Chicago: University of Chicago Press, 2021.

Moyer, Paul B. *The Public Universal Friend: Jemima Wilkinson and Religious Enthusiasm in Revolutionary America*. Ithaca: Cornell University Press, 2015.

Mueller, Max Perry. *Race and the Making of the Mormon People*. Chapel Hill: University of North Carolina Press, 2017.

Nagy, Ron. *Precipitated Spirit Paintings*. Hendersonville, NC: Galde Press, 2006.

———. *Slate Writing: Invisible Intelligence*. Hendersonville, NC: Galde Press, 2012.

Nagy, Ron, and Joyce LaJudice. *The Chronicles of Lily Dale: Free Thinkers and Spiritualism—Courage and Determinism—The Early Years*. Self-published using CreateSpace Independent Publishing Platform, 2017.

———. *The Spirits of Lily Dale*. Lakeville, MN: Galde Press, 2010.

———. *Spirits of Lily Dale*. Hendersonville, NC: Galde Press, 2017.

Natale, Simone. *Supernatural Entertainments: Victorian Spiritualism and the Rise of Modern Media Culture*. State College: Pennsylvania State University Press, 2017.

Neihardt, John G. *Black Elk Speaks: The Complete Edition*. Lincoln: University of Nebraska Press, 2014.

Nobisch, Maxwell Stevenson. "'To Free Thought, Free Speech, and Free Investigation': The Cultural Landscape of Lily Dale, New York." PhD. diss., University of Georgia, 2020.

Odgen, Emily. *Credulity: A Cultural History of Mesmerism*. Chicago: University of Chicago Press, 2018.

Owen, Alex. *The Darkened Room: Women, Power, and Spiritualism in Late Victorian England*. Chicago: University of Chicago Press, 2004.

Owen, Suzanne. *The Appropriation of Native American Spirituality*. New York: Bloomsbury, 2011.

Parsons, Elaine Frantz. *Manhood Lost: Fallen Drunkards and Redeeming Women in the Nineteenth-Century United States*. Baltimore: Johns Hopkins University Press, 2010.

Perciaccante, Marianne. *Calling Down Fire: Charles Grandison Finney and Revivalism in Jefferson County, New York*. Albany: State University of New York Press, 2003.

Pike, Sarah M. *New Age and Neopagan Religions in America*. New York: Columbia University Press, 2004.

Pond, Mariam Buckner. *The Unwilling Martyrs: Story of the Fox Family*. London: Spiritualist Press, 1947.

Puglionesi, Alicia. *In Whose Ruins: Power, Possession, and the Landscapes of American Empire*. New York: Scribner, 2022.

Raboteau, Albert J. *Slave Religion: The Invisible Institution*. Oxford: Oxford University Press, 1978.

Reitano, Joanne. *New York State: Peoples, Places, and Priorities*. New York: Routledge, 2016.

Richter, Daniel K. *The Ordeal of the Longhouse: The Peoples of the Iroquois League in the Era of European Colonization*. Chapel Hill: University of North Carolina Press, 1992.

Rowe, David L. *God's Strange Work: William Miller and the End of the World.* Grand Rapids: Eerdmans Publishing Group, 2008.
Seeman, Erik. *Speaking with the Dead in Early America.* Philadelphia: University of Pennsylvania Press, 2019.
Shandler, Nina. *The Strange Case of Hellish Nell.* Cambridge: Da Capo Press, 2006.
Shilling, Ruth. *Through a Medium's Eyes. About Life, Love, Mediumship, and the Spirit World.* Vol. 3. *Neal Rzepkowski, MD.* West Kingston, RI: All One World Publishing, 2018.
Smith, Adair Martin. "Native American Use of Eagle Feathers under the Religious Freedom Restoration Act." *University of Cincinnati Law Review* 84 (2018): 575–94.
Smith, John Howard. *The First Great Awakening: Redefining Religion in British America, 1725–1775.* Lanham, MD: Fairleigh Dickinson Press, 2014.
Smiths, David D. "The Frontier Army and the Destruction of the Buffalo, 1865–1883." *Western Historical Quarterly* 25, no. 3 (Autumn 1994): 312–38.
Starr, Paul. *The Social Transformation of American Medicine: The Rise of a Sovereign Profession and the Making of a Vast Industry.* New York: Basic Books, 1982.
Steiger, Brad. *Medicine Talk: A Guide to Walking in Balance and Surviving on the Earth Mother.* New York: Doubleday, 1974.
Taylor, Alan. *The Divided Ground: Indians, Settlers, and the Northern Borderland of the American Revolution.* New York: Knopf, 2006.
Tetrault, Lisa. *The Myth of Seneca Falls: Memory and the Women's Suffrage Movement, 1848–1898.* Chapel Hill: University of North Carolina Press, 2014.
Tosh, John. *A Man's Place: Masculinity and the Middle-Class Home in Victorian England.* New Haven: Yale University Press, 2007.
Trafzer, Clifford E., and Joel R. Hyer. *Exterminate Them: Written Accounts of the Murder, Rape, and Enslavement of Native Americans during the California Gold Rush.* East Lansing: Michigan State University Press, 1999.
Tromp, Marlene. *Altered States: Sex, Nation, Drugs, and Self-Transformation in Victorian Spiritualism.* Albany: State University of New York Press, 2006.
———. "Spirited Sexuality: Sex, Marriage, and Victorian Spiritualism." *Victorian Literature and Culture* 31, no. 1 (2003): 67–81.
Troy, Kathryn. *The Specter of the Indian: Race, Gender, and Ghosts in American Séances, 1848–1890.* Albany: State University of New York Press, 2017.
Ulrich, Laurel Thatcher. *The Age of Homespun: Objects and Stories in the Creation of an American Myth.* New York: Doubleday, 2001.
———. *A House Full of Females: Plural Marriage and Women's Rights in Early Mormonism, 1835–1870.* New York: Knopf, 2017.
Urban, Hugh. *New Age, Neopagan, and New Religious Movements: Alternative Spirituality in Contemporary America.* Berkeley: University of California Press, 2015.
Walker, David. "The Humbug in American Religion: Ritual Theories of Nineteenth-Century Spiritualism," *Religion and American Culture: A Journal of Interpretation* 23, no. 1 (2013): 30–74.
Walkowitz, Judith. *City of Dreadful Delight: Narratives of Sexual Danger in Late-Victorian Britain.* Chicago: University of Chicago Press, 2013.
Walton, John K., ed. *Histories of Tourism: Representation, Identity and Conflict.* Bristol, UK: Channel View Publications, 2005.

Warren, Louis. *God's Red Son: The Ghost Dance Religion and the Making of Modern America*. New York: Basic Books, 2017.

Weisberg, Barbara. *Talking to the Dead: Kate and Maggie Fox and the Rise of Spiritualism*. New York: HarperOne, 2005.

Wernitznig, Dagmar. *Going Native or Going Naive? White Shamanism and the Neo-Noble Savage*. Lanham, MD: University Press of America, 2003.

White, Barbara A. *The Beecher Sisters*. New Haven: Yale University Press, 2003.

White, Ethan Doyle. *Wicca: History, Belief and Community in Modern Pagan Witchcraft*. Liverpool: Liverpool University Press, 2022.

Wicker, Christine. *Lily Dale: The Town That Talks to the Dead*. San Francisco: HarperSanFrancisco, 2003.

Williams, Glenn. *The Year of the Hangman: George Washington's Campaign against the Iroquois*. Yardley, PA: Westholme, 2005.

Index

abolitionism, 7, 28–30, 55, 70–71, 103, 124
  women's rights and, 92–93, 98–99, 103
alcohol, 8–9, 11, 116–123, 129, 149, 194n1
  Lily Dale's prohibition of, 119–120, 133, 136, 139–140
  madness and, 126, 130–131
  spiritualists' use of, 118, 122, 127, 131–133
alcoholism, 29, 77, 117–118, 126–132
Alden, Willard, 3, 17, 36–37, 107, 120, 179n5
American Association of Spiritualists (AAS), 62, 124
American Indian Movement (AIM), 144, 157, 166–167, 197n3
American Indian Religious Freedom Act (AIRFA), 153, 157
American Revolution, 19, 23–24
American Society for Psychical Research (ASPR), 52, 53, 78, 80–82
Andrews, Lynn, 159–160, 166, 20n56
Anthony, Susan B., 96, 110, 111–112, 141
  opinion on Spiritualism of, 93–94, 114–115
  suffrage work of, 98–100, 105–106, 137
  visits to Lily Dale by, 89–90, 91, 101, 103, *107*, 111–112, 136
assimilationism, 150–151, 160
auditorium, 2, 39–40, 84, 89–91, 103, 115
Aurora Guest House, 39–40, 43, *44*
automatic writing. *See* slate writing

Babcock, Elnora, 88, 98, 104
Bangs sisters, 74–76, 107

Index

Banner of Light, The, 32–33, 50, 93, 105, 150
   Lily Dale according to the, 34–35, 37, 66
   scandal reported in, 73, 78, 124
Barrett, Harrison D., 50–51, 56, 62, 103, 104
Bear Tribe Medicine Society, 158–159, 164, 165, 201n77
Beecher, Heny Ward, 124, 182n35
Beecher, Lyman, 103, 124, 134, 137
Black Elk Speaks, 155–156, 157–158, 201n74
Blake, Lillie Devereux, 98, 104
Blavatsky, Helena Petrovna, 154, 155, 199n36
Braude, Ann, 30, 45, 48, 55, 62, 93
Brehm, Marie C., 138
Britain. *See* United Kingdom
Britten, Emma Hardinge, 31–32, 33–34
Buffalo, NY, 10, 15, 21–22, 28, 70, 87, 162
   authors' relationship to, 9, 12, 40, 142, 180n15
   proximity to Lily Dale of, 15, 35, 53, 120
Bundy, John C., 73, 75–76, 126, 130
Burned Over District, 2, 10, 16, 26–27, 49, 92

California, 95–96, 108, 115, 130, 151
   suffragist activism in, 94, 110, 112–113
camp meetings, 95, 179n4, 179n7
   Methodist origins of, 22–23, 32
   Spiritualist adoption of, 32–38, 95, 137, 183n61
Capron, Eliab, 47, 69
Carrington, Hereward, 42, 52, 53–54, 78–84, 87, 184n6
Cassadaga Lake Free Association (CLFA), 17, 50, 101–102, 196n65, 197n71
   development of, 41, 96–97, 105–106
   founding of, 3, 18, 29, 35–38, 95
   temperance and, 119–120, 135–138
   See also Lily Dale Assembly

Cassadaga Lakes, 2, 14, 16, 121
Cassadaga Spiritualist Camp (FL), 120, 160
Cassadagan, The, 109, 121
Castañeda, Carlos, 156–157, 158, 159
Catt, Carrie Chapman, 109, 136
Cattaraugus Reservation, 143, 162
Center for Inquiry (CFI), 87
Cercle Harmonique, 56
Chautauqua County, New York, 17, 35–36, 95, 100, 104, 120
Chautauqua Institution, 2, 53, 90, 100, 123, 135, 137
Chicago, Illinois, 75, 135
Chief Ho-To-Pi, 164
Children's Lyceum, 63, 97, 179n2
Chinquilla, 148, 160–162, 200n61
Christianity, 45, 57–60, 132–134, 153, 155
   Indian policy and, 149–150
   revivalism within, 26–28, 122
   See also Protestantism
Christian Spiritualism, 59–60
Civil War, 12, 24, 31, 94, 98, 176
conservatism, 16, 57, 109, 123, 133–134, 136
   within Spiritualism, 124–126, 132
conversion (religious), 22, 25, 26, 84, 149, 156
   to Spiritualism, 30, 33, 46, 69, 94, 125, 169
Cook, Florence, 127, 139
Corinthian Hall (Rochester), 46, 67, 77, 185n17
cottages, 37, 60–61, 63, 83, 105
   as venues for mediumship, 3, 40–42, 43, 48, 54, 169
Cottrell, Flo, 47
COVID-19 pandemic, 1, 2, 169, 176
Cowen v. Lily Dale Assembly, 58–59
Cox, Robert, 29, 48
Cross, Whitney, 22, 25–26, 181n30, 182n35
cultural appropriation, 7, 63, 154, 157–158, 162–164, 201n74

Davis, Andrew Jackson, 31, 154
Dawes Act, 150, 152
death, 9, 15, 31, 124, 171, 173
Declaration of Sentiments, The, 92, 110
Deloria, Vine, Jr., 157, 162, 167
D'Espérance, Madame. *See* Hope, Elizabeth
domesticity, 41, 43–45, 51–53, 62
Doolittle, Harriet, 95
Douglass, Frederick, 28, 30
Doyle, Sir Arthur Conan, 46–47, 51, 69, 78
drunkenness. *See* intoxication
Duncan, Helen, 51

ectoplasm, 42, 69, 123
Eighteenth Amendment, 133, 136, 139
emotion, 15–16, 22, 40, 126, 171–172
entertainment. *See* recreation
environmentalism, 155–156
Erie Canal, 20–22, 24–26, 28
Everett, Henry, 103, 106, 107, 112
Everett, Josephine Pettengill, 103, 105, 107, 112, 115
Everett, Leolyn, 107
exposés, 73–74, 77–78, 81–82, 129, 184n6

femininity, 45–46, 49, 50–51, 62–63, 130, 187n76
feminism, 57, 88, 92, 98, 118, 133
  Lily Dale as locus of, 96, 104–105, 135–138
  Spiritualism and, 29, 50, 62, 124, 173
  See also Women's Rights movement
Fetters, Abby, 131–132
Finney, Charles Grandison, 25–26, 30, 182n35
First Great Awakening, 22, 122–123
Fixen, Laura, 137, 138
Florida, 108, 120, 148, 159, 160, 201n72
Fourier, Charles, 28
Fourteenth Amendment, 98, 104, 142n49
Fox, Kate, 67, 69, 78, 123–124, 189n43
  alcoholism of, 76–77, 126, 129

Fox, Maggie (Mrs. Maggie Fox Kane), 69–70, 72–73, 124, 188n16
  repudiation of Spiritualism by, 76–78, 126–127, 173, 189n43
  visit to Lily Dale by, 47, 66–67, 172–173, 187n2
Fox, Nettie Pease, 34, 35
Fox cottage, 46, 47–48, 65–67, 87, 110–111, 172, 185n17
Fox sisters, 11, 29–31, 46–47, 51, 78, 93
  criticisms of, 66–72, 123–124, 126–127, 130, 172
  fraud, 10–11, 67, 124, 162, 170, 172–173
  exposure of, 73–81, 126, 128–129, 184n6
  Spiritualist responses to accusations of, 72–73, 82–83, 134
  Spiritualists' self-policing of, 61, 70–71, 84–87, 132, 139–140
free love movement, 124–126, 132
French, Elizabeth J., 134
frontier, 16–18, 23–25
Furness, Horace Howard, 72, 80

gatekeeping, 40, 56–59
gender, 24, 62–63, 98–99, 181n24
  challenges to, within Spiritualism, 45–46, 55–56, 92–93, 123, 138
  See also women
Genesee River Valley, 20, 23
Ghost Dance religion, 151–154, 156
Gilman, Charlotte Perkins, 91, 111, 112, 137, 139
Graham, H. H., 74–75, 76
Grandmother Spider, 143, 164, 197n2
Great Spirit (Wakantanka), 145–147, 156
grief, 9, 15–16, 117–118, 171–172

Handsome Lake, 149
Hanny, Marguerite, 59–60
Harper, Ida Husted, 111, 112, 113, 114
Haudenosaunee, 18–20, 22, 141, 143–144, 149, 167
Hazard, Thomas R., 72

health, 35–36, 122, 148–149, 154
Hiawatha, 147, 148
Hicks, Elias, 30
historians, 47, 50, 115, 129, 174, 176
  authors as, 4, 15–16, 172–173, 179n1
Home, Daniel Dunglas, 46, 48
Hooker, Isabella Beecher, 91, 103–104, 109, 114, 134, 136
Hope, Elizabeth (pseud. Madame D'Espérance), 84–86, 132
Howe, Julia Ward, 99
Howell, Mary Seymour, 105, 112, 115, 136, 138
Hull, Moses, 125
Hydesville, NY (Rochester rappings), 29–30, 45–47, 51, 65–67, 92, 172
  See also Fox cottage
Hyslop, James, 53, 68, 80–81

Indian policy, 150–151, 153
Indians. *See* Native Americans
Indigenous Americans. *See* Native Americans
industrialization, 7, 12, 18–22
Inspiration Stump, 2, 4–7, 53, 89, 169
intentional communities, 12, 16, 33, 35–36, 41, 173
  See also utopianism
intoxication, 74, 76, 85, 122–124, 126–128, 132–133
  as spiritual tool, 118, 152–153, 155
investigation (psychic), 74–75, 87, 161, 173
  Fox sisters' experiences of, 11, 30–31, 67–70
  Lily Dale's experiences with, 42–43, 52, 61, 73–74, 80–83, 184n6
  Seybert Commission, 71–72, 73
  Spiritualists' requests for, 70–73, 78–79
Iroquois Hotel, 11, 120–121, 141, 180n14, 194n9, 202n5
Isaac, Howard, 162, 163, 201n68

Jones, Stevens Sanborn, 74
Jonson, Joseph, 54
Julia's Bureau, 86–87

Kane, Eisha Kent, 66, 70
Keeler, Pierre L. O. A., 80

Ladies' Auxiliary (Lily Dale), 63, 138
LaDuke, Vincent (pseud. Sun Bear), 158–159, 162, 163, 164, 165–167, 201n74, 201n77
LaJudice, Joyce, 36, 173, 174, 197n71
Lake Pleasant camp, 33–34, 36
Lakota religion, 151–152, 156–158, 163–164, 166–167
  See also Native American religion
Laona Free Association, 95, 97
Lease, Mary Ellen, 136, 137
lecture circuits, 94–96, 97, 100, 108, 135
Leolyn Inn, 36, 47, *117*, 120, *140*, 141
  ownership of, 107, 112
Leolyn Woods, 2, 3, 7, 107, 115, 142
Liberator, The, 70–71
Light, 73, 76, 77, 128
Lillie, John T., 62–63, 108
Lillie, Mrs. R. Shepard, 49, 108
Lily Dale Assembly, 47, 55, 101–102, 121, 169
  gender parity within board of, 57–58, 62–63
  public relations challenges of, 53, 81–83, 122, 134, 138–140
  real estate transactions of, 3, 35, 36, 40, 55, 107, 148
  residency requirements of, 2, 43, 55–60
  response to fraud accusations by, 53, 73–75, 80–83, 170
  See also Cassadaga Lake Free Association (CLFA)
Lily Dale Assembly, Inc. V Hanny, 59–60
Lily Dale Museum, 48, 76, 89–90, 143, 144, 160, 174–177
  authors' experiences in, 11–12, 39, 65, 118, 142, 168–171
Lowe, Louisa, 131

madness. *See* mental illness
Maplewood Hotel, 47, 53, 107, 116, 118, 140
  historic events at, 2, 82, *102*, 106, *117*

Marion Skidmore Library, 1, 9, 37, 97, 115, 174
Marriage, 93, 125
materializations. *See* physical mediumship
McCoy, Mrs. M. T., 54, 79
media. *See* Spiritualist media
medicine, 9, 69
medicine men. *See* shamanism
medicine wheel, 153, 157–159, 162–164, 166, 201n68, 201n74
mediums, 43, 85, 95, 123, 139, 173
   abuse of, 72, 77–78, 124, 126–127, 130–132
   accusations of fraud made toward, 11, 73–74, 80–81, 126, 128
   passivity of, 46, 49, 86, 122, 131
   See names of individual mediums
mediumship, 6–7, 70, 94–95
   celebrity and, 29, 51–53, 66–67, 75–76
   demonstrations of, 3, 41, 42, 46, 53, 68, 169
   self-doubt of own's own, 67, 76–78, 85–86, 127, 173
   transgressive nature of, 29–30, 48–50, 55–56, 92
   women's dominance of, 45–46, 49–50, 57, 62, 123
   See also physical mediumship and "true mediumship"
Mellon, Annie Fairlamb, 129, 139
mental illness, 75, 122, 126, 127–132
mesmerism, 69, 97, 130, 154
Methodism, 3, 32–34, 100, 122–123
Millennialism, 28, 154
Millerism, 26–27, 29
Moore, Hugh, 81–82
Mormonism, 27–28, 154
Morris Pratt Institute, 125–156
Mott, Lucretia, 101, 110
mythology, 35–36, 149, 163, 172, 199n36

Nagy, Ron, 11, 17, 36, 65, 121, 168, 197n71
   authors' relationship with, 9, 39, 88, 142, 170

Natale, Simone, 44, 67, 185n17
Nation, Carrie, 118, 138
National American Woman Suffrage Association (NAWSA), 99–100, 104, 109–113
National Colored Spiritualist Association of Churches (NCSAC), 56–58, 186n54
National Spiritualist Association of Churches (NSAC), 50, 56–60, 62, 106, 119, 126, 140, 187n71
Native American religion, 142–145, 149, 151, 165–167
   bastardization of, 156–160, 166–167
   regulation of, 151–153, 157, 199n32
   See also Lakota religion
Native Americans, 18–19, 101, 149, 197n3
   appropriating the culture of, 7–8, 63, 142–144, 164, 186n51
   commercializing the culture of, 142, 147–148, 158–160
   identity politics of, 155–156, 160–166, 197n1, 201n73
   New Age religion's origins in culture of, 155–158, 167
   reliance of Lily Dale mythology on, 35, 143–144, 159–160
   white violence toward, 12, 149–153, 160
nature, 3, 16–17, 34–36, 107, 155–156
New Age religion, 144, 153–167
New England, 19–20, 22–24, 36
New York City, 21, 25, 53, 77, 146–147
New York State, 10, 18–22, 35–36, 119, 143
   political activism in, 106
   religious radicalism in, 2, 16–19, 22–31, 92
New York State Constitutional Convention, 103, 104–106
   See also Women's suffrage
Nickell, Joe, 87–88
Nineteenth Amendment, 113–114, 194n90

Nitsch, Twylah Hurd, 162, 198n4, 201n68, 201n71, 201n72
　See also Wolf Clan Teaching Lodge
Norman, A., 78–79

Octagon House, 81, 98, 105
Oneida community, 28–29
Onset Bay, 33–35, 81, 84
Orvis, Anna, 135
Oskenonton, 143–149, 160–161, 167, 186n51

Palmyra, New York, 27–28
pan-Indianism, 157, 201n74
parapsychology, 71–72, 78–83, 173, 184n6
performance. *See* spectacle.
persecution, 27, 75–76, 160
Pettengill, Abby Louise, 101–103, 109, 112, 113, 114–115
　activities at Lily Dale of, 81, 103, 105, 108, 109, 111, 137
　Alden property ownership by, 36, 107
　feminist reform of, 91, 106, *107*
Peyotism, 152–153, 156
phenomena. *See* physical mediumship
physical mediumship, 42–43, 75, 84–85, 127, 129, 179n3
　Lily Dale Assembly's banning of, 3, 42, 60–61
　popularity of, 66–69, 80–84
　vulnerability of, 11, 53–54, 69–70, 78–85, 123, 132
Pierpont Grove, 33–34, 183n61
pioneering. *See* frontier
place, 1–4, 10, 45, 97–98, 115, 169, 176
　spirituality of, 7–9, 34, 90, 110, 172
plastic shamanism, 143, 162–163
political equality, 51, 92–93, 95–97, 105, 113, 134
　Lily Dale activism for, 97–98, 100–103, 106, 110
Political Equality Club, 98
Pomfret, New York, 2, 37, 119, 168
Post, Amy, 46, 69, 93, 94
Post, Isaac, 46, 69, 93, 94

preaching, 22–26, 32, 96, 108, 110, 122–123, 149
prostitution, 25–26, 93, 124, 125, 133
Protestantism, 24–28, 32, 33, 56, 154
　See also Christianity
psychiatry, 130
Public Universal Friend, 23–24

Quakerism (Religious Society of Friends), 24, 30, 46, 50, 93, 94, 122

race, 7, 35, 40, 98–99, 113
Ramsdell, Josh, 16, *17*, 18, 174
readings. *See* spirit communication
recreation, 33–35, 42, 68, 76, 83, 139,
　Victorian culture of, 3–4, 7, 42–45, 83, 173, 179n7
Red Jacket, 160, 161
reform, 28–30, 92–94, 122, 126, 132–134, 138
　Spiritualism as vehicle of, 55, 91–94, 96–98, 102, 115
　See also temperance movement, women's rights movement, and women's suffrage
religion, 23, 86, 92, 155
　freedom of, 30, 49, 100, 153, 157, 199n32
　See also Christianity, Protestantism, and Spiritualism
Religio-Philosophical Journal, 73, 74, 76, 124–125, 126, 130
Religious Crimes Code, 151–152
religious revivalism, 18, 22–23, 25, 157
Richmond, Almond Benson, 73–75, 136, 196n65
Richmond, Cora L. V. (Scott), 49–51, 56, 94, 104, 111, 185n30
Rochester, New York, 20–21, 25–26, 29, 46–47, 67–68, 93, 110–111
　See also Hydesville, NY
Rzepkowski, Neal, 143, 164–165, 197n2

Sabol, Robert, 59–60, 187n64
salvation, 22, 24–25, 150
San Francisco, 95, 112

Sanger, Margaret, 113
Sawyer, Mattie Brown, 125
Scheu, Jacob, 120–121
Scheu, Louisa, 120–121, 194n10
science, 68–69, 71–72, 94, 173
Scott, Cora. *See* Richmond, Cora L. V.
séances, 48–49, 54, 81–82, 110, 129, 160
    conversion as precipitated by, 30, 34, 47, 84, 94
    entertainment value of, 42–45, 61, 68
    mediums' vulnerability during, 51, 131–132
    See also spirit communication
Second Great Awakening, 23–32, 38, 68, 123, 179n4, 181n30
    social reform during, 28, 92, 115, 126, 154
Seneca Falls convention, 2, 28, 30, 92–93, 110, 114, 191n6
Seneca Indian Historical Society, 163, 201n72
Seneca Nation, 3, 19, 20, 143, 160
    Twylah Hurd Nitsch and, 162–163
separate spheres ideology, 41, 43–45, 49, 62
Seventh Day Adventism, 27, 125
Sewall, May Wright, 88, 136
sexuality, 46, 93, 122–123, 125–126, 130
Seybert, Henry, 71, 72, 73
Seybert Commission, 71–74, 80, 196n65
Shakers, 23, 28, 191n7
shamanism, 69, 151, 156, 158–159, 166–167
    See also plastic shamanism
Shaw, Rev. Dr. Anna Howard, 99–100, 102, 105–106, 110–113, 136–137
Showers, Frederica Hurst, 127–128
Showers, Mary Rosina, 127–128
skepticism, 10, 47, 66, 80, 123–124, 126–127
    role of physical mediumship in, 43, 78, 84–85
    Spiritualism as inviting of, 68–70, 87–88

Skidmore, Marion, 96–98, 100, 101–103, 105–109, 115
slate writing, 42, 50, 70, 72–74, 80–81, 86–87
Smith, Ashbel Grattan, 37, 38
Smith, Joseph, 27, 35–36, 192n40
spectacle, 42, 44–47, 123–124, 147–148, 160–161
    popular demand for, 7, 46, 51, 80
    skepticism attracted by, 67–69, 77–78
spirit cabinets, 54, 173
spirit communication, 29, 46, 103, 151–152, 160, 164–165
    message services as a means to, 4–7, 39, 89–90, 175–176
    Spiritualism's foundation in, 15, 29–31,
    transgressive nature of, 48–50, 92–93
    under test conditions, 42–43, 74, 79, 85–87
    See also séances, slate writing, spirit paintings, spirit photography, spirit rappings, and spirit trumpet
spirit healing, 31, 122, 124
spirit paintings, 76, 107, 144, 160, 174
spirit photography, 53, 69, 78–79
spirit quests, 143, 156, 157, 199n36
spirit rappings, 29–31, 32, 46–47, 64, 66–67, 93–94, 110
    skepticism of, 69–70, 72, 77, 126, 172
spirit trumpet, 3, 42, 54, 70, 79, 83
spiritualism, 7–8, 10–11, 68, 92, 160
    challenges to legitimacy of, 66, 70, 82, 122, 125–126, 130–132, 134
    decline of, 42, 57–59
    home as the site of, 43–45, 47–48
    institutionalization of, 55–56, 60–61
    Maggie Fox's repudiation of, 76–78, 126–127
    origins and growth of, 18, 29–34, 47–, 65, 67–68
    scientific inquiry and, 31–32, 60–61, 70–72, 88
    transgressive nature of, 49–51, 62–63, 92–93, 95–96, 123
Spiritualist media, 72–77, 93, 124, 127, 161

Stanton, Elizabeth Cady, 92, 93, 98–99, 101, 103, 110
Stead, William Thomas, 86
Stone, Lucy, 99, 103, 105, 136
Stowe, Harriet Beecher, 103, 114
Sun Bear. *See* LaDuke, Vincent.
Sunflower, The, 6, 37, 41, 121, 197n71
Sunny Brae ranch, 96, 110
Support and Protection of Indian Religions and Indigenous Traditions (SPIRIT), 166
Swain, Adeline Morrison, 134
sweat lodges, 143, 153, 156, 157, 163, 164, 165
Swedenborgians, 31, 154, 199n34

table tipping, 3, 42
Teachings of Don Juan, The, 155, 156–158
temperance movement, 55, 99–100, 118–122, 132–139, 173
theology, 28, 30, 58–59, 200n57
Theosophy, 154–156
trance mediumship, 42–43, 51, 84–85, 94, 131–132, 155
Transcendentalism, 154, 155
Trefny, D. P., 75
Tromp, Marlene, 86, 129
"true mediumship," 61, 71, 77, 84, 127, 139.
   See also mediums and fraud
Twing, Carrie E. S., 137, 174

Underhill, Leah Fox, 29, 69, 76–78, 123
United Kingdom, 45, 48, 122, 127, 133, 148
Universal Association of Spiritualists (UAS), 124–125
University of Pennsylvania, 71, 72
utopianism, 2, 15, 24, 28–29, 151, 175
   See also intentional communities

Vermont, 4, 22–23, 27, 40
Victorianism, 10–11, 53, 86, 179n7
   gender norms of, 41, 43–45, 48–49, 62, 123, 129–134

Warne, George B., 53, 81, 82–83
Watson, Elizabeth Lowe (Libbie), 49, 91, 98, 108
   reform work of, 111–113, 115, 135, 137
   Spiritualist ministry of, 94–96, 110
Weisberg, Barbara, 70, 77
white supremacy, 40, 56–57, 60–61, 98–99, 149–152
Wigwam Indian Village, 142–143, 144, 148
wilderness. *See* nature
Wilkinson, Jemima, 23–24, 29
   See also Public Universal Friend
Willard, Frances, 99, 118, 132–133, 137
Wind Daughter, 158, 164–165
Wolf Clan Teaching Lodge, 163–164, 201n77
women, 45, 118–119, 133–134, 184n7
   Lily Dale Assembly's marginalization of, 55–57, 60, 62–63, 138–139
   Lily Dale's target demographic, 4, 103–104
   mediums who are, 57, 85–86, 123, 126, 130–131
   Spiritualism as liberation for, 41, 44–45, 49–51, 62–63
   See also feminism, Women's Day, women's rights movement, and women's suffrage
Women's Christian Temperance Union (WCTU), 99–100, 114, 120, 132–138
   suffrage reform and, 105, 111
Women's Day, 63, 96, 98, 113–114, 138–139, 176
   suffrage activism during, 100, 104, 107, 109
women's rights movement, 45, 63, 91–95, 110, 133–134
   discord within the, 98–100, 103
   Lily Dale as a hub of, 96–97, 104, 108, 114–115
   See also Seneca Falls convention

women's suffrage, 91, 97–101, 112, 173–174, 194n90
 Lily Dale's dedication to, 89–91, 94, 103–104, 106–115
 temperance women and, 134–138
 See also New York State constitutional convention

Wood, Catherine Elizabeth, 129
Woodhull, Victoria, 124–126
Wounded Knee massacre, 151–152, 156, 157

Yankees, 20, 26